May 2005

Ron McIntyre

The ATTITUDE
of LEADERSHIP

The ATTITUDE of LEADERSHIP

TAKING THE LEAD AND KEEPING IT

KEITH HARRELL

WILEY

JOHN WILEY & SONS, INC.

Published by John Wiley & Sons, Inc., Hoboken, New Jersey.
Published simultaneously in Canada.

For general information on our other products and services please contact our Customer Care Department within the United States at (800) 762-2974, outside the United States at (317) 572-3993 or fax (317) 572-4002.

Wiley also publishes its books in a variety of electronic formats. Some content that appears in print may not be available in electronic books. For more information about Wiley products, visit our Web site at www.wiley.com.

Library of Congress Cataloging-in-Publication Data:

The attitude of leadership : taking the lead and keeping it / [ed. by] Keith Harrell.
    p.   cm.
    Includes bibliographical references and index.
    ISBN 0-471-42024-7 (cloth)
    1. Leadership   I. Harrell, Keith D.
HD57.7.A77   2003
658.4′092—dc21

                                             2003002600

Printed in the United States of America.

10 9 8 7 6 5 4 3 2 1

To all the leaders in this world
who are making a difference by leading
with integrity, respect, and the faith
to trust the calling and purpose for their life.
And most important, to God for giving me everything—
life, knowledge, wisdom, and the ability to do His work.

PREFACE

Do you sometimes get discouraged by reading yet another headline about a CEO gone bad?

Do you wonder if there are still ethical leaders who practice the old-fashioned values of integrity, service, and accountability?

The reassuring answer to that question is a resounding YES. In fact, this book features more than 20 such leaders from a cross-section of industries who are respected by their peers and revered by their employees. Why? They are visionary motivators who lead by example and practice what they preach. What a concept.

However, I don't simply describe what these respected captains of industry have to say; in addition, I examine their best practices, ask thought-provoking questions to prompt you to evaluate whether you are following their lead, and provide specific suggestions on how you can apply these ideas in your own workplace.

What I've discovered through my interviews with these outstanding individuals is that:

- Anyone can be a leader. You don't have to be in a management position to positively influence others.
- Everyone should become a leader because it gives us multiple opportunities to pay our rent on this earth by giving back.
- Becoming a leader is the key to personal and professional fulfillment which is directly proportionate to the difference we make in the lives of others.
- Leadership is contagious, in the best sense of the word. A commitment to be our best and to inspire others to be their best sets up a leadership legacy that motivates others to respond in kind.
- Effective leadership is a by-product of having and demonstrating the right attitudes. The timeless characteristics of honesty,

integrity, and accountability are what inspire people to trust and follow their leader—not because that person is their boss.

Life Is 50 Percent What We Make It, 50 Percent How We Take It

In my previous book, *Attitude Is Everything*, I shared my philosophy that how we approach life determines how we fare in life. You are about to discover that the same truth applies to business.

If you would like to reflect upon your own leadership skills, if you'd like to find out what works and what doesn't work for other leaders, if you'd like to plan how to improve your ability to positively impact others, you are in the right place because that's what this book is about. The ideas you're about to read are timeless and universal. You can apply them whether you run your own small business, direct a large corporation, head up a department, or manage a team of 30 employees.

You may be wondering, "There are hundreds of business books crowding the shelves. Why is this one worth reading?" Good question. I know you're busy, so I've done my best to fill this book with insightful, practical, motivating insights you can apply immediately. I've purposely kept the chapters short, so you can dip into them and derive real-life value—even if you have only a few minutes to spare.

Here are some other reasons I believe this book will be worth your valuable time:

1. *The leaders featured are all role models of integrity.* The primary criteria for inclusion was not financial success, industry clout, or name recognition. The primary criteria was that these individuals have proven track records of professional success and, even more importantly, they be congruent, walking-talking examples of servant-leadership. You will like these individuals. You'll be intrigued by their unique how-I-got-to-be-this-way stories, and you'll be favorably impressed with how they live their values on a daily basis—on and off the job.

2. *This book gives hope.* In this day and age of disturbing scandals about Enron and WorldCom, many professionals have become disillusioned. They are yearning to know, "Is integrity passe? Are

there any executives left who still believe in and practice personal accountability? If executives like this do exist, are their organizations thriving as a result of their inspired leadership?" The answer is yes and yes. This book gives reaffirming proof that these attitudes of leadership are not a Pollyannaish pipe dream—they are a reality that is available and advantageous for every one of us.

3. *This book has the ring of truth.* To respect a book, you need to know that its ideas are not abstract concepts or esoteric, academic theories conjured up by an author who has no real-life experience in the field. Our featured leaders have all "been there, done this." They've been through crises where they've had to lay off people. They've walked into companies that were about to go under and turned them around. They've dealt with employees who were less than motivated. You can trust their insights because they've been gleaned from actual experiences.

4. *This book is meant to be shared.* Since this book is about leadership—that is, positively influencing others to do and be their best—you are encouraged to share this book with your staff so you're all on the same page, so to speak. Perhaps employees could read a chapter a week, and you can use the chapter-ending questions to lead a meaningful discussion at your staff meetings on how employees are practicing, or not practicing, those specific qualities in their jobs. Perhaps you could assign a different chapter to each staff member and ask them to report back so you get different points of view while giving them an opportunity to hone their public-speaking skills (an important part of being an effective leader). The point is, don't keep this book to yourself. Share the intellectual wealth of these interviewees with others so more people will benefit.

5. *This book focuses on how you can apply these ideas.* The purpose of education is not knowledge; it's action.

I hope you enjoy this book and find it an interesting read. More importantly, I hope you follow up and put these ideas into practice so you reap real-world results. Each chapter ends with questions to help you examine whether or not you're using these techniques in your own life. If you're not currently using these techniques, these questions can help you determine how you could. You may be thinking, "I already know this." That's not the point. The point is, "Are you doing them?"

As Johann Goethe said, "Knowing is not enough, we must apply. Willing is not enough, we must do."

It has been a pleasure and a privilege for me to get to know these extraordinary leaders. I hope you too will find it a pleasure and a privilege, I wish you a positive journey as you take the lead in your life by developing the attitudes for successful leadership.

KEITH D. HARRELL

ACKNOWLEDGMENTS

While writing this book, I was honored and extremely grateful to have the outstanding help and support of many talented people. I want to express my utmost thanks to:

Matt Holt, my editor, for his vision, feedback, and expertise and his wonderful staff at John Wiley & Sons.

My literary agent Jan Miller.

Shannon Mizer-Marven for doing what you do best.

Wes Smith for your initial work on this project.

My sister Toni Malliet, who has always been a strong leader. You never cease to amaze me with your special gift and talents.

Sam Horn, author of *Take the Bully by the Horns: Stop Unethical, Uncooperative and Unpleasant People from Running and Ruining Your Life*, you are a master writer and I know this project would not have been as successful without your wisdom and insights.

My office manager Donna Cash for her countless hours, your patience and your ability to go above and beyond the call of duty. You are one of the main forces in the successful leadership at HPS. I thank God daily for your attitude-is-everything attitude, commitment, and excellence.

I want to thank these leaders for their time and commitment to be interviewed and the valuable insights that they shared with me personally. Your success and leadership principles are truly making a difference: Dr. Richard Valinsky, Jeff Rich, Sue Cole, Sharon Denson, Judge Greg Mathis, and Chris Grady.

And finally, thanks to many individuals who have in their own special ways contributed to the creation of this book: Ralph Bianco, Oscar Camejo, Bobbie Christmas, Lisa Daniel, Arabella Grayson, Monisha Harrell, Deborah Johnson, Doug Smart, and Carolyn Zatto.

CONTENTS

You Never Know

Harvey Najim, President and CEO
Sirius Computer Solutions

How was Harvey Najim able to build a $250 million company in five years? Why do his hundreds of employees revere him? At least partially, Harvey credits his philosophy of "Do the Right Thing for The Right Reasons . . . Because You Never Know." Read on to find out how he was first introduced to this idea.

"Ever since I was knee-high to a grasshopper, my father often took me to work with him at his wholesale candy, syrup, and tobacco business. He had a set regimen of what we were supposed to do, and if there was "nothing" to do, he'd find something. One sweltering summer day, he ordered my cousin and me to move 250—yes, 250—four-gallon cases of soda, sweep underneath them, and return them to their original places. As you can imagine, the work was hot, hard, and thankless.

"I complained, mumbling out loud that the job was a pointless task and not worth doing. After all, no one would ever know or care if dust settled underneath the cases. My father told me, 'Son, it's important to do the right thing, whether or not it will ever get noticed. If you do the right thing for the right reasons, you will never regret it, and you never know what will happen as a result.'

"Guess who showed up later that afternoon: the health inspector. Guess what he asked my dad to do? Right. Move the soda cases aside, so he could see if the facilities were thoroughly cleaned. Dad did, they

1

were, and I learned a lifelong lesson that I continue to practice in my personal and professional life."

Can You Get Past the Pig?

"When I graduated from high school, my parents lined us four boys up. I was the oldest, and my parents decided I should be a doctor, their second son should be an engineer, and their third son should be a lawyer. The youngest was selected to run our family business. My two middle brothers followed my parents' wishes. My youngest brother and I didn't . . . for good reasons.

"I had no interest in medicine, but in the beginning, I honored my parents' plans for me, because they wanted me to have 'Doctor' in front of my name. I went to an excellent medical school, Washington University in Saint Louis, Missouri. In my second-year biology lab, we were dissecting a pig, and, well, there's no way of getting around it, I passed out. My professor kindly and wisely suggested that if I couldn't get past the pig, I probably wouldn't make a good doctor. He was right, of course, and I concluded that medicine was not my field.

"I graduated with a degree in mathematics and was also a commissioned second lieutenant, thanks to my involvement in ROTC. Next, I worked for Boeing Aircraft while studying for my master's degree in night school. The Vietnam War started, and I went on active duty as a first lieutenant in San Antonio. By a fluke, I was assigned to a base near San Antonio, where I trained as a data processing officer. I found computer science fascinating, and I seemed to have a natural talent for it, because of my math degree and my interest in math. Two years after, I got out of the military, IBM hired me, and the rest is history. I had found my calling."

High-Tech Should Be High-Touch

"I may be the sole shareholder in my company, but I'm clear that if employees are to have a stake in the success of Sirius, they have to know every day that their efforts are acknowledged and appreciated. It's not important for a leader to be the smartest person in an organization; it is important for a leader to genuinely care about the people in an organization. For employees to know it, you've got to show it.

"Once or twice a day, I walk around and talk with people throughout the company. I'll ask how they're doing and what they're working on. I pass on compliments from their supervisors. I make it a point to know the name of everyone who works for me. I know when their work anniversaries are, whether they're married and have kids, and who just got back from having surgery. People don't care how much you know until they know how much you care.

"My interest is genuine, and it pays dividends. We don't lose many good employees, hardly any at all. I think this family atmosphere is one of the reasons we've received the IBM Leadership Award for the fourth straight year. No other IBM partner has ever earned the award more than two years in a row. We may be high-tech, but we're also high-touch, in that we stay connected with each other through frequent communication and contact."

Life Is Like a Chair

"I go to every employee orientation to talk to our new-hires about the things I believe in, which include (1) we're in business to make money, (2) work hard and play hard, (3) take time for family and friends, (4) always strive for excellence, (5) give back to the community, (6) develop a passionate attitude about what you do, (7) support your team to build synergy, and (8) have a relationship with God.

"I believe life is like a chair with four legs. The four legs are your work, your hobbies, your family, and your relationship with God. If one of those legs gets smaller than the others, the chair of life gets off center, and you will be off balance.

"I tell employees about the time Mother Teresa of Calcutta was interviewed after receiving the Nobel Peace Prize. The reporter asked, 'Why do you do what you do? How can you bear to have children die in your arms? Don't you get discouraged when you realize you can prolong only a few people's lives for a little while, because you'll never be able to completely eradicate hunger and disease in these people?'

"Mother Teresa said, 'I just try to do all I can, every day, with all I have.'

"That interview left an indelible impression on me, and I try to share that message with employees. This is what we're trying to do here at Sirius: Do all you can, every day, with all you have—and keep your chair of life in balance."

Stay the Course and Maintain Trust

"Immediately after September 11, 2001, I wrote a letter to employees assuring them that everyone in our company was safe, and their jobs were secure. I wanted them to know it was okay to be concerned. I told them I understood if some of them were sitting at their desks with a sick feeling in their stomachs, because I was feeling the same way.

"Sometimes there's a perception that CEOs don't cry, that CEOs don't have the same kinds of problems other people do. That's not true. We all have the same feelings and problems. People sometimes put the CEO of a company up on a pedestal, but I think it's more important for CEOs to have the strength to reveal their vulnerability. Admitting to our emotions makes it okay for employees to express theirs.

"At the same time, leaders need to set an example of moving forward. That's what I was trying to do with that letter. I had a heavy heart the night of September 11. I went to bed and couldn't sleep, so I got up and jotted down my thoughts. I wanted employees to know I was thinking of them, and that even though things seemed to be in turmoil, the company was going to stay on course.

"Open communication establishes a climate of trust. Even though we're a private corporation, I run our business as though it were a public company being scrutinized by shareholders, market watchers, and Wall Street professionals. By being up front with all our facts, we're showing we don't have any secrets.

"Every quarter I send a message to employees and report on the state of our business. I don't hide things in my quarterly messages; I face them head on. I tell what our revenues are and how we're doing regarding profitability. I report our current challenges and address anything else that's pertinent to our industry. If I perceive that employees are worried about the economic environment, I give my take on that. By picking up on issues when they're minor irritations, we prevent them from becoming major challenges."

The Fewer, the Better

"When I got ready to start my business 22 years ago, I went to see a man who was a pillar in the business community and asked his advice on how best to build a company. He told me to remember two key things: 'Number one, hire good people. Number two, hire damn few of them.' With that, he got up and walked out of the meeting, leaving me sitting there. As you can imagine, he made quite an impression.

"Not only have I never forgotten his succinct suggestions, I have verified its wisdom, time and again, in the last two decades. It's so important to be thoughtful and thorough when hiring people, to ensure they'll be good matches for the organization. I've learned from first-hand experience that it's better to have one high performer in a job than three or four so-so performers.

"Haste in hiring people backfires in myriad ways. By the time we realize we've hired unproductive individuals, we've invested time and money in training, motivating, monitoring, and counseling them. Once we conclude they're not working out—or not working, period—we have to go through the costly, time-consuming process of terminating them, and then start the hiring process all over again.

"Disciplining or firing employees can be particularly challenging when you're a people person. It's important that I don't let long-time personal relationships overrule or interfere with my making necessary business decisions. As a matter of fact, I have a hat rack in my office, because I collect logo caps, so if a staff member isn't performing and I need to confront him or her about it, I may actually put on my CEO cap, so the person understands I'm acting in that role. I may say, 'Don't take what I'm saying personally. Take what I'm saying seriously. I'm trying to be helpful-critical, not critical-critical.'

"If I have to terminate someone, I try to do it in a way that preserves that person's dignity. I may say that from what I've observed in that person's performance, he or she may not be right for this company, and that the company may not be right for the person. I'm not saying the employee is wrong and the company is not right, just that the situation isn't working out for either of us. My method allows employees to leave with their self-respect intact. In fact, with only a few exceptions, a number of the people I've had to let go still stay in touch, which is testimony to the fact that it's possible to make smart business decisions while still maintaining friendships."

Go for the Gold

"Every morning I get up and I think, 'Today, every one of our competitors is trying to figure out how to take market share away from us.' If I didn't believe that, I wouldn't work as hard as I do. I want our employees to bring that same type of zeal to their jobs. I want them to have competitive spirits that drive them to be their best, so we can continue being number one in our industry.

"I don't want to be second at anything, because no one remembers who got the silver or the bronze medal. You remember who got the gold. I want our company to get the gold medal every year, and I want employees who want that, too. I'm very competitive. I don't want to leave anything on the table. When I get up to shave, I never want to look in a mirror and say, 'I wonder if I could have . . .' or 'I wonder if I should have . . .'

"If our industry is growing at 3 to 4 percent a year, which is what all the pundits are predicting, I'd like us to grow 15 percent a year. I expect employees to work hard and to perform at a high level, and I demand the same thing from myself. I arrive before everyone else does, and I work an hour later than everyone else does, because if I don't set the example, who will?"

Complacency Is Not an Option

"Of all the jobs leaders have, one of the toughest is to make sure that complacency doesn't set in at any level. If you see an organization with a great deal of vim, vigor, and vitality, I guarantee you the CEO has a great deal of vim, vigor, and vitality. If you see an organization that is complacent and lethargic, you can bet the CEO is, too.

"I was watching the opening ceremonies of the Winter Olympics with my wife the week before our 2002 annual meeting. The theme of our event that year was 'Get in the Game,' and I was trying to come up with an innovative, attention-getting way to address the issue of vigorous, ongoing effort for my closing remarks at the Awards Banquet.

"I'm a math major and a numbers guy, and I couldn't get over the fact that the athletes had trained for many years, and possibly a lifetime, to get into the Olympic Games, yet the games lasted only 17 days; most of their events lasted only minutes; and there would be only three medal winners for each event. When the Winter Olympics were over, though, the athletes would go back home, where they would have four years to rest, prepare, train, and fine-tune their skills before coming back to compete."

Win the Work Olympics

"I realized that Olympic athletes have four years to 'get into the game.' In my remarks to employees, I made the point that we don't have the luxury of taking four years to gear up for our next international performance. We don't have down-time in our business. Our season ends on December 31, and the next season starts on January 1.

"I told them it was my hope that the three days of training we'd just had would provide them with the key initiatives, education, and team plays for them to 'get into the game' for our upcoming year. If those Olympic athletes could make a commitment to train for four years to get ready to do something for 17 days, then I hoped our employees would use what they'd learned in the previous three days to go out and work hard for the next 365 days.

"My analogy seemed to work. In fact, an IBM executive who was at that meeting told me, 'It was special to see the overwhelming thrill and emotion in peoples' eyes as they ran down that red carpet and high-fived, danced, and hugged when they got their awards. The validation gave them a sense of accomplishment, pride, conviction, and determination to do it again.'

"Exactly. That's one of the goals of a good leader, to motivate troops so they're ready to go at it again, willingly and enthusiastically."

The Power of One

"I found another analogy that offers insight into the importance of always striving for our best. I think it's important to keep informed about what's happening in the world, so most days I read our local paper, the *New York Times*, the *Wall Street Journal*, and *USA Today*. Years ago, I was reading the sports section, and I saw a list of the top 25 golfers on the pro tour, along with their average golf scores and income for the year.

"What amazed me was that the twenty-fifth ranked golfer made $25,000 and change, with an average round of 70.1, and the top-ranked person made $625,000 with an average score of 69.2. The difference was nine-tenths of one stroke!

"That article motivated me to talk with my employees about the power of one. It was such a clear example of how doing one thing your competitors don't do—or doing it better than your competitors—can make the difference between being number one or number twenty-five. If we want to be the best, then achieving that goal is as straightforward as making one more sales call before we go home, working one extra hour a day, or producing one more proposal or quote.

"The power of one means being early for meetings, returning voice mail messages and e-mails right away, taking the time to write a thank-you letter to a client or a personal note to a coworker. It means having standards that are nonnegotiable and that we practice around the clock. We can't just put in a little extra effort two hours a day on Monday, Wednesday, and Friday. We've got to do it seven days a week, 24 hours a day, and 52 weeks a year.

"Employees want a strong sense of destination, and it's the leader's job to make sure that happens. Our competitiveness and our clarity about being number one in our industry, and our commitment to doing what it takes to make that happen, means we all know exactly where we're going, and we're driving ourselves there."

Keith's Attitude Check

A number of our interviewees talked about the importance of matching talents with job requirements so we're well suited for our work, but no one said it quite as interestingly as Harvey Najim.

Think back over your own career. Did you start off in one profession, only to discover you couldn't "get past the pig?" Were you pressured to go into a specific career, only to find out it wasn't for you? Did you, like Harvey, have the courage to get out of that line of work and find the profession that did suit you?

Maybe, like Harvey, you discovered your calling through a fluke. Perhaps you tried several types of jobs before you settled into one that was a natural match for your abilities. You may still be searching for your perfect match. In fact, you may know you're not in your right field now, but you feel locked in. Are you really? I'm about to show you other ways to break out, shine, excel, or otherwise find what puts a sparkle in your eye and a bounce in your step.

Is Your Ladder against the Wrong Wall?

There's a famous saying, "You don't want to get to the top of the ladder and find out it's leaning against the wrong wall." I believe that if our ladder is against the wrong wall—if we're in a profession that doesn't match our personality, style, and skills—we won't ever be able to get to the top of the ladder.

If our heart's not in our job, perhaps we shouldn't be in that job. If, for whatever reason, we're doing work that is not in alignment with our values or aptitude, we're operating at a compromised capacity, and we're operating with dissonance and complacency. We'll never be our most effective as a leader, if we are forcing ourselves to dissect pigs that repel us.

You might think, "What you're saying may be true, but it's easier to stay than to change. It's easier to tell people to change than it is to make the change yourself. I don't have the freedom to seek work that suits me. What about my mortgage? Who's going to pay the bills and put my kids through school? I've got 20 years in; I'm not going to sacrifice my tenure or my job security. I can't disappoint my family or let people down."

Leaders Come in All Sorts of Packages

All your objections may be true. Even so, your job is not the thing you do. Question yourself this way: "Where in my life could I serve in a leadership role where I'd be doing something congruent with who I really am?" Leaders come in all sorts of packages, and many organizations need leaders. You can be a leader coaching your son's soccer team. You can be a leader by running for the board of your local community association. You can be a leader by volunteering to chair a fund-raising committee or an event for your church or civic organization. You can even start a volunteer organization yourself.

If you want to contribute to society and make a difference for as many people as possible, figure out your strengths, what you love to do, and how you can purposely place yourself in a position to add the most value. As Albert Einstein said, "Try not to become a man of success, but rather to become a man of value."

Become a person of value—that's one of the messages of this book. Anyone can be a leader. Anyone can add value. Everyone should be a leader. Everyone should do his or her best to add value. Being a leader is up to us. We can't wait for other people to put us in leadership positions or give us leadership opportunities. It is our responsibility to seek congruent leadership roles, so we can make the biggest possible contribution to life, while here on earth.

Are You Operating with Open-Book Management?

Harvey Najim talked about his open-book management style, where he reveals revenues and honestly addresses issues that arise regarding competition, the market, world news, and the future. Think about how you communicate in times of crisis. Do you shrivel at the thought of having to face employees with news of a bad quarter, cutbacks, or other signs that associates may perceive as failures? How can you turn the messages around, so employees feel empowered and driven to overcome obstacles and setbacks? If you don't inform your employees when the company faces a challenge, how can they help you surmount it?

ATTITUDE ACTION PLAN

- Are you working in an industry or capacity that inspires you?
- If you find that you are not working in the field you love, what is your action plan for finding the field that will excite you so much that you will find yourself driven to succeed?
- Do you look for ways to serve your community in a leadership role?
- Do you keep your employees informed of the company and department status?
- What do you do to ensure that your employees know that you care, so they will care?
- How do you show your employees the value of dedication and putting out a little extra effort?
- Who works for you? Do you have the fewest, but the best people possible?
- What do you do for your employees to help them "get past the pig" and find the field, job, or capacity that most inspires them?

Brief Biography

Harvey Najim, president and chief executive officer of Sirius Computer Solutions, founded the company in 1980 under the name Star Data Systems. His innovative business vision led it to become the largest IBM midrange eServer reseller in the world, with revenues exceeding $255 million. The company's more than 335 employees share Harvey Najim's unwavering commitment to excellence at 34 locations nationwide.

In February 2001, IBM awarded Harvey Najim the highest honor ever given to a Business Partner. Bob McCormick, vice president of Business Partners Americas presented IBM's Lifetime Achievement Award to Najim. At that time, IBM estimated that Sirius had contributed more than $1.2 billion in revenue since becoming an IBM Business Partner.

Harvey Najim graduated from the University of Wichita with a BA in mathematics in June 1964. He attended the President's Class at the Wharton School of Finance in June 1990, as well as the Owner President's Class at Harvard University in October 1994.

Prior to founding Sirius Computer Solutions, Harvey Najim served the IBM Corporation for 13 years in technical, marketing, and management capacities. In his early career, he worked for Boeing Aircraft in the Industrial Engineering Department. Najim also served his country in the United States Army as a first lieutenant, assistant chief of Data Processing, at HQ Brooke Army Medical Center while stationed at Fort Sam Houston.

Harvey Najim has served on numerous IBM Business Partner Advisory Councils and the Avnet Computer Marketing's Advisory Council and has participated in several task forces with IBM. He serves on the board of directors of J.P. Morgan Chase Bank in San Antonio and is the former chairman of the board of directors of San Antonio Federal Credit Union. He is also a former member of the board of directors of Junior Achievement, Respite Care of San Antonio, and the American Society of Computer Dealers. He continues to be recognized for his outstanding leadership in campaigning for the United Way of San Antonio and Bexar County, Texas.

The Magic of Belief

Mark E. Miller, President and COO
Equifax

A convincing trend emerged from our interviews with executive leaders. We learned that their parents almost always had positive attitudes and strongly influenced their children. Many high-ranking Americans remember affirmations repeated throughout their childhood, such the one Mark Miller heard from his parents: "Anything worth having is worth working hard for."

Do you ever think of the power of words, and how parental words can carve their way into the mind of a child? Do you recall words from your childhood that still affect you today?

Mark Miller certainly does.

"I grew up in a little town called McDonough, outside of Atlanta. Living in a small town, I played everything, following the seasons. Whether it was basketball, football, or baseball, we had lots of healthy competition, and I always received encouragement from my parents.

"My mother always said I could do anything in the world I wanted to do. I tried to tell her it wasn't true. I said, 'I can't fly. I can't get up on the roof and fly.'

"She just shook her head and said, 'You can do anything.'

"Luckily, we lived in a one-story house, so I never tested my negative theory. Instead, I incorporated her positive beliefs into my life, because I heard them so often, they became a part of me."

Make the Magic Begin

"My mother had read a book that influenced her, when I was young, and I've still got a copy of it in my office today. It's *The Magic of Believing* by Claude M. Bristol, and it was published in the 1940s. The message in Bristol's book captured Mother's imagination and inspired her, and she lived by his message that if you believe, anything is possible.

"As an example, I was playing Little League baseball, and we had a game against the team that was in first place. Those players were much bigger than the ones on my team. We were 9 and 10 years old, but the members of the other team already had facial hair. They were bigger, stronger, and faster, and I didn't think we could beat them.

"My mother had read that book, so she put up signs all around our house. The signs said, 'Beat the Giants' and 'You Can Do It,' and motivational things like that. She wanted me and my fellow teammates to see them.

"At first I was embarrassed, but as the days passed leading up to the game—the final game of the season—the messages permeated my brain. By the time the day arrived, I believed we could win. I'll never forget that day as long as I live. We went out and beat that team 8–2. We won through belief alone, and that realization made a big impact on me. It's the way I've conducted my affairs ever since. If you believe in something, you put your heart, your mind, and your sweat equity into it; you can make a difference."

Step Up to Bat

"My coaches and teachers were a good influence, too, but mostly I'd say my mother gave me the most inspiration. She had to overcome some vision problems early in life, but to meet her, you'd never know it. She does not let it hinder her. She's untraditional, in that she's not afraid to speak her mind and step up and be counted. She's a positive influence on everyone who comes into contact with her.

"When you look at my experiences in corporate life, I realize how much she inspired me. It's sometimes easier not to raise your hand, not to step up or be counted. People allow themselves to be affected by fear or uncertainty. Sometimes it's easier to be a wallflower, do your job quietly, and, you hope, effectively, but I've found that the only way you have an opportunity to grow is by going the extra mile, volunteering for that extra assignment.

"Most companies that follow tradition innately give you what I'll call a template that says, 'Here's how you can do well. This is the booklet we follow at our corporation. Plug into that success formula, and you'll do okay here.'

"What's really important, though, is to take that formula to the next level. Paint outside the lines. I always tell people, 'Look, I was not in any way preordained for my assignment here, but I was given the opportunity with a great company to make a difference. I had good ideas, and people were willing to listen and give me an opportunity to foster those ideas.' I want others to come up with their own ideas."

Your Chance to Make a Difference

"No matter what role you take in any organization, whether it's your church, your company, or your community, everybody has an opportunity to make a difference. It doesn't matter if you're gregarious or introverted, whether you work in the mailroom or the boardroom. You have a chance to make a difference in the organization. That's what meritocracy in an organization is all about. Meritocracy is a system that gives everybody opportunities based on their abilities, rather than their positions, background, or alliances. People willing to put in energy and passion are the ones who will lead the organization in the future. When we put these beliefs into practice we unlock creativity, more ideas coming from every corner of the organization. We're going to have a competitive advantage, as a result. Great people, fostering creativity and innovation, that's the only competitive advantage that's sustainable.

"It's performance orientation, and I try to stimulate that every time I come in contact with our people. This continual improvement is not just about the senior leadership team or me. It's about each of us. Step up and be counted. Make a difference, regardless of your job description or job title, and our company is going to be wildly successful, and we're going to make dreams come true for our investors, employees, and other stakeholders. I tell our people, 'It's a fairly simple formula, if we do these things well, we will grow. Through growth, there will be great new jobs, promotions, and opportunities to lead. For you, there's going to be growth. There will be promotions and opportunities to lead.' That's pretty darn exciting. That's why we all get up in the morning."

Get Outside Yourself

"One of the greatest things we can do during our time on earth is to be a part of something bigger than ourselves, whether it's a corporation, a town, an organization, or a charity. If you can make a difference in the group of people you like and enjoy being around, you're going to have a great deal of gratitude and satisfaction about your life. That realization inspires people to go the extra mile."

Challenge Tradition

"Leadership is about courage, and part of that courage is the courage to evolve. It's the courage to allow someone to challenge you, because he or she sees a better way. My mother was unorthodox for the times, and her strong belief system worked for her. I think it's unorthodox today to challenge the way things have always been done, to face down conventional wisdom in a way that moves the ball forward. That's what I'm constantly challenging people to do.

"If you love your business today and choose not to change it constantly and update it, then five years from today, you're not going to like it very much. You have to challenge yourself to face reality and deal with that reality in a rapidly changing business environment. I've been lucky enough to be surrounded by great people, and I've been lucky enough or smart enough to get out of their way."

Build a Dream Team

"Surround yourself with the best and the brightest, as I have, and you can accomplish anything. Put a lot of attention and time into making sure you have the right people in the right jobs. Give them the tools they need to succeed, and then you have to be comfortable delegating, allowing them to go out and do their jobs. Give them the latitude they need to get the job done, holding them accountable for the results. It's all part of a performance culture.

"Speaking of accountable people, I love to read biographies of great leaders. Leaders such as Theodore Roosevelt, Winston Churchill, and Abraham Lincoln inspire me. Some historians say Lincoln was the least-qualified president to ever enter the White House, but he had an unlimited capacity to grow and to learn, and he never gave up or lost his sense of humor. There are some wonderful lessons in history, and they apply today in a very real way."

Keith's Attitude Check

When Mark speaks, his vision resonates powerfully through what he says, how he says it, and his body language shows it. He believes it, practices it, and lives it, and that's why he's compelling and motivating. His message comes from his very pores. With that kind of conviction, he has become driven by a message, leading others to reach for and attain higher and higher goals.

He proves through his day-to-day dealings with people that the status quo is just a beginning, not an end. It's a platform to stand on, while you look for ways to improve yourself, your business, your attitude, and your methods of dealing with others. He surrounds himself with good people and then turns them loose to find ways to improve their own jobs and the company, because if you're not improving, you're falling behind.

Mark holds the unshakable belief that anything is possible, and therefore he doesn't put limits on himself or his team. During the compilation of this book, I watched Mark's career soar even higher, as he rose from president and CEO of Galileo International, a division of Cendant Corporation, to become the president and COO of Equifax, Inc., a S&P Fortune 500 Company, responsible for leading operations and management of offices in North America, Latin America, and Europe.

He walks the walk, steps up to the plate, takes on more and more responsibility, and reaps the rewards and benefits. At the same time, his employees also learn, grow, and progress, because of his philosophy of setting stretch goals. He gives people the tools and latitude to succeed, holding them accountable for results and knowing when to get out of the way.

The magic of belief lives in him and shows in everything he accomplishes, and he passes that magic to all with whom he has contact.

You Must Believe It to Achieve It

I don't know who was the first person to say, "If you can believe it, you can achieve it," but these words echo through the hearts of many children today, and as a result, the children who believe they can go to college "miraculously" go to college. The ones who think they don't have a chance, find their negative beliefs fulfilled, as well, and that's truly unfortunate.

"People have power when people think they have power," said William Wyche Fowler, an American politician. Mark Miller thinks he has power. He has an unwavering belief that he can do anything, and therefore, he can.

When you have an attitude of belief, you cannot be swayed from your goal. The formula of "belief equals success" is so simple that people sometimes overlook it. If you believe in something, though, your whole attitude takes on that belief.

When you were an infant, for example, chances are you saw other people walking, so you innately believed you could walk, too. As a result, you pulled yourself up on a table leg or a chair leg, and you were rewarded with cheers from your parents. You kept pulling yourself up, day after day, until the muscles in your legs developed. You gained balance, strength, and confidence, and one day you let go of that chair leg and took your first steps. After that, you kept taking one or two steps at a time, and even though you fell down, you kept getting up, until you mastered the skill of walking. Children have the power of belief. Why should we lose it when we get older? We don't. It's there. You just have to find it in yourself.

Find your belief. Can it be that simple? Yes, it is. Think about it. If you want to climb a mountain, even though you have never before done anything so athletic, the desire begins with the belief that you can do it. Once you believe you can do it, you prepare yourself. You read books on how to climb mountains. You acquire the necessary equipment. You train with skilled people. You pick a good team to assist you, and in the end, you climb that mountain.

If you believe you can be a great leader, you surround yourself with the right people, you read about and follow the leadership qualities of other great leaders, and you take the action needed to become a great leader. Soon you are the leader you believed you could be.

Be Positive

Avoid thinking negative thoughts that hold you back. Instead, create a positive action plan, one based on the belief that you can meet your goals. Self-doubt, frustration, fears, and anger serve as barriers to your goals. Every time you have a negative thought, say, "Cancel that thought," and replace it with a positive one.

Let's say you want to expand your company into other states. Write down your goal as if it is already under way, because in truth it is. Keep it simple, but specific. Imbed a deadline in it. Look at it. Read it. Internalize it. Keep the written goal in your wallet, so you can look at it dozens of times a day.

Your goal might be as simple as this: "I open four new stores in four other states by September 30."

Human nature sometimes works against us, and you might have the urge to look at your written goal and think, "Sure, I'd like to expand my company into four other states by September, but I'll never be able to supply all those stores with merchandise." When a negative thought like that pops into your mind, say, "Cancel that thought! The way to supply all those stores will become clear to me by the time I need to know."

The next time you get a negative thought, an effective way to eliminate it is to say something positive out loud. You can't hang onto a thought while you are speaking. Try this exercise: Take a moment and count to 10 silently to yourself, and let's assume that's your thought. Now before getting to 10 shout out loud I love my family and attitude is everything. Notice that you are no longer focused on counting to 10. The next time you find yourself thinking bad thoughts, say something positive out loud. By doing this, you are reprogramming your mind and changing your thoughts, which are the two key factors in changing your beliefs.

As a leader, if you want better results, start with your programming, the things you read, the things you watch on television, the things you say, and what others say to you. Your programming creates your belief and your belief creates your attitude.

Use positive thoughts, trust in your belief, and you can achieve anything.

ATTITUDE ACTION PLAN

- What are your beliefs? Do they stem from your childhood, or did you create them yourself? How can you make them stronger and more rewarding?

- What beliefs do you want to instill in your children, your coworkers, your employees, or your fellow members of an organization? What messages do you give them? How can you improve on those messages?

- Do you demonstrate your beliefs through your actions? Do you believe you can improve your situation, job, or organization? Do you find ways to continually improve?

- If you find that you have negative beliefs, what is your action plan for turning them into positive, self-fulfilling ones?

- Have you surrounded yourself with people who are capable and willing to grow and reach for more, every day? Do you stay out of their way and let them do their job and constantly improve themselves and the company?

- What message would you like to see every day, that would empower you and remind you to believe in the magic of belief? Write it down and study it. Post it on your mirror and on your desk and put a copy in your wallet.

Brief Biography

Mark E. Miller is president and chief operating officer of Equifax, Inc. He was named to this position in June 2002. He is responsible for leading operations with the management of North America, Latin America, Europe, Direct to Consumer and Technology reporting to him.

Since October 2001, Mr. Miller served as president and chief executive officer of Galileo International, a division of Cendant Corporation, Parsippany, New Jersey, and from January 2001 until October 2001, he was president and chief operating officer of Cendant's Travel Division. Previously, Mr. Miller served as president and chief operating officer of Avis Rent a Car from June 1999 until January 2001, and from 1997 until June 1999, he was president and chief executive officer of PHH Arval, a vehicle management company, and Wright Express. Before that, from 1994 until 1997, he was president of General Electric Capital Financial, Salt Lake City, Utah, and held sales management positions with American Express Company, Washington, DC, from 1984 until 1994. He began his career with Eastern Airlines in Atlanta, Georgia, in 1982.

Mr. Miller earned a bachelor of science degree in business administration in 1982 from Jacksonville State University.

What Are Your Bloodstream Beliefs?

Robert D. Bates, President
Jefferson Pilot Benefit Partners

Jawaharlal Nehru pointed out that "there is only one thing that remains to us, that cannot be taken away: to act with courage and dignity and to stick to the ideals that give meaning to your life." Ideal is defined as "a standard of excellence; an ultimate objective or aim of endeavor." Bob Bates' leadership is founded on a bedrock of ideals that are seamlessly integrated into how he operates. Reflect on what your "Bloodstream Beliefs" are while reading this interview with Bob.

"One of the keys to effective leadership is operating with what I call 'Bloodstream Beliefs,'" explained Bob Bates. "It's not just that we believe in these values, they're in our blood. We can't not do them because they're so central to who we are. These Bloodstream Beliefs are the basic tenets by which we work. We don't just 'mouth' them, we live them.

"One of our primary Bloodstream Beliefs is the concept of 'fair play.' I grew up in a small town of 6,000 people and I worked from the time I was young. One of my favorite jobs was being a golf caddy because it gave me an opportunity to see all kinds of people in action. I just had a penchant for observing people.

"I realized at an early age that the people I respected had a sense of fair play. They didn't hedge on the rules, they honored them. They didn't cover up mistakes so they could win; they freely admitted their mistakes because they knew the difference between right and wrong.

"I think that's one of the reasons our company has been so successful. Our sense of fair play means we do what's right, even it that's not always what's easiest or most expedient. Integrity starts with 'right thinking,' and we choose to do what's right because that's what we stand for."

Superstars Don't Win Games

"Growing up, I played a lot of sports. I was fortunate to be selected captain of my football, basketball, and baseball teams, and another lesson I learned early on is that superstars don't win games. They may win individual scoring awards—but it's the TEAM that wins the game. In sports, you find out firsthand that teamwork is not just an abstract concept, it's a reality. You can have a great quarterback, but if the linemen don't protect him, he's going to get sacked. You can have a great running back, but if his teammates don't block for him, he'll be thrown for a loss. You see this again and again in pro sports. A team will lose its star player due to an injury and they'll actually play better without him. As a captain, I learned that I could use my leadership skills to set the group up for success but they're the ones who actually deliver the results.

"I've carried that concept into our organization. Everyone in our company knows he or she plays an important role in our success. A Bloodstream Belief is that every employee is valued and appreciated. One of the ways we show that belief is to reach out to each other and give 'encouraging words.' I think that's one of the reasons we have such amazing employee loyalty. We have 6 percent turnover in an industry that averages more than 20 percent turnover."

The Double-Up Philosophy

"Years ago, I read a book that had a profound influence on my life. You know how sometimes the right word at the right time can give you perfect clarity about what needs to be done? I was facing a particularly demanding situation, and Napoleon Hill's *Think and Grow Rich* did that for me. He has a section that addresses how to deal with challenges, and he states that (I'm paraphrasing) 'In any great endeavor, there will be a bleak point in time in which you are tempted to give up because you're so disappointed and exhausted . . . and that's the exact point in time in which you need to redouble your efforts to see things through.' He said that many people stop only steps away from victory, and that if they can just intensify their resolve and persevere through their dark night of the soul, they can prevail.

"Well, I took that message to heart," said Bates. "It gave me courage to persevere back when we were starting this now-$800-million company from scratch, and it gives us the courage to keep fighting the good fight when our company faces daunting circumstances or is in the midst of radical change."

Discipline Is Not a Four-Letter Word

"My mother and father were both hard workers and they taught me how rewarding it can be to do a job well," Bates continued. "Instead of shying away from hard work, I learned to welcome it. Another of our Bloodstream Beliefs is that discipline—doing what needs to be done whether we want to or not—is the attitude for getting results.

"I believe that discipline is the antidote to dysfunction. If we're to operate optimally, we need to be in top shape. That's why I eat right, get my rest, and exercise regularly (every morning at 5 A.M.—yikes). The saying that 'Fatigue makes a coward of all of us' is true. I don't particularly like getting up at 5 A.M. to exercise, but I do it because I know I will not be able to be my best or work my hardest if I don't."

The Best Cost-Reduction Program Is Not Cutting Back on Customer Care

"Another of our Bloodstream Beliefs is to take first-class care of our customers. The importance of this was demonstrated on my first trip to Hawaii. After a five-hour flight from the mainland and a long drive to our destination hotel, we finally arrived. As we walked into the lobby, we were intercepted by a smiling hostess who handed each of us a glass of fresh-squeezed orange juice after draping a fragrant flower lei around our neck. It was such a simple thing, but it had a profound effect on me. My tired, frustrated state of mind was instantly replaced by a sunny disposition. Her aloha spirit and positive attitude infused me and I was motivated to respond in kind. I still remember that moment of grace as if it had happened yesterday.

"We strive to give that same quality of service to our customers. One of my favorite things to do is to walk through our call center and watch our employees handle calls—because they're all smiling. That's one of the things we look for when we're hiring people—do they have a warm, genuine smile and the right attitude?

"I was walking through the other day when a pleased-as-punch employee stopped me to tell me about a positive response she'd just received. She had answered the customer's questions and resolved the situation in minutes. The customer was quiet for a few seconds and then asked, 'Did you feel that?' Puzzled, the employee asked, 'Feel what?' 'The hug I just gave you,' the satisfied customer replied. Now that's First-Class service.

"I shudder when I read in the newspaper that a company is laying off 10 percent of its service staff because it's going through tough times. The problem is, the volume of work is staying the same but now it's being handled by fewer employees. This is a formula for disaster. Those employees will be overloaded and overwhelmed—and frustrated, unhappy employees cannot give the quality of service you want.

"We have found that the best cost-reduction program is giving quality customer service. Our data and track record prove this. Taking good care of the customer reduces errors and decreases the number of complaints. Simply said, our customers don't have to call or write back to correct mistakes that shouldn't have been made in the first place. As the saying goes, 'If you don't have time to do it right the first time, when are you going to have time to do it over again?' Our commitment to getting it right the first time is a point of pride with us, and it positively impacts our bottom line on a daily basis.

"I think people want to be proud of where they work, and our policy, our Bloodstream Belief, of doing things right the first time is something they can support. It goes back to our belief in fair play. We find that by giving our customers what they want, they give us what we want."

Keith's Attitude Check

When you get right down to it, Bloodstream Beliefs are simply about doing the right thing, regardless. I was working at IBM when the first major downsize in the company's 65-year history occurred. Were we frightened? Worried? Angry? Of course we were, but I take my hat off to IBM because the company did its best to communicate to every employee why this business decision had to be made. Our leaders met with us to reiterate that we were valued and to explain in detail how they were going to support us by retraining us for other opportunities inside and outside the company.

The company helped us to adjust to the reality that there was life after IBM by paying for us to work with an outplacement consulting firm. My outplacement counselor helped me develop the business plan I still use today. My experience with IBM through this tumultuous time demonstrated that it's possible for leaders to transcend tough times and still maintain integrity as long as they practice the values that cause their employees (or former employees) to continue to hold them in high regard.

What Kind of Leader Are You?

I've personally been the beneficiary of Bob's first-rate customer service on more than one occasion. I met Bob for the first time when I traveled to Omaha to speak before a group of his sales managers. After I'd given my presentation, Bob came up to congratulate me on doing a fine job and mentioned he would like to stay in touch.

About a week later, a handwritten thank-you card arrived in the mail. I was impressed. Many leaders at that level would delegate that task or not do it all. Highly placed executives juggle dozens of million-dollar decisions on a daily basis. Who has the time to write a personal note? Well, Bob does. It's just another example of his thoughtfulness. Two months later, I was invited back, this time to speak to the entire company. Guess what? Bob followed up with another handwritten thank-you note.

When I called to thank him in person, he was out of his office, however, his assistant told me this above-and-beyond thoughtfulness was normal behavior for Bob. She told me, "It's not unusual for employees to come in on a Monday morning and find a voicemail from Bob asking how their son did in his high school football game. If he knows someone has a family member with a health challenge, he'll follow up with a personal phone call to see how they're doing. Each month, he takes employees with a birthday in that month out to lunch as a group to celebrate their special day."

Carmelia Elliott said, "Make yourself a blessing to someone. Your kind smile or pat on the back just might pull someone back from the edge." Bob makes himself a blessing to his employees, and everyone he encounters, on a daily basis. In the midst of his busy, demanding day, he takes time to be kind.

It's easy for multitasking leaders to get caught up in pressing obligations and become irritable or impatient. Sometimes, without really thinking about it, we take out our accumulated tension on the people around us. We walk around with a furrowed brow, narrowed eyes, and clenched jaw. Could we, instead, make a conscious effort to be considerate of others? Could we set aside time, even if it's only 15 minutes a day, to make those personal phone calls or write those handwritten notes to let people know we're thinking of them and are thankful to them? Taking the time to share some "encouraging words," as Bob calls them, might be just what they needed to hear that day to keep them going.

Synergy Beats a Superstar Every Time

Bob brought up an interesting point about how some teams actually perform better without their superstar. You may be thinking, "How can that be?" I've experienced it myself. When a player on a team is supremely gifted, other players often start slacking off their effort.

They may not get the ball as much so they become complacent, or they become reliant on their superstar "carrying" them so they feel they don't have to perform at the top of their game. Sometimes, resentments set in because the superstar gets a disproportionate amount of the attention and credit.

The group dynamics change the instant the superstar gets injured or is taken out of the game for some reason. Now, teammates have to produce. They can no longer afford to be lazy or give partial effort. The responsibility to win is back on their shoulders, and they often respond accordingly. They become reenergized and recommitted to giving their all. They start paying attention and caring again.

Synergy may be defined as "the total effect being greater than the sum of the effects taken independently." In other words, five (basketball), nine (baseball), or eleven (football) players working together will always produce better results than one individual working alone, even if that individual is spectacularly talented.

Do you have a superstar on your team? Do you have someone who outperforms the others in his or her department? Do you have an employee who is so gifted at what he or she does that other coworkers pale in comparison? What do you do to make sure that individual is rewarded for his or her contributions while keeping the emphasis on group effort? What do you do to make sure other team members don't feel undervalued or overlooked? What do you do to make sure your "linemen" (your frontline people) get as much attention and appreciation as your "quarterback" (your managers)?

Are You Playing by the Rules?

Bob talked fondly about his "caddy" days and how he learned to respect the players who honored the rules, even when it added strokes to their score.

Golf has become my favorite hobby these past few years, and I second his observation that you can tell a great deal about people from the way they honor, or don't honor, the rules. You've probably heard people say that how we play golf is a metaphor or reflection of our personality. If you have a quick temper, it's sure to show up when you duck hook your drive into the lagoon. If someone's dishonest, chances are you'll see him giving himself a better lie when his ball lands in the rough. If someone has integrity, he'll politely refuse that mulligan when he accidentally taps his ball off the tee on a practice swing.

I was taken aback one time when I played in a charity tournament with someone who played fast and loose with the rules. I saw this individual kick his ball out from behind a tree when he thought no one was watching. On several holes, he said his score was a double bogey instead of the triple bogey he had actually shot. As we progressed through the 18 holes, his "gimmee" puts got longer and longer until he was giving himself puts that were a good 3 to 4 feet away from the hole.

There's No Such Thing as Part-Time Honesty

You may be thinking, "What's the big deal? It was just a round of golf." However, I could tell the other members of the foursome (myself included) were thinking, "If this guy pulls these type of pranks on the golf course, what types of pranks does he pull in business?"

Honesty can't be turned on and off like a faucet. We can't be honest sometimes and not others. Or, actually, we can be honest sometimes and not others—but no one will trust us. How can they? They won't know when we're telling the truth and when we're not. As German author Friedrich Hebbel said, "Remember: one lie does not cost you one truth, but the truth."

On the other hand, I'm fortunate to have a regular golfing buddy who is scrupulously honest. Even when we're having a relaxed, casual round, even though we've known each other for years and we're good friends, he always plays by the rules. It's just the way he is. As Bob says, when you live your values, you can't not do them.

As you can imagine, I trust this friend implicitly. I have never had any cause to question his honesty because his actions are testimony to the fact that he acts with integrity, no matter what. He has what I call a *truth track record*.

Do You Have a Truth Track Record?

What's your truth track record? Can people count on you to "tell it like it is"? Have you told white lies because you thought it was in the best interests of employees? Hedging the truth, even when done with the best of intentions, often backfires because it means people will forever wonder if we're "spinning" the facts.

The good news is, even if we've been less than honest in the past, we can "come clean." Pull a *mea culpa*. Mea Culpa means "my fault" in Latin. People will often forgive us for past transgressions if we confess and proclaim our intention to do better.

Whether it's in golf or in leadership, we can wipe the slate clean and have a fresh start if we announce to our playing partners or employees that, from now on, they can count on us to play by the rules and tell the truth. They may be skeptical at first and it will take time for them to see from our actions that we mean what we say. However, it is possible for anyone to establish a track record of truth over time if they consistently keep their word, even when it's tempting to do otherwise.

It comes down to this. Do you want to be trusted? Then tell the truth. People may not enjoy hearing it; but they'll give you credit for having the courage and decency to tell it.

ATTITUDE ACTION PLAN

- What is one of your Bloodstream Beliefs?
- What is a value you have that is so integral to who you are, you can't not do it?

- How did you acquire that Bloodstream Belief? Who or what instilled it in you?

- When was the last time you reevaluated your Bloodstream Beliefs? If you were to update them, which value would you add, delete, or change?

- How do you role-model and teach your Bloodstream Beliefs to the people you lead?

- Have you ever been on a team in which the superstar got all the attention? How did that affect the team and your motivation/performance?

- What is one specific thing you do to make sure ALL members of your team get the recognition and appreciation they want and deserve?

- How did it make you feel?

- Did it motivate you to do more business with them?

- What do you do as a leader to inspire your employees to give quality customer service?

- What is one of your favorite service success stories about your organization?

Brief Biography

Robert D. Bates received a BS degree in Electrical Engineering from the University of Missouri. His business career has provided a wide range and depth of experience beginning in the textile industry in 1964 with companies such as Dupont, Roanoke Mills, and Virginia Apparel Corporation. He entered the insurance business in 1972 as an agent with Paul Revere Insurance Company and rose to chief marketing officer and vice president of sales and marketing. He joined Business Men's Assurance Company of America in 1981 as senior vice president of sales, was appointed to the board of directors in 1984, and advanced to executive vice president of insurance operations in 1987.

Mr. Bates joined Guarantee Life Insurance Company in 1989 as president and chief executive officer and was named chairman of the board of directors in November 1990. In December 1999, the Jefferson-Pilot Corporation acquired Guarantee Life. He is now the president of Jefferson Pilot Benefit Partners. Benefit Partners markets ancillary (nonmedical) group insurance products including life, long-term and short-term disability, and dental as well as voluntary employee benefits. He also serves as a member of the Jefferson Pilot Financial Management Committee.

Active throughout his career in industry organizations, Mr. Bates is past chairman, board of directors, Life Insurance Marketing and Research Association (LIMRA); past chairman, Agency Management Training Council (AMTC); past chairman, Life Underwriters Training Council (LUTC); past director, Health Insurance Association of America (HIAA) and secretary, 1996 to 1998; and past director, American Council of Life Insurance (ACLI). He is currently a director of McCarthy Group, Inc., an investment banking company.

Within the community, he has served as chairman, Greater Omaha Chamber of Commerce; chairman, Mid-America Council, Boy Scouts of America; chairman, United Way of the Midlands; and is currently director, Henry Doorly Zoo; trustee, Joslyn Art Museum; a member of the Board of Governors, Ak-Sar-Ben; and member STRATCOM Consultation Committee.

Mr. Bates and his wife, Judy, have a son and daughter and six grandchildren.

Turn Soft Science of
Management into Hard Science

Jean Cohen, Vice President
Ritz Carlton

Jean Cohen reports that hiring employees who find pride in their work is important, and clearly stated goals and procedures keep those employees on track. The combination delivers the powerful punch that keeps her organization performing at its peak.

"One of the toughest challenges facing a leader is in developing pragmatic systems for supervising performance. The ability to reliably produce excellence depends on our ability to turn the soft science of management into a hard science.

"We try to do that at the Ritz Carlton by institutionalizing our daily activities while maintaining a humanistic philosophy. We have systemwide procedures to help us manage our time resources, human resources, and material resources."

A Measure of Success

"Hotels are 24/7 operations, which means we could work 18 hours a day, and it still wouldn't be enough. So many different responsibilities compete for our attention that we've developed a method to objectively assess what's most important, so we can stay focused on our high-payoff priorities.

"We identify the critical success factors of our job annually. We review them with our direct reports to get consensus that they're accurate and in alignment with our organizational goals and values. We then create measurable outcomes and map out the action steps we must take to achieve them. We check our progress every quarter and review our factors and outcomes, to make sure they're still appropriate. For example, during the Gulf War, we needed to adjust our goals to allow for the downturn in the travel industry.

"Having clarity about our goals helps me figure out what projects are truly deserving of my time and attention. A staff member may propose a great idea, but if I see it's going to compromise the achievement of one of our stated goals, I am able to say 'No.' The system holds me accountable and keeps me on track. Having measurable outcomes helps me make objective, instead of subjective, decisions about how I allocate my time and attention. It keeps me from responding impulsively to whatever crosses my desk."

It's a Match

"One of the keys to being a good leader is matching the right person with the right job. Someone can be brilliant; however, that person will underperform if put in the wrong position.

"Once again, Ritz Carlton doesn't leave things to chance. We have a comprehensive program called Talent Plus that identifies each individual's traits, temperament, and talents. We then search for a job in which the required skill sets are a match for that individual's personal profile. Obviously, the system is not foolproof; however, it is right more often than not, and it is rewarding to see people who were struggling start to soar when they're placed in the right position.

"We all have aces and spaces. It makes sense that if you're an extrovert and love working with people, you'll do better in marketing than in accounting. My responsibility as a leader is to help staff members find their true north, their correct positions within the company, so they can shine in their jobs and become top performers. Everyone benefits when that happens."

Service Is Not Servitude

"One of the characteristics we look for in our employees is the understanding that service is not servitude. For example, we want our housekeepers to feel a pride of ownership, to feel 'This is my room.' We don't want workers to think they're relegated to a meaningless job and that cleaning is demoralizing, because that attitude will be reflected in the quality of their work. If you take pride in your work, you never get bored, because you always care about what you're producing and understand how you're contributing.

"Our motto is 'We are ladies and gentlemen serving ladies and gentlemen.' That approach and expectation is true for everyone who works here, which is why we take the selection process so seriously. Every potential employee goes through four to six interviews before being hired. Our housekeepers interview with our general manager and with the head of Rooms, in addition to the director of Housekeeping. Why? We understand housekeepers have a direct impact on our bottom line, because they have direct contact with our guests. We're very careful about who we hire, because we want every associate to feel a sense of ownership about our hotel and its success. It doesn't matter whether you're a dishwasher or the director of marketing, we want you interested in our profit-and-loss statements. We want you committed to making every guest a repeat guest."

Continuous Communication

"We believe one of the keys to consistency is constancy. We have meetings every day for every shift. Each meeting starts with a message from our president. That message is given to every employee in every one of our 50 hotels. Everyone is in the loop. We have 20 basic principles that contribute to delivering five-diamond service, and we review one each day. When we've run through all 20, we start all over again at the beginning. Repeating the basics ad infinitum incorporates them into our attitude and behavior so we follow them automatically, without thinking.

"Next, we share special head's-up reports on VIP arrivals, certain guest preferences, employee celebrations, local news, and so on. It's particularly telling that we both give and receive information in these meetings. Suggestions are constantly solicited on how we can improve our service and our properties. Including everyone in these briefings demonstrates our belief that there is no separation between employees. These daily get-togethers are tangible proof that everyone counts, that we care what each employee thinks, and that we care enough to make sure every employee feels included and informed."

Keith's Attitude Check

I agree with Jean Cohen that if we want something to happen we need to attach a number to it. I learned a long time ago when I was at the IBM sales school that the secret to manifesting goals is to make them measurable. It wasn't enough to say I wanted to increase my sales. I had to decide and write down exactly by what percentage I wanted to increase my sales. It wasn't enough to tell my supervisor I had a good month. I had to be specific about how exactly this month compared to the previous month. I had to state what I did differently to produce that increase.

Only by quantifying our standards can we accurately gauge our progress. Do you have measurable goals for yourself as a leader and systems set in place for your staff to establish measurable goals for themselves? Do you review them regularly, like Jean, to make needed adjustments?

It's about Time

Are you sometimes so overwhelmed by all your work responsibilities that you don't know where to start?

A friend introduced me to the concept of triage. If you've ever watched the TV dramas *M*A*S*H* or *ER*, you may be familiar with the concept of triage, but it was new to me, especially in relation to business. Simply put, triage is the sorting and allocation of treatment to patients (especially battle and disaster victims) according to a system of priorities designed to maximize the number of survivors.

If the emergency room is swamped with patients, the staff does a quick triage to assess the relative severity of each patient's condition, to determine who requires the most immediate care, who should be attended to first, second, third, and so on. Ideally, everyone would get immediate care, but in the real world, especially if you're short staffed, that is not always possible. That's why you hear complaints from people who go to the emergency room when their situations are less than urgent. If you go into the emergency room with a cut on your hand, you may have to wait for treatment while others get care for breathing problems, heart attacks, strokes, and other life-threatening conditions, even if they arrive after you.

Similarly, when we're swamped with priorities, we should also do a quick triage to assess the relative importance of our various demands, so we can decide what to attend to first, second, and third. The key, as Jean demonstrated, is to (1) identify our critical success factors, (2) compare all the tasks that are competing for our attention to those success factors, (3) weed out the tasks that are not urgent or not in alignment with our success factors, and (4) prioritize the remaining tasks, so we know what to do and in what order.

When we plan our day, we take our plans one step further and prioritize, giving each task an A, B, or C priority based on urgency as well as relationship to our overall goals. Prioritizing on paper helps us clearly see that many of our tasks can be put off, passed off, or dropped off, especially those that are of the lowest priority.

Everything on our two-page To Do list seems urgent, until we take a moment to think about each task. Many of us work in organizations that have been forced to downsize, so we're perpetually short-staffed, but most of us are not without some help. By triaging our tasks, we determine which responsibilities can be delegated, which can be delayed, which can be done only by us, and which don't really need to be done at all. This system of triage helps us be as effective as possible, despite a heavy workload. It saves us much frustration and time.

Do You Triage Your Time?

Want an example of someone who's good at triaging his time? A friend was suffering from a terrible toothache and went to her dentist, who extracted the troublesome tooth. Later that afternoon, she received a call from her dentist. Her heart sank because she thought the only reason he would be calling was to deliver bad news. Perhaps he had missed part of the tooth or discovered that further surgery was required.

Instead, Dr. Shimakawa asked solicitously, "How are you doing? Are you feeling any discomfort?" He was making a courtesy call! The only reason he had phoned was to follow up and make sure she was doing okay. My friend was so impressed by the dentist's rare display of above-and-beyond customer service that she asked what had prompted him to call. He explained, "Our goal is to treat our patients so well, they want to come back, and they want to recommend us to their friends. I found that I could fill my waiting room with the best magazines, a big television, and a Nintendo; I could play soothing music; I could buy the latest high-tech equipment and newest computer billing programs, but those things weren't what our clients really wanted. They wanted to know we cared about them as an individual, that they weren't just my 10 o'clock appointment or the patient in Room Three.

"My staff and I agreed that the best way we could get across the message that we care was to set aside a half hour at the end of every day and personally call the patients who had treatment that day. Instead of trying to jam in more appointments, I use that time to connect with my patients. The feedback has been tremendous, because what we do is so rare. Those 30 minutes a day on the phone do more to produce repeat business than any other investment we make. It has become a high-pay-off priority."

What a clear example of a leader who invested the time to figure out the best use of his time! Many of you are familiar with the Pareto Principle, or the 80/20 Rule that states that 80 percent of the value comes from 20 percent of the items or activities. Have you identified your 20 percent? Is there one particular activity you do as a leader that has exponential payoff? What is that?

Is Service a Privilege or a Pain?

How do you instill in your team the philosophy that serving others is a privilege and a pleasure? I worked in a restaurant while I was going to school, and my grandmother instilled in me the pride of ownership. It didn't matter if I was busing tables or cleaning the floor; she demanded that I do the job well. Sloppiness was simply not an option.

That lesson has stuck with me. I can't comprehend the notion of slacking off and doing a halfhearted job in the hope no one will notice or care. It's said that character is reflected in how we behave when no one is watching. What my grandmother taught me is that excellence is what we do all the time, not just when someone's watching. We do it because we want to be excellent. She taught me that doing a high quality job of serving others is an opportunity to make a difference. It's not something to be ashamed of; it's something to welcome.

Do you have a screening process to determine if potential employees have a service attitude? When you interview people, do you ask open-ended questions about how they feel about serving others? Their answers are often quite revealing and can help you determine whether they will be intrinsically motivated to do their best, no matter what.

Communicate, Communicate, Communicate

It always amazes me when I ask leaders how often they meet with their employees, and some reply, "We're too busy to have meetings." Yikes! It reminds me of the adage, "If we don't have time to do it right the first time, when are we going to have time to do it over again?" I point out that if they don't take the time for meetings up front, they're going to take more time to correct the mistakes and misunderstandings that happen because things weren't clarified and communicated correctly from the beginning.

Jean explained the commitment her organization has toward hosting meetings every day for every shift. Instead of being dissuaded by the logistical complications such meetings present, the executives at Ritz Carlton understand that daily meetings are time, money, and effort well spent. Instead of just saying that consistency is important, instead of just saying that communication is important, they put their meetings where their mouths are. They understand that frequent, regularly scheduled briefings set up two-way communication, so there is a give-and-take of information. Some organizations talk about staying connected; this organization does it from the top down and the bottom up. Their daily meetings are proof that the organization lives its values and practices what it preaches.

I was told years ago three of the strongest words in the world to motivate anybody are "I love you," and that four of the strongest words to motivate anybody are "I love you, too," and five of the strongest words to motivate anybody are "I am proud of you." As an effective leader, you can't be hesitant to express words that have been proven to motivate.

ATTITUDE ACTION PLAN

■ Do you have systemwide procedures to manage your time, human, and material resources?

■ What is an example of one pragmatic way you turn the soft science of management into a hard science?

■ What are three critical success factors of your position?

■ How do you review these critical success factors by yourself and with direct reports to make sure they're accurate and in alignment with organizational goals and values?

■ Do you have measurable goals and specific action steps to achieve them?

■ When you have many different responsibilities competing for your attention, how do you triage your time and decide what to attend to first?

■ Have you identified your high-payoff priorities?

■ Have you set up a system to make sure you make time for your high-payoff priorities, no matter what?

■ How would you describe your attitude about service?

■ How have you established a corporate culture in which employees provide high quality service willingly and voluntarily?

■ What is one specific thing you do and/or your organization does to turn every customer into a repeat customer?

■ Do you have a special selection process to help you hire employees who will be intrinsically motivated to do their best?

■ How often do you hold meetings with your staff? How are those meetings scheduled and structured?

■ If you don't meet frequently with your team, why not? What are the deterrents and what are the consequences?

■ Have you set up two-way communication within your organization or department?

Brief Biography

Jean Cohen is the regional vice president for the Ritz-Carlton Hotel Company, LLC. She oversees 13 luxury hotels located in major cities throughout the East Coast and Midwest.

Her responsibilities include Ritz-Carlton hotels in Boston, Cleveland, Dearborn, Pentagon City (Arlington, Virginia), Philadelphia, St. Louis, Tysons Corner (McLean, Virginia), New York City, Baltimore, and Washington, D.C.

A hotel executive with nearly 25 years of hospitality-industry experience, she most recently served as general manager of the Marriott Marquis Hotel in New York City's Times Square. Among her other positions, Jean Cohen was general manager of the American Automobile Association (AAA) five-diamond-rated Ritz-Carlton, New York, on Central Park South. She worked for Marriott International for more than a decade.

Jean Cohen has held positions on the boards of the Hotel Association of New York City and Mayor Rudolph Guiliani's Midtown Committee. She is a member of La Chaine des Rotisseurs and NYC and Company.

A graduate of Northeastern University with a degree in accounting and finance, Jean Cohen holds a master's degree from Harvard University in business.

A native of Boston, Massachusetts, Cohen currently resides in Manhattan with her husband, Steven Cohen.

Excellence Is Not an Act—It's a Habit

Nido Qubein, Chairman
Great Harvest Bread Company

Like many leaders, Nido Qubein (pronounced *Needo Coo-bane*) learned from a valuable role model at an early age. His father, an import/export merchant, died when Qubein was 6 years old, and his mother reared him, instilled valuable lessons in him, and modeled the life of common sense and perseverance. Qubein grew up in the Middle East and came to America at the age of 17 with no knowledge of English, no contacts, and only 50 dollars in his pocket. He chose to attend Mount Olive College, a Baptist school in Eastern North Carolina, because its name was similar to the biblical Mount of Olives.

"My mother had only a fourth-grade education, but she had a PhD in disciplined common sense. She stayed up day and night to work hard to feed us, clothe us, and instill in us values for living and principles for life. Ever since I was a little boy, I heard my mother say things like, 'If you want to be a great man, you must first work side-by-side with great people. Who you spend time with is precisely who you become, so pick your friends carefully.'

"Thanks to my mother's timeless wisdom, I discovered at an early age that good habits are hard to develop and easy to live with, and bad habits are easy to develop, but hard to live with. I discovered that for the timid, change is frightening; for the comfortable, change is threatening; for the confident, change is opportunity. After much observation, I concluded that the source of confidence is competence, and the only way to develop competence is to habitually do more of the activities that move us closer to our goals, and to habitually eliminate the activities that keep us from getting closer to our goals."

Live and Lead with Intentional Congruence

"The word success can be defined in one word, *balance*. When we are spiritually, mentally, socially, physically, intellectually, and economically balanced, we are successful. To attain balance, we must daily engage in activities that are intentionally congruent. If life is the base of our jigsaw puzzle, then we want to make sure all the pieces of that puzzle fit into it synergistically, so the total sum of our efforts is truly a sparkling body of efficiency, effectiveness, and contribution.

"Life is a phenomenal opportunity for us to do good, be good, do more, and have more, so we can give more. It matters to me that I contribute something of measure to the world and to the people I come in touch with—my family, my community, and my professional associates. I don't live to be successful; I live to be significant."

Give for the Giving, Not for the Getting

"I worked 10 hours a day to help pay my way through college. At the end of my second year, the college president came up to me and said, 'Nido, I know you think you are paying your way through school, but the truth is, there is a chasm between the money you owe the school and the money being paid the school. You might like to know that a doctor in a neighboring city has been picking up your tab.'

"I asked to meet the doctor, so I could thank him or her for the enormous kindness and generosity. The college president told me, 'That's what makes this extraordinary. The doctor wishes to remain anonymous.'

"I went back to my dorm and cried my eyes out. That day I made a commitment to God. You see, we make decisions with our brains, but we make commitments with our hearts. That's why commitments are longer lasting and harder to break. I made a commitment that some day I would do something worthwhile; I, too, would start a scholarship fund to help other people the way I had been helped. To this day, I do not know who that doctor was, but his or her actions inspired me to found a scholarship program that has allowed us to give more than 500 young people an opportunity to receive a college education."

Investment in People—Money Well Spent

"The most significant part of my existence other than my family, my faith, and my friends, is that scholarship foundation that we began in the early 1970s. We've given more than two million dollars to deserving young people. There is nothing you get out of that, except the satisfaction of knowing it matters that you live, it matters that you work, it matters that you achieve, because you can turn right around and do something good with it.

"Service to others is what drives me. I've discovered that the more you give, the more you get—as long as you don't give merely so you will get. The Scottish theologian, William Barclay, said, 'Always give without remembering; always receive without forgetting.' If we could live our lives that way, we would become stewards of all that is good—we become candleholders and candle lighters."

Leaders as Candle Lighters

"My housemother in college was a candle lighter in my life. The woman was more than 65 years old, and she had no financial means other than $100 a month from her Social Security check and an equal amount from the college. This 'mother-in-residence' enriched our lives just by giving us an opportunity to be in her presence. I could talk to her about anything, because she was such a good listener.

"When I was a junior in college, I saved $350, thinking it would be enough to buy a car. Much to my disappointment, the cheapest working car I could find cost $700. I told my housemother about it, and I said I guessed I was going to have to work even longer to get enough money to afford a car.

"The following month, I got my bank statement. Lo and behold, my balance was not $350 as I thought, but $700. I thought, 'Man, I love this country. The bankers don't know how to add.' Then it dawned on me. Could she? Would she? Did she?

"I ran to ask my dorm mother if she had put the money in my account. I'll never forget what she said. 'I've decided it is much better to invest my money in the life of a budding young man, than it is to park it in my savings account.'

"Stories like these do not just influence our behavior; stories like these affect, microcosmically, the very heart of who we are and what we stand for. They mold us, so our mission to serve becomes so subconscious that we do it without focusing on it. Serving becomes an integral part of who we are."

Ethical Leadership Makes a Difference

"Sometimes, people ask me if the attitude that 'leadership is an opportunity to serve' is becoming increasingly rare. Cynics read about the scandalous behavior of some of our nation's CEOs and say it proves that power corrupts. Skeptics conclude that the majority of our leaders have become arrogant, greedy, and out for themselves.

"I don't believe that at all. I surround myself with leaders who believe wholeheartedly in what I just spoke about. Let me give you an analogy. The only airplanes you ever hear about are the ones that crash. You don't hear about the thousands of airplanes that take off and land safely every day. It's the same with business. Ethical leadership may not be romantic. It may not make good editorial copy to talk about the millions, or at least the thousands, of leaders engaged in wholesome, integrity-based business every day. We talk about the headliners who are morally bankrupt, but there is an enormous body of leaders who really want to make our world a better place in which to work and live."

Leaders Preach What They Practice

"We've all heard the saying, 'Pretty is as pretty does.' Well, that talks about external beauty, and I preach the exact opposite of that. I tell my two daughters, 'Pretty does as pretty is.' I ask a simple question about leadership, 'Which comes first, the doing state or the being state?' I submit that you are, therefore you do—not you do, therefore you are. We have to practice what we preach, yes, but more importantly, we have to preach what we practice.

"Mother Teresa embodied this concept. She was wholeheartedly invested in her work. She didn't try to be a leader, she simply was. She sought to do nothing but good, and ultimately will be remembered for generations to come as a person who changed the world for the better."

Leaders Have Healthy Egos

"Mother Teresa didn't do what she did to be noticed or recognized. She modeled a leader with healthy self-esteem. Leaders need to have positive self-esteem, because when you feel good about yourself, you want to enhance yourself. When you're confident, you seek to enrich your soul, heart, and brain, so you can do and be your best. Leaders need a strong sense of self, so they can stand the test of time and survive adversity.

"Ego is different from self-esteem. If ego means that when God created us he created someone intelligent, and with this intelligence, we have a duty and responsibility to make things better, then that ego is serving a higher purpose. If ego means we do what we do so other people will notice us, it reflects immaturity. If we put ourselves in leadership positions or try to make a pile of money to prove we are special, that attitude is unhealthy. Why do some people who make a million dollars a year wonder, 'If I'm so darn successful, how come I'm so darn miserable?'

"Are we seeking happiness or fulfillment? Happiness is to fulfillment as chat rooms are to chats. Happiness is to fulfillment as virtual reality is to reality. I want the real thing. I want reality, and I want my chats face to face. Fulfillment is not based on accumulating or acquiring; it is based on being productive, adding value, serving, and making a difference. We don't get happiness by having something. We get happiness by becoming something."

Leadership Is Not about Numbers

"When we talk of successful leaders, we sometimes miss the point. If you asked Donald Trump what success is, he might say, 'Making a lot of money.' If you asked Ted Turner what success is, he might tell you it's building a media empire. If you asked Hank Aaron what success is, he might say beating the record of Babe Ruth. If you asked Mother Teresa, she would probably have said, 'Feeding the hungry, tending the sick, and clothing the cold in the streets of Calcutta.'

"Successful leadership is not transactional leadership. It is not the numbers we achieve at the end of the quarter in a public company. It is not how many employees we have. It is not how many products we invent. All of those things are transactional. To me, what really matters is to transcend transactional leadership to pursue transformational leadership. Transformational leadership speaks for the lives we touch, the people we grow, the environments we nurture. When we have all of that, we have a state of being, and that state of being somehow, some way, creates for us the state of doing.

"Leadership is not about managing a process according to standards and plans; it's about being someone who inspires and grows people. That's the number-one characteristic for being a good leader: being other oriented."

Knowledge Alone Is Not Power

"Every single day, before I go to sleep, I ask myself, 'What did I learn today that I did not know yesterday?' We have to become better tomorrow than we are today, just to stay even. As I express it to my audiences, 'If you are as good today as you were a year ago, you are worse off.'

"We might be walking, talking encyclopedias, but good leaders that would not make. Knowledge is like food in the grocery store. It does not become useful to us intellectually and emotionally until we cook it, eat it, digest it, and it breaks down and enters our bloodstream. Only when we absorb knowledge, digest it, understand it, learn it, and act upon it does it become nutritious to our ongoing growth as a leader."

I Can See Clearly Now

"In his later years, retail entrepreneur J. C. Penney said, 'My eyesight may be dimming, but my vision has never been greater.' As leaders, we must have a clear vision of who we are, what we want to become, and how we plan to get there. Clarity of vision means asking ourselves if we're pursuing a course of action that is leading us to a destination that is consistent with our values. To find clarity as an individual, we ask from a personal perspective, 'Who am I, and what matters to me? What do I want to accomplish, and why is that important to me? Are my answers to these questions in balance physically, mentally, spiritually, and economically? If I were able to achieve Utopia, why would that matter? What piece of it would I value the most?'

"As an organization, we must ask, 'Who are we? What matters to our company? What do we want to accomplish, and how does that help our company survive and thrive? Are our answers to these questions in balance physically, mentally, spiritually, and economically?'"

Hard Work, without Smart Work, Doesn't Work

"Being willing to work hard is the equivalent to being willing to breathe oxygen, so you can survive. It is like being willing to eat food every day, so you can sustain yourself physically. Working hard, in and of itself, is never sufficient. Some people work diligently, but their absence of clarity and vision means their hard work doesn't produce maximum achievement, or even above-average performance. Some people may clock 40 hours a week, but if you factor in all the unproductive events of the day, such as chatting with friends, holding or attending ineffective meetings, reading and answering personal e-mail, and the like, those people might actually be working only 20 hours.

"The happiest people in the world are the ones who are most productive, the ones who get the most done. The best leaders help their employees improve efficiency by increasing their knowledge, skill level, and thinking ability through training. We can't just expect employees to become geniuses by telling them to become so; we have to train them how to act like geniuses. It's naïve to believe that by simply lecturing people, they can learn skills.

"We live our lives and do our work at one of three different levels: the disciplined level, the causal level, or the sloppy level. If we examine dynamic leaders in life, whether they are captains of industry or captains of the armed forces, we find they are highly disciplined. We want our employees to be highly disciplined, so they must be highly trained. We can't adhere to a 'Let's do such and such and see what happens' approach; we must establish a clear vision, apply a thought strategy, and provide practical systems.

"Doing those things develops employees' minds and gives them an intellectual technology that allows them to have more insight and impact. Employees will be able to look at problems and solve them faster, so they can get from Point A to Point B more quickly and with better results. The practice helps them operate at maximum efficiency, what I call consistent execution."

Hire the Best—Keep Only the Best

"One of the biggest challenges facing leaders is dealing with employees who are not operating effectively, executing consistently, or adding value. This confrontation can be avoided to some degree by (1) hiring the best people; (2) developing people so they remain the best; (3) conducting regular performance appraisals to gauge how people are measurably contributing to the organization; and (4) monitoring, directing, correcting, and counseling people on how to better contribute to the organization.

"If, after all this, a person doesn't cut it, we must fairly and squarely find a way to let the person go. The least we owe any person is the truth. It will be better for the organization, but it will also be better for that employee, because trying to fit people in where they don't belong is not doing them any favors."

Balance Gratitude and Growth

"The best leaders lose themselves in worthwhile endeavors. They have a clear definition of why they live, why they work, and why they serve. They are driven, not merely by goals or tasks, but also by a consuming desire to contribute. They are not content to be satisfied with mediocrity. They are appreciative of the opportunities they're given, and they express their gratitude for those opportunities by giving back. In fact, they're highly aware of the blessings in their life and actively acknowledge and honor them.

"There is an interesting dynamic, a positive tension, between always trying to improve and being content with our current circumstances. On the one hand, leaders are always trying to polish, innovate, and become better. On the other hand, they need to be grateful for all that's right with their lives, instead of being constantly needy or greedy. In striving to be more, it's important not to overlook what we already have. The way to maintain a healthy balance between gratitude and growth is to count our blessings daily and then multiply them by perpetuating them for others.

"I have been blessed to know good people. I have been blessed to have a good mind. I have been blessed to have a healthy body. I have been blessed to live in America. I acknowledge that I often drink from wells I did not dig. I often warm myself from fires I did not build. I travel across bridges I did not construct.

"My life's hope is that, like others have done before me, I can somehow contribute to digging wells that quench the thirst of those in need; that I can build fires of kindness, so others can warm themselves from the flames of my stewardship; and that I can construct bridges, so others can travel across the chasms of life more successfully and fruitfully."

Keith's Attitude Check

Were you fortunate enough to have a parent with a PhD in common sense? As I've shared in other chapters, my mother and grandmother instilled in me the attitude that I could do anything and be anything I wanted, if I was willing to work hard enough and persevere through adversity. Even though I had to overcome stuttering when I was young, and although I faced health challenges during college, the adults who led me "lit my candle" at an early age and fanned the flames of my desire and determination to be the best I could be.

I was fortunate to have caring adults in my childhood who started me on the path to healthy habits. As Ralph Waldo Emerson said, "We are all looking for someone who will make us do what we can." Who was the person in your childhood who made you function at capacity, instead of allowing you to slack off and turn your back on your potential? What healthy habit did you develop when you were young? Have you continued that good habit, or did it, somehow, get cast aside along the way?

Are You Intentionally Congruent?

Congruence means someone or something is in a state of agreement or harmony. Are you, as Nido Qubein suggested, deliberately engaging in activities that move you closer to your goals? Or are you indulging in activities that conflict with your goals?

I go to church at least a couple of times a week when I'm in Atlanta. Why? It keeps me congruent with who and how I want to be. It gives me an opportunity to associate with the quality of people I want to connect with. It immerses me in my faith, so I am able to behave in ways congruent with being a Christian. I do it because my minister's words remind me of the importance of acting with integrity, no matter what the circumstances.

Sometimes, when I've been on the road nonstop for a long time, I feel a little tired, and it would be easy to forego going to a service. It is tempting to think, "I'll go next week," or "I'll make up for it by going to the evening service." That's when my clarity kicks in and reminds me that going to church keeps me in alignment with my goals. Off I go, doing what I should do to remain congruent with my life plan. I call this response a *habit activity*.

Working out is another of my habit activities. Many times I don't feel like working out; in fact, it's often the last thing I want to do, but I do it anyway, because it keeps me mentally and physically fit, which is congruent with my vision of the quality of person I want to be. As Nido Qubein said, I've made this commitment with my heart. It was not a decision I made only with my head. I'm clear that going to church and staying healthy matter to me, and both activities help me and my company survive and thrive. As Walt Disney said, "It's easy to make decisions when you know what your values are."

How Is Your Mindsight?

J. C. Penney's quote, "My eyesight may be dimming, but my vision has never been greater" is insightful (sorry, couldn't resist that pun). Do you have a clear vision of who you are, what you want to become, and how you plan to get there? I call that vision *mindsight*. Seeing with our eyes is eyesight. Visualizing with our brain is mindsight. Have you clarified what matters to you and why? Is your organization clear about what it wants and how it plans to accomplish it?

Maybe, like Jean Cohen of Ritz Carlton, you have morning meetings, even if you're at 100 percent occupancy, because the gatherings support your commitment to maintain frequent, two-way communication.

Ask yourself, too, if you've developed a harmful habit activity that doesn't serve you. For example, do you say you want to be healthy, but you still smoke? Do you say you want to be fit, but you keep putting off that trip to the gym? Do you say you want to have a wholesome family life, but there is just so much to do at work that you cannot take time to attend your child's baseball game?

Being out of balance is like having a flat tire. You can, if you want, still get where you are going, but the ride is rougher and the going is tougher.

An attitude of leadership starts with change and being honest with yourself.

Has it been easy maintaining balance and congruency in all areas of my life? No, it hasn't, but with proper discipline, focus, and faith, I'm changing and growing every day.

When you change and grow to be more congruent in all areas of your life, then and only then, you will experience the master plan that enables you to fulfill the calling and purpose for your life.

How Are You Investing in People?

As individuals, we have the option of investing in people by giving them money. Like Nido Qubein, we can establish scholarships that enable deserving youngsters a chance to get a college education. We can lend money to a relative who is starting a new business. We can financially support individuals who are down on their luck, or we can donate to a worthy cause and help innocent victims of a natural disaster.

As leaders, we invest in people by giving our time and talent. One definition of the word *scholarship* is "a fund of knowledge and learning." How are you providing a scholarship of knowledge and learning for your employees? How are you passing on your lessons learned in an effort to save people from unnecessary trial-and-terror learning?

Remember Nido Qubein's story about his dorm mother who said she would rather invest her money in the life a young person than park it in a savings account? Are you sharing your expertise and experience with others, or are you parking it in your brain? Did you ever stop to think that it's selfish to keep all your insights to yourself? If you can save people time-consuming mistakes and misunderstandings by revealing your insights, aren't you helping them? Passing along knowledge is not a form of arrogance, a subtle statement of "I know and you don't." Instead, enlightening others is service. You are saying, "This is what I've learned, and I'm going to share it, in the hopes it is of value to you."

Just as that anonymous doctor was a financial benefactor to Nido Qubein, we can be intellectual benefactors by freely sharing our intellectual capital, so other people don't have to reinvent their job wheel. We can feed the minds of fellow professionals by sharing the fruits of our mental labor. We can grow young employees by giving them insights and information that help them become more effective, productive, and focused.

Positive Leaders Are Positive Magnets

When I first went to the National Speakers Association Conference in August 1992, I noticed a very well-dressed man who throughout the conference always seemed to have a crowd around him. By the end of that conference, I not only knew the man's name was Nido Qubein but I had heard from very reliable sources he was a man of integrity, character, and faith. Over the years, I've gotten to know him personally and everything I had heard about him is true. He is someone who has made a positive mark on my life that cannot be erased.

ATTITUDE ACTION PLAN

- Are you providing intellectual nutrition?
- Are you congruent?
- Do you write about your lessons learned in business journals?
- Do you lecture at a local college, continuing education program, or MBA program?
- Do you have protégés? Do you actively mentor people in your profession?
- How are you transforming the minds of the people who work with, around, and for you?
- What is a specific way you teach what you have been taught?
- Leadership is not about numbers; it's about touching lives. Who can you touch today?
- As Margaret Fuller said, "If you have knowledge, let others light their candles at it." How are you going to pass on your knowledge, so people can learn something today that they didn't know yesterday?

Brief Biography

Nido Qubein is chairman of Great Harvest Bread Company with 200 stores in 35 states and Canada. He's also chairman of Creative Services, Inc., an international consulting firm, through which he delivers more than a hundred presentations a year to corporations internationally. He's also chairman of McNeill-Lehman, Inc. and Business Life, Inc. and is a director of BB&T Corporation, the tenth largest financial institution in the United States.

Qubein, a graduate of Mount Olive College, received his bachelor's degree in business from High Point University, and received an MBA from the University of North Carolina in Greensboro in 1971.

An active speaker, author, and consultant, Qubein has delivered many presentations in the past 30 years. He has written numerous books, including *Achieving Peak Performance* and *Stairway to Success,* and recorded scores of audio and video learning programs, including a bestseller in effective communication published by Nightengale-Conant and Berkley.

Nido Qubein is the recipient of an Ellis Island Medal of Honor, an award that honors immigrants and their descendants for their contributions to America. Previous award winners include civil rights torchbearer Rosa Parks and Nobel Peace Prize winners Jimmy Carter and Elie Weisel. Since 1972, the Qubein Foundation has granted more than 500 scholarships worth more than two million dollars. Former president of the 4,000-member National Speakers Association and founder of the National Speakers Association Foundation, Nido received its highest award, the Cavett (known as the Oscar of professional speaking), was inducted into the Sales and Marketing International Hall of Fame, and was awarded the prestigious Golden Gavel Award from Toastmasters International.

Nido lives in High Point, North Carolina, with his wife Mariana. They have four children.

The Leadership Legacy

Mel Blount, CEO and President
Mel Blount Youth Homes

As with many of our interviewees, Mel Blount says his parents were pivotal in shaping his citizenship. Mel, the youngest of 11 children, grew up in Vidalia, Georgia, in a close-knit family that emphasized giving back to the community and being productive. His mother didn't want her children to grow up and become sharecroppers, so she constantly told them how important it was to get an education, so they would be able to support themselves.

She gave them the most important education they'd ever receive— the education on how to become humanitarians.

Leaders Walk the Extra Mile

"I remember my parents walking miles to a sick neighbor's house, after a hard day's work, to cook, clean, and take care of them. They would then walk back late at night and get up at dawn the next morning to head out to the fields to work. It was the norm for them to reach out and help others. I grew up with a sense of the importance of being involved in and contributing to our community. Over and over, my parents told me, 'It's not what you say, it's what you do that counts.'

"I was fortunate to have some natural athletic talent, but my coaches kept telling me that if I wanted to excel, I was going to have to work harder than everyone else. Not just work hard, work harder than anyone else, because if I didn't, my competitors would be working harder than me, which meant they would be better than me. That lesson served me well throughout my football career. It's the first trait we try to instill in the kids at our youth camp. Our mission is to help them realize they can turn their lives around, if they're willing to work hard, focus, prepare, and perform."

There's No Excuse for Excuses

"Many of the kids at the youth camp come from difficult circumstances, but I don't think we do them any favors by letting them get away with excuses. We start off with little things, like we insist they be punctual. Some of these kids have overwhelming problems, so it would be pointless to try to change everything at once. We start with chores they can learn quickly, and they get some satisfaction from doing something tangible and doing it well.

"My goal isn't to be popular or to get them to like me. The best medicine doesn't always taste good. As my parents taught me, what matters is not that we're buddy-buddy. What matters is that we try to be fair and firm; we try to be a good person; and we hold the people around us accountable for being good. Being firm means expecting the very best out of people and letting them know we're not going to accept anything less than the best.

"Another part of being a good leader is being available to people when they need you. People have to feel like they can come to us at the eleventh hour when they need comfort, guidance, or direction. They need to know we connect with them from the inside out as a person, and nothing else matters. Those are the types of things that make kids and adults feel they can trust us."

More to Success Than the Super Bowl

"Even in the midst of winning NFL championships with the Pittsburgh Steelers, even with the money and the rings, I knew it wasn't the material things that mattered. What mattered was whether I was at peace with myself. What mattered was whether I was proud of who I was. What mattered was whether I had a sense of purpose.

"I got clear about having a sense of purpose the day I returned to my small hometown after our first Super Bowl win. All my nieces and nephews went to their schools and told the local kids that 'Uncle Mel' was back. Kids came out to our farm and gathered around, clamoring for my picture, my autograph, and to hear all about the game. When I looked into their eyes, though, I could tell they wanted more than that. They really wanted to be noticed. They were crying out to be seen. They knew there was a big world out there, and they hoped someone would care enough to come into their lives and help them, as Martin Luther King said, 'do better and be better.'

"That revelation inspired me to start my youth ministry. I knew how fortunate I had been to have caring role models in my life who had lifted me up; now it was my turn to lift others up. My successful career in football had given me an 'opportunity for impact,' and I decided I was going to make the most of it."

Leaders Paint a Picture of the Future

"A leader who had a lifelong impact on me was Jimmy Thacker, the football coach at Lion's Industrial Senior High School in the early 1960s. Our school was segregated and poor. Each of us had to furnish our own equipment, down to our shoes and socks, because the school couldn't afford to support its athletic programs.

"Coach Thacker had a daily ritual. He had us sit in a circle on the field, while he read newspaper articles about the successful exploits of former Lion's High students. To this day, I remember sitting back on the grass and picturing the thrilling touchdown pass, the last-minute touchdown catch, or the 50-yard run that won the game. While Coach related all those successes to us, every one of us in that circle sat there and thought, 'Someday, Coach is going to be reading about me.' He planted in our minds seeds of what we could be. He painted a picture of our future that did not include segregated schools or soiled, torn uniforms. He painted a picture of our potential, and he planted in us the desire and determination to make our big dreams come true."

Leaders Capture and Create Imagination

"One reason Coach Thacker's reading of those articles captured our imagination was that we weren't just hearing what he said, we were seeing it, visualizing it in our minds. If we really want to motivate people, we can't just talk to them; we need to create word pictures they can visualize. If we want people to go beyond their current abilities, we must paint a mental picture, so they can imagine what success looks like. Only then will they buy into the idea and believe it's possible for them.

"I try to paint a picture of success for our kids to see. I read articles about graduates of our program who bought into the philosophy of our program and went on to lead successful lives. I tell the stories of former residents who turned their lives around and got their high school diplomas. I tell them about the young men who left determined to go to college and make something of themselves. I tell them about Aaron, one of three young men pictured on my book, who now proudly serves his country in Afghanistan with Operation Enduring Freedom.

"I hope those kids are sitting there thinking, 'Someday he'll be reading about me.' I hope they're picturing themselves out in the world, making a difference, adding value.

"That's the leadership legacy. When someone has a great influence on you, like my parents and coaches had on me, you are compelled to do the same for others. You are driven to honor and pass on their gift by trying to be a positive influence on as many people as possible."

Keith's Attitude Check

Did you grow up where neighbors helped neighbors, and it was the norm to contribute to your community? Was the concept of humanitarianism—concern for human welfare, especially through philanthropic activities—instilled in you at an early age?

Good leaders, by definition, are humanitarians, because they're concerned about the welfare of their employees, and they show it every day. When I think back to my days at IBM, one thing that struck me first about the leadership at our sales school was that the leaders genuinely cared about our welfare. They invested themselves in giving us all the knowledge and skills necessary, so we could succeed. Would your employees say you care about them? In what specific ways do you show that you care?

Dare to Be Unpopular

Mel Blount understood that it's more important to be respected than to be liked. Good leaders care more about productivity than popularity.

When I think back about the people who influenced me, they weren't always the nice, supportive, encouraging types. Some of them were hard, demanding types who stretched me past my limits. I didn't like some of them at the time, because they wouldn't let me slide or slack off. I'm indebted to them, though, because they didn't let me be lazy.

Are there people working for you who are not being all they could be? Are you letting them get away with subpar performance? Do you realize you're not doing them any favors by not holding them account-able? Fulfill your role as a leader and tell them, "No more excuses." They may not like you for it now, but they may thank you for it later.

Material Things Can Be Immaterial

Maurice Sendak said, "There must be more to life than having every-thing." Blount knows this to be true. In the midst of the money, the rings, the fame, and the attention, he was clear that life is about giving everything, not having everything.

Every year *People* magazine publishes its "Fifty Most Beautiful People" issue, and every year it's full of people who seem to have every-thing—and it's not enough. Many of those great-looking people talk about their substance abuse problems, their depression, their multiple divorces, their angst, their eating disorders, their lack of self-confidence; you name it. The only truly fulfilled interviewees talk about their ser-vice to others or their involvement in some worthy cause that gives them the satisfaction that they're making a difference. Obviously, there's a clear distinction between *a* good life and *the* good life.

If you work with young people, chances are many of them have bought into society's current emphasis on having more stuff. Every time teens turn on the television, listen to the radio, and log on to the Internet, they're bombarded with materialistic images that shout that happiness can be had, if you simply buy this object immediately. Credit card number please. Part of our responsibility as leaders is to help young folks realize the truth of Maurice Sendak's and Mel Blount's philoso-phy: Happiness is achieved through taking advantage of our opportuni-ties for impact, not through taking advantage of our opportunities to buy the latest gadget.

Who's Crying Out to Be Seen?

One of the easiest things to do as a leader is to overlook the workers who quietly get their jobs done and never cause any problems. When we're managing many people, we sometimes take our silently efficient employees for granted and focus only on trying to turn around the troublemakers. The squeaky wheels not only get the grease, they often get the whole can of oil.

A friend who owned several retail stores complained to me of a particularly difficult employee whose sour attitude was wreaking havoc with customers and coworkers alike. The owner had done everything she could to rectify the situation. Over a period of several months, she met with the disgruntled employee several times, sent her to expensive training programs, and even rearranged her work schedule, in attempts to mollify her. Nothing worked.

One of the other employees finally pointed out that the owner was ignoring all the staff members who were earning every penny of their paychecks, and lavishing a disproportionate amount of attention on the one negative employee. The owner realized she was right; it was past time for her to start paying attention to the many employees who were behaving well, instead of concentrating on the one employee who wasn't.

The good employees had been silently crying out to be noticed, and it was her job as a leader to recognize their contributions instead of overlooking them in her misplaced focus on the ill-tempered staff member.

Think about your staff. Do you know of anyone who has silently been doing great work, and for whatever reason, you've failed to recognize and reward it? In a way, do they get penalized for their conscientiousness? Does the fact that they never cause any problems actually work against them, because the only time your employees hear from you is when they do something wrong?

If you discover you are mistakenly concentrating on the negative employees, rather than on the ones giving their best performance, can you vow to change your reaction? Can you make it a daily habit by focusing on something positive your people do. Keep your eyes open, always looking for the things they do right. Promise yourself that you'll notice their efforts and results, instead of overlooking them? Just like Mel's nieces, nephews, and hometown children hoped he would reach out and notice them, your employees hope you'll reach out and notice them.

We address in other chapters the importance of having a clear vision for our organization and ourselves. Mel Blount's story shows us how important it is for that vision to be something we can vividly picture with our minds. Can we see ourselves in this future? Are we thinking and hoping, "Someday that will be me?" When we have a vision, we can reach our goals.

Plant Pictures of Prosperity

Back in the 1970s, long before the term "cyber" referred to computers, Dr. Maxwell Maltz wrote a book called *PsychoCybernetics*. As a plastic surgeon, he noticed that even after he repaired disfiguring scars, a percentage of his patients still felt ugly and complained that he had done nothing for them. Others whose scars were not completely reparable reported feeling beautiful and thankful for the work he had performed. He gradually realized that his patients' attitude, their self-image, made all the difference in the world. If they saw themselves as attractive, they were. If they visualized themselves as permanently disfigured, then they continued to feel that way, even if surgery dramatically improved their appearance. He took his theory one step further and performed studies on athletes, to see if their visions of themselves made any difference in their performance. He had one set of athletes simply sit in a chair and envision themselves succeeding, time and time again, making a touchdown or shooting a basket or hitting a powerful tennis serve. He had others practice their sport without visualization. A third set did both—they visualized success in their sports, and they also practiced. He learned that the athletes who visualized their success improved their performance, even without physically practicing. The ones who practiced also improved, to some degree. By an overwhelming majority, though, the ones who combined practice with visualization showed the best overall improvement.

When I was a salesperson at IBM in the Office Products Division selling primarily IBM typewriters, copiers, and word processing equipment, my branch manager Al Martin used to tell us to go out and test drive a new car, go look at some new houses on the weekend, he would even mention there's a lot of water in Seattle maybe some of you ought to go out and buy a boat. He would say get a picture of what you are looking at, for example, that brand new car, put a picture of it on your desk, make a copy of it to put on your refrigerator, put it on the visor in your car. He would say look at the picture several times a day, visualize yourself owning it. What's going to help you pay for that brand new toy is selling a lot of IBM equipment. He would take us through that same process, visualize making those sales calls, getting those appointments, getting those demonstrations, and closing those deals.

What we believe we can do, what we envision ourselves being able to do, we miraculously can do.

ATTITUDE ACTION PLAN

- How do you plan to plant pictures of prosperity in the minds of your employees, your children, your colleagues, and the members of the committees you chair?

- Do you read about the accomplishments of successful employees at your annual meetings?

- Do you share past triumphs in employee orientations?

- Do you feature staff success stories in your publications?

- Do you paint an image of a bigger, brighter future, so that your associates can clearly visualize it?

- How do you plan to give back to your community?

- Do you have your own clear vision of where you want to be, where you want your company to be, and where you want your associates to be in one year? Two years? Five years?

Brief Biography

Mel Blount is the president and CEO of The Mel Blount Youth Home in Vidalia, Georgia, which assists young boys to become productive members of society. Longing to do more, in 1989 Mel established another youth home near Pittsburgh, Pennsylvania, in the rural location of Claysville, Pennsylvania. Mel's vision is to establish more youth homes throughout the United States. His compassion, service, and perseverance have already given many young men the opportunity and the desire to pursue their potential to the fullest.

Mel received a football scholarship, and in 1970 he graduated with a BS degree in physical education from Southern University, in Baton Rouge, Louisiana. Recruited by the Pittsburgh Steelers, he spent his entire professional football career with the same team. After retiring from playing football, Mel continued to be involved with the game. From August 1983 to May 1990, Mel was the director of Player Relations for the NFL. In 1990, he assumed a position as a consultant and member of the National Football League Commissioner Player Advisory Board.

Mel Blount was enshrined in the Pro Football Hall of Fame during his first year of eligibility. During the same era, he was appointed president of Mountaineer Magic Entertainment, Inc., an association related to horse racing in Chester, West Virginia. Mel had been an avid horseman since his childhood days on the farm. In 1990, Mel won the Cutting Horse Championship in the Open Division at the Florida Cutting Horse Association Show. As a businessman and sportsman, Mel has been involved with the horse industry by breeding and raising thoroughbreds and quarter horses.

Shortly before retiring from the Pittsburgh Steelers in 1983, Mel thought frequently of what his life's work should be. He had seen too many boys lost to a system that was failing them, and he decided to make a difference.

Mel serves on the board of directors of numerous organizations concerned with the youth of this country. In 1989, he was spokesperson for Safe and Sound, an organization involved in the prevention of child abuse. Mel has received many awards for his commitment to community service including:

Vectors Pittsburgh—Man of the Year Award 1990.

Boy Scouts of America, Pittsburgh—Service Award.

Dapper Dan Pittsburgh—Al Abrams Award.

National Conference of Christian and Jews—Peoplehood Award.

NAACP—Human Rights Award 1991.

Named 524th Daily Point of Light by President George Bush.

Named one of Eight National Heroes by *U.S. News & World Report.*

Walter Camp Football Foundation—Man of the Year Award 1992.

Honorary Doctorate of Humane Letters from Southern University.

Selected one of the Ten Most Caring People in America by The Caring Institute.

Author of the book, *The Cross Burns Brightly.*

NFL 75th Anniversary All-Time Team.

Martin Luther King Jr. Humanitarian Award.

Inducted into the World Sports Humanitarian Hall of Fame.

NFL Alumni—Spirit Award.

NFL Alumni Order of Leather Helmet and Community Service Award.

Mel is always looking for ways to help our youth, and he is a strong believer in Socrates' belief that: "the individual protected and nurtured by society has an obligation to society."

Do You Have an Infectious Passion?

Jo Jerman, Vice President of Sales
Merck & Co., Inc.

In my "Attitude Is Everything" keynote speech, I tell my audience that enthusiasm is a powerful word, and that the English word *enthusiasm* is derived from the Greek word *enthousiasmos*, which means "inspiration." The two root words, *enthous* and *entheos*, mean "God or spirit within." Jo Jerman definitely has enthusiasm, a wonderful spirit, and a passion that comes from within. She typifies enthusiasm.

"If you want people to do what you want them to do, you're going to have to inspire them. You're almost going to have to *infect* them, with your passion.

"One thing I learned early on is that no matter how smart you were, how rich you were, or where you came from, success in life boiled down to perseverance. The second thing I learned is success is all about honesty; it's all about being true to yourself and true to others, following through on commitments. The third thing I learned is that people will always want to follow you, *if* you have a positive, upbeat, optimistic, can-do attitude. If you have those things, if you can make people believe, and if people believe in you, they'll want to follow you.

"When I was in high school, there were a couple of folks who seemed to succeed all the time. I watched them closely, and I learned that it wasn't about their innate ability. It was about their head. It was about their attitude. It was about what *they* thought they could do. They had incredible determination, an unswerving drive to be at the top of their game, be it academics, acting, sports, politics, or whatever.

"More than my fellow students, the person who had the most influence on me in my school years was my dad. He instilled in me the belief that no matter what I wanted to do, I could achieve it. He showed me that I didn't have to follow any kind of traditional path; my path was up to me. My father told me, 'Whatever you choose to do, as long as you work at it, if you're honest, if you're ethical, if you're positive, and you have a can-do attitude, you can do it.'

"In college, one of my sociology professors also had a powerful impact on me. He brought a tremendous amount of energy, and enthusiasm to a subject I wasn't particularly attracted to. But the next thing I knew, I found myself wanting to work very, very hard for the man, because he believed so much and tried so hard. I found myself energized just walking to his class! I found myself excited about the subject and eager to learn. His enthusiasm was that infectious. As a result, I not only learned about sociology, but I also learned the value of enthusiasm.

"Since I've been at Merck, I've held a number of different positions. These experiences were terrific for me. I'm delighted that I had them, because I learned a tremendous amount along the way. I also learned that I love selling, and I love working with people. Those two things are great energizers in my life. I love managing salespeople, and I love all the concepts and practices of leadership—the whole journey—because I am never at the finish line. There is always more to learn about leadership.

"I learn something new about myself every day. I learn something new about leadership every day. I learn something new about how to enhance performance every day, how to motivate people, how to inspire people.

"God has really blessed me beyond belief with a loving family, a good job, working for a terrific company, and great people to work with. I'm so thankful for those things! How great it is to enjoy what you do everyday!"

Everything Is About People

"The more time I spend on earth, the more I realize that everything is about people. True leaders know this. Life is all about relationships. Business is all about leadership. Leadership is all about inspiring people. That's the only sure path to success. I don't care if you're running a sales organization or if you're the CEO of a bank, it all comes down to people.

"It may sound simplistic, but if you hire the right people, when you have the right people working for you, your life becomes easier. But let me back up and say that managing performance and coaching for advanced performance is difficult. It requires courage. It requires conflict management. Most people find those things too time consuming. Many people would rather let things go, than address difficult, yet important issues. If someone isn't ever going to be an 'A' player, you shouldn't have them working for you. 'A' players always get the job done and get it done right! I am happy, delighted, and blessed with a team of 'A' players. They're such smart people. They're so motivated to excel that they inspire me to aim even higher.

"I've also learned how to delegate. As a matter of fact, I've learned it is much better to have people who are closest to the work to do the work. If issues come up, if projects need to get done that affect associates or representatives, the smartest thing I could do is involve a task force of people who are closest to the work. They're going to give me the best solutions. Ever since I caught on to that important idea, I no longer ever assume that I know the best answer. When I delegate to the people who are closest to the work, guess what? I always get a better solution."

Ninety-Percent Rule

"People in corporate America value data. They value the hard facts. But sometimes you just can't find all the facts, so you've got to go by your instincts. Over the years, I've learned to trust my instincts, because you know what? Generally, they're pretty good. I'm not going to say mine are perfect, but generally, because of my experiences, because I've got valuable people that I can talk to, I have a pretty good sense of which way I need to go. The key is doing it. When you run a sales organization, it's better to be 90 percent right and on time, than to be 100 percent right and late! Don't let analysis paralysis set in!

"When you're running a sales organization, you don't always have time to stop everything and delve deep into research, because the customers you need to see are seeing other salespeople. So, one of the things I do first is I try to get as much information, good information, as quickly as I can. Then I come up with the pros, the cons, and what reactions will result from my actions. I try to think through each scenario.

You can never be 100 percent predictive about people, because everyone is different. You've got to learn to trust your gut, though. Be timely. Your people are looking to you to lead."

Control What You Can

"Regardless of the business you're in, things are hitting you all the time that you have absolutely no control over. When people worry about things they cannot control, they lose their grip. Fear and worries will color our decisions and can even affect our health, so my motto is, 'I'm only going to worry about what I can control . . . everything else will take care of itself.'

"Just because I have that motto, that does not mean I won't give input where I think it can have impact. That's not the case at all, but there is no sense in me wasting good energy and good brain cells worrying about something I can't influence.

"I've noticed that salespeople often have a tendency to spend a great deal of time worrying about things they can't control, such as what the competition is doing. You can't worry about that. You have to concentrate on *your* sales call. The best pros in sales have a laser focus.

"I hope that when people speak of me, they point to my energy and my optimism. Folks will tell you that I advise my sales teams to control what they can control and forget about the rest. What is it that is within our control? Every day of your life you can control your actions and your attitude. The right actions done with the right attitude is powerful. That formula will always deliver.

"If you can't be passionate about what you do, then you shouldn't do it. Life is too short to waste a moment of it. You have to be passionate, and you've got to do everything to the best of your ability every day."

Keith's Attitude Check

When you are passionate about what you do, people will follow you. My life as been an example of what Jo Jerman describes as an "infectious passion." I know that each one of my successes was achieved when I was passionate about what I believed in and what I was doing. Enthusiasm and passion are infectious. Other people catch your enthusiasm; it spreads and is transmitted to all the people around you.

Passion and Enthusiasm Are Contagious

In many of my presentations, I perform an exercise that demonstrates the power of enthusiasm. I divide the audience into two sides. I make side one visibly larger. I challenge each side to stand up for five seconds and cheer, to give themselves and their families a round of applause. I ask them to use their voices and bodies and to really get into it. Invariably the first side, the larger side, always does an excellent job, but what I find is that passion and enthusiasm of the first side inspires and motivates the second side, the smaller group, to do even better. The cheers and shouts from the second side invariably match or exceed those of the larger side. Passion is infectious.

My successes came about when I was passionate about my endeavors, whether it was basketball, my sales and marketing career at IBM, my professional speaking career, or my family. My strongest support came when others could sense and feel my passion. Each of us can attest, without a doubt, that it is easy to follow someone who is positive, upbeat, and optimistic and has a "can-do" attitude. I believe it was my can-do attitude during a high school semi-final basketball game that led us to victory. We were a team with a 22–0 record, and we were in the final minutes of the game. We were behind by 8 points with only 3 minutes left in the game, and my team seemed paralyzed. That's when my coach called a time out. I came to the huddle pumped up, fired up, and excited. I was passionate and enthusiastic when I yelled out, "Give me the ball." My enthusiasm and passion convinced my coaches and my teammates that I had the solution. For the next several plays, my team ran the offense through me. I scored, we scored, and we won the game. Looking back on that night, anyone of my teammates were capable of leading us to victory, but no one else at that moment had my level of passion and enthusiasm. When I released it, it became infectious and the whole team caught it and that's what propelled us to win. That same enthusiasm is the principle behind Jerman's leadership philosophy.

Jerman also explains that everything is about people. Leadership is about people. I have said, "People don't care about how much you know, until they know how much you care." When you want the best, you have to give your best. I thank God for one of my managers at IBM, who recognized my talent, nurtured and supported me, and gave me the opportunity to showcase my abilities as a speaker and trainer. He saw the perfect fit, and I found my purpose and my passion. I began to want the best, and I then gave my best. I earned more support than I'd ever had before from my manager and the other managers in the office. They saw I had a purpose and a passion, and they bought into my dream and personal vision.

Although Jerman states that hers is a simplistic concept, you also need to develop an "A" team. When you have the right people in your life, the right people working for you, your life does become easier. Your "A" team should consist of the people with whom you share the greatest trust and confidence. I have always said wise women have been the core of my "A" team. My grandmother, my mother, my sister, my aunts, and my office support staff are sound, supportive, and skilled. My "A" team has been composed of mentors who have been willing to give me constructive feedback to improve my performance. I am the product of many loving, supportive, creative, productive, and dedicated people.

Another key issue that Jerman brings to the forefront is to "control what you can control," or as the saying goes, "Don't sweat the small stuff, and it's all small stuff!" Charles Mayo tells us that most people worry too much. He states that 40 percent of all worries involve things that have already happened; 30 percent never will happen, 12 percent are worries over unfounded health concerns, and 10 percent are over daily nothings. In other words, 92 percent of the things we worry over are things over which we have no control. Our worry does not repair, resolve, or replace anything. Instead, it often leads to high blood pressure, heart attacks, poor performance, and lack of concentration.

We may not have control over many of the circumstances in our lives, but we can control how we respond to them. Attitude is a choice. You can choose which attitude you will have, and as Jerman will tell you, if you want to be successful in leadership, you must have a positive, upbeat, can-do attitude with a passion that is contagious.

ATTITUDE ACTION PLAN

- Take a few moments to think about and list the things in your life that you are passionate about. Make separate lists for home, work, church, recreation, volunteer work, and so on.

- How does your behavior change when you are doing the things for which you have a passion?

- How do you feel, when you have passion about your work, project, or relationships?

- Transfer those feelings to other events and things. Make those passionate behaviors a part of your daily routine, especially when you are in a leadership role.

- Observe others as they catch your enthusiasm and grow in passion.

- Do others comment about your passion?

- Keep a list of the positive feedback you receive from others and work even harder to duplicate those behaviors in other areas of your life.

- Be certain you have an "A" team working with you.

- Define membership into your team. What characteristics do you want from members of your "A" team?

- How do you, as a leader, support those who support you?

- For one day, keep a journal. Write down everything you worried about or stressed over. At the end of the day, sit down and put the list into two categories: things you could have controlled and things over which you had no control. How much of your day did you spend sweating the small stuff?

- If you find you worry too much, write down this manta: "There may be things in my life that I cannot control, but I always have control over how I respond to life."

Brief Biography

Jo Jerman is the Vice President of Sales, Southeast Region Business Group, at Merck & Co., Inc. She received her BS in sociology from the University of North Carolina and took Continuing Business Education courses at Harvard Business School. In her 25 years at Merck & Co., Inc., she has held many other positions.

Before she joined Merck & Co., Inc., Jerman was a medical social worker at Duke University Medical Center.

The North Carolina Chapter of the Arthritis Foundation honored her with a Community Service Award.

Say No to "Yes People"

William (Gus) Pagonis, Head of Logistics Group
Sears Roebuck and Company

With 29 years of military service, Gus Pagonis, a three-star general, knows how to motivate troops and instill loyalty. Recruited by Sears, Roebuck and Company a decade ago to turn the Logistics Organization around, Gus accomplished the goal, and with minimal turnover rate in his immediate staff. Some people have never had the benefit of military management, so you may find it even more fascinating to learn how the military trained this leader how to lead.

"I don't want copycat staff members who think like me. I want to be able to count on the fact that employees will disagree if they see things differently. If something is wrong, I don't want people playing ostrich, afraid to tell me. Integrity is the price of admission to my team, and that means speaking up for what you think is right. I'm careful not to kill the messenger. I assume that my staff members have valid reasons for their opinions, so I hear them out to discover what I don't know or am overlooking. The best decisions are made when you collect and consider differing data, and the only way to ensure you do that is to welcome honest feedback."

Keep a Page on Every Employee

"My parents were Greek immigrants who came to this country with no money and no job, but with a positive attitude. They started their own small hotel with a restaurant/bar and worked around the clock to make it successful. I started working alongside them in my early teens. Dad really impressed me, because he made it a point to learn the background of every employee. He didn't do it in a suspicious or intrusive way; he did it because he wanted to understand and accommodate their circumstances.

"For example, he knew which one of his employees had no car and had to use public transportation. He knew who had a handicapped child that needed to be picked up by a special bus. He knew who was married, who was not, and who was paying alimony. His knowledge of their circumstances allowed him to build their work schedules around their particular needs. With his awareness of their factors, he could treat each employee with dignity and not put anyone in situations that conflicted with personal requirements.

"The Privacy Act of 1974 limits our ability to ask for or acquire information about our employees' personal lives. I understand the need for that policy, and I follow the letter of the law so I'm in compliance; however, I don't think it's smart to follow regulations blindly if they violate common sense. I keep a page on each of my direct reports. I know more about them than the HR director does. Like my father before me, I inform myself, so I can better serve my employees. I don't think my tactic is an invasion of their privacy; I think it's an opportunity to honor their individual idiosyncrasies. By knowing who my employees are, I'm better able to be empathetic to their special needs and match them with work responsibilities that are aligned with their particular circumstances.

"An example of this idea in action took place in the Gulf War. As commanding general of logistics, I was in charge of supplies for our troops, everything from tents to toilet tissue. When I put myself in the shoes of the men and women who were far from home in daunting, desert-like circumstances, I realized that a little thing like having ice-cold soda could make a big difference in morale. We made it available, because it was one small way we could let our armed forces know that we understood what it was like for them, and that we cared."

Are You Fit for Business?

"Twelve noon to 1 P.M. is gym time for me. I run and swim every day, because I think it's my obligation to stay fit. Simply said, we can't be as effective as we want or need to be if we're out of shape. Working out is, literally and figuratively, an attitude; it's an opportunity to work out accumulated stress and tension, so we return to our jobs re-energized.

"I work out for myself, but I also do it to send a clear message to employees that fitness isn't frivolous. I don't want employees eating lunch at their desks. Working nonstop for eight to ten hours makes for a long, tiring day and it's a recipe for exhaustion. I want my staff members to understand that exercising in the middle of their day isn't taking time away from their work; it's investing time to make them more effective at their work.

"I'm also out of the office at 5:30. I could stay until 8 or 9 every night, because there's always work to do, but I want my employees home with their families, and that means I have to set the example and be home with mine. Part of being fit for business is keeping balance in our lives, and that means not getting swallowed up by our work responsibilities."

Keep It Short

"I believe in stand-up meetings. It's one of the best ways to keep people focused. Instead of people lounging around a table and having meandering discussions that go nowhere, when they stand up at a meeting, they stay on their toes, so to speak. As a result, we move through our agenda quickly and effectively.

"I also have a policy that messages must be kept to the size of a three-by-five-inch card. The limited space disciplines us to distill our communication, so we get right to the point and don't waste each other's time with details that aren't necessary to the discussion. Editing memos to a single index card is hard at first, but it becomes easier with time, and it's a skill that dramatically increases everyone's effectiveness. By forcing ourselves to weed out what's superfluous, we transfer information in 3 minutes, instead of 30.

"Keeping briefings short has other benefits for leaders. The simpler the communication, the clearer it is, and the more easily it's understood at every level. Furthermore, when we tell our people *everything*, they can't remember it all. What's worse, telling them everything leaves no room for innovation. Comprehensive instructions that cover every eventuality relegate people to following our explicitly laid-out instructions. On the other hand, a succinct communiqué with parameters, but without the particulars, is the essence of leadership. It gives people an opportunity to incorporate their expertise and experience and act accordingly. In other words, long, detailed messages are autocratic, while shorter messages are democratic, because they encourage adaptation, which results in ownership."

Act on 70 Percent

"Decisiveness is one of the most important characteristics of leadership. If our division is facing a problem, my first step is to seek the advice of my managers. Their front-line experience with the situation usually generates incisive options on how to proceed. I consider their input, and then I don't hesitate to make a decision.

"I don't believe in conducting exhaustive research and waiting until I have 100 percent of the facts, because the extra time taken to get that additional information is not time well spent. I'd rather act when I have 70 percent of the facts, because I anticipate that we'll need to make course corrections as circumstances change anyway.

"Macho leaders think they have to be right all the time. That attitude often means they're reluctant to admit mistakes and change a decision once it's been made, because they think they have to be beyond reproach. I count on changing decisions after the fact, because it means we're building in flexibility to adapt to unanticipated events as they unfold."

The Vacation Test

"One of the factors taken for granted in the military is that you're always training your replacement. As an officer, you'll usually be rotated to new assignments every one to three years, so it is your job to prepare someone to do your job.

"I've tried to transfer this philosophy to the civilian world. There's an easy test to gauge how well you're training your replacements: Answer this question: When you're on vacation, how well does your team function? If your team can't get along without you, you're not doing a good job as a leader. You may be incredibly competent and talented. You may be respected, liked, and appreciated. You may be a hardworking model of integrity, but if you've made yourself indispensable, you're not doing your job as a leader.

"A leader's job is to get results through his or her people. A leader's job is not to do all the work alone. One of my chief responsibilities is to train my subordinates to be autonomous. When I see that my staff members are working effectively without me, I'm fulfilling my function as a leader."

Keith's Attitude Check

I can relate to Gus Pagonis's belief that our effectiveness as a leader depends on whether our people function well when we're gone. My effectiveness as a speaker depends on whether participants function better after I'm gone. It's nice when people tell me they enjoy my keynote speeches, but it's even nicer when they get in touch weeks or months after the fact and tell me they're still using the tools I've imparted.

Leadership is about producing exponential results. One person, no matter how brilliant, can get only so much done. One leader, motivating others to be and do their best, can get exponentially more done.

Likewise, a speaker who delivers a fascinating presentation creates an interesting and intriguing hour for the people in the room. A speaker who delivers a thought-provoking presentation that causes people to do things differently, however, creates an exponentially beneficial impact on the people who attend as well as on all the people that attendee knows, at that time and in the years ahead.

Have you made yourself dispensable as a leader? Do you train the people who report to you to think creatively and allow them the autonomy they need to get the job done? If not, you're doing them and the organization a disservice. One of my biggest challenges as an entrepreneur happened when I first started my business and hired my first employee. I was so hands-on about how I thought the office systems should function and operate that I crippled productivity, because I never gave my staff encouragement or the proper training. I learned that I stifled creativity, instead of promoting it, as the leader of the office. My micromanagement in turn not only caused internal friction, but also caused me to lose focus on key aspects of the business that needed my full attention.

My grandmother used to say, "If you have a thoroughbred, let it run." I had some good people working for me, I should have just given them more training and let them run. Leaders train their people to work independently but to function interdependently. An enterprise should never be totally dependent on its leader to keep the operation functioning.

Are You Dispensable?

What was your answer to Gus's question: When you're on vacation, how well does your team function? If your office or company runs fine without you, good for you, because it doesn't mean you're not adding value. It means you've done a good job preparing your employees to be autonomous.

But as a leader a question you should ask yourself, are your worried, are you fearful that if you train your employees to well, help them grow too much that they may take over your position or leadership role. If so, what insecurities do you need to address?

I was privileged to work with a leader who taught me a wonderful way to help people be resourceful. He said replace the words, "I think" with "What do you think?"

If my office manager, comes to me with a problem and I solve it for her, guess where she's going to head the next time she has a problem? Straight to my office. Instead of giving answers and telling people what I think, I try to give guidance by asking what they think. When others learn to think through and solve their own problems, they get more work done, they sense that you trust them, and they are happier at their jobs.

Don't you want your employees to be resourceful, to be able meet and handle any situation? Of course you do, and that's why you have to let them ponder alternatives, implement minor changes, and deal with challenges on their own.

Honestly assess whether you are training your people to be dependent or independent. Are you yielding to the temptation to do things yourself, instead of teaching your people how to do things themselves? If so, how are you going to foster resourceful within your team? Are you going to replace "I think" with "What do you think?" Will you teach them to think for themselves? Are you going to resist the temptation to rush in and rescue, and instead hold them accountable for resolving their own dilemmas?

The Battlefield of the Mind

Another management friend of mine feels like there's a war going on and her military-type leadership enables her to win her battles. She says, "When there's a war a leader needs to show up and it doesn't matter whether you are president, vice president, director, or secretary. The question is when it's time to lead can you lead?

You may not feel that your workplace or office is a battlefield, yet the market and competitors create minor skirmishes and major attacks, so many of the same battlefield tactics apply to business.

Gus Pagonis has been very effective using a militaristic management model—minimize the frills and maximize the results—to turn around a major corporation. While his approach may appear austere to civilian personnel, it's a personal style that suits his personality, background, and training. Does your leadership style encompass your "best practices"?

When leading, the key is to play to your strengths. No doubt about it, Gus is still a three-star general leading the troops to victory.

I read a book several months ago by Joyce Meyers entitled *The Battlefield of the Mind* which reminded me of the importance of maintaining the right mind-set and the right attitude. Whether your battlefield is at work or at home, the biggest battle you need to win as a leader is the battle in your mind. Being mentally tough today and staying focused is a key discipline that must be embraced. One way to win the battle in your mind is to monitor and control your internal dialog. Negative self-talk, negative communication programs your subconscious mind which leads to defeat. If you don't manage what you say to yourself, surrender. The battle is already lost. I recently read that a psychologist stated that upwards of 80 percent of our internal conversation is negative. Unless you eliminate the negative words and thoughts in your mind your chances of victory will be limited.

ATTITUDE ACTION PLAN

- Do you create an environment where employees can share honest feedback without fearing negative consequences?

- While honoring the Privacy Act, do you make appropriate efforts to get to know who your employees are "outside the office"?

- In what ways do you accommodate the special needs of employees and gauge the results? Are people more willing to pitch in? Has productivity increased? Has absenteeism declined? Have communication channels improved?

(continued)

Continued

- Being physically and mentally fit are two hallmarks of leadership. Have you set the example for your organization? If your business does not currently support physical fitness, what tangible steps will you take to create an environment conducive to regular workouts?

- Assess the effectiveness of meetings. What make changes do you need to implement that will make your meetings more productive?

- Assess and modify internal memos and communications for clarity and effectiveness. What suggestions will you make to staff members to improve communications?

- Adopt decision-making strategies that empower employees and allow for flexibility. When someone asks you what you think about an idea, do you always say, "What you think?"

- Train employees to lead by allowing them autonomy. Do you hire the best, and then get out of their way?

- If you left on a vacation today, would your operation continue without you? What steps are you going to take each day to help team members grow in self-sufficiency, so you will be dispensable?

Brief Biography

William (Gus) Pagonis was elected head of the Supply Chain for Sears, Roebuck and Company in November 1993. He is responsible for establishing policies and procedures for the flow of inventory from vendor to store as well as for vendor relations, transportation, distribution, international logistics, home delivery services, and the integration of information systems to cement it all together. He functions as the single point of contact for all Sears Logistics for more than 2,500 stores, including a network of strategically positioned distribution centers. In addition, he is president of Sears Logistics Services, Inc., a wholly owned subsidiary of Sears.

Prior to joining Sears, Pagonis served in the U.S. Army for 29 years, retiring with the three-star rank of Lieutenant General. Pagonis is widely recognized for his logistical achievements, particularly during Desert Shield/Desert Storm. As General Schwarzkopf's logistics commander, he functioned as the single point of contact responsible for all logistics (food, shelter, fuel, ammunition, transportation, contracting) for the Gulf War.

A native of Charleroi, Pennsylvania, Pagonis completed undergraduate and graduate studies at Pennsylvania State University. He is the author of *Moving*

Mountains: Lessons in Leadership and Logistics from the Gulf War, published by Harvard Business School Press.

The military awards and decorations Pagonis has received include The Distinguished Service Medal, Silver Star, Legion of Merit, Bronze Star Medal with "V" device, King Abdul Aziz Zad Class Medal (Saudi Arabia), Merit and Honor medal (Greece), and the Gold Cross of Honor of the Federal Armed Forces (Germany). His most recent civilian recognitions include being named a 1994 Distinguished Alumni of Pennsylvania State University and receiving an Honorary Doctor of Public Service from the Washington and Jefferson College, Washington, Pennsylvania, in May 1997. He has been listed in Marquis *Who's Who* since 1992.

Gus and his wife Cheri Pagonis have two sons: Lieutenant Colonel Gust Pagonis, U.S. Army, and Robert Pagonis, a chef who graduated from the International Culinary Academy in Pittsburgh, Pennsylvania.

CAPSIZING

Don Wood, CEO
80/20

Downsizing, or to put a positive spin on the term, rightsizing, has become a common solution for organizations seeking a profitable balance of people and productivity. Perhaps CAPSIZING would stir up profitable productivity. Don Wood's ability to "cultivate an atmosphere of productivity by sensing an individual's zeal for involvement and nurturing it for growth" is the heartbeat of his leadership attitude and the organization's success. The atmosphere itself is motivating.

"The role of a coach is to get everybody to do what they don't want to do, so they can enjoy the benefits. I have a very successful company, and all my employees are doing well. I pay them really well, the ones that I keep. My job is to make sure they do what they don't want to do so they can enjoy the benefits. The end result: our dollars per employee are more than double the national average for our manufacturing category.

"A former chairman of Jaguar once said, 'You learn the hard way that you can hire their hands and their heads, but you can't hire their hearts.' That's an earned position. You lead people; you manage things, and you really have to be able to differentiate. I deal with this every day."

Stupid Is Forever, Ignorance Can Be Fixed

"Our company abides by the motto: Stupid is forever, ignorance can be fixed. We feel that stupidity is over at the competition, not here. I work only with smart people. I insist on smart. I don't even care about their academic credentials. Education doesn't necessarily make them smart. I need smart people.

"My immediate staff is under 30 people. Only one of those staff members has a four-year degree. The rest are all high school graduates. I pay them well because they do the work, come in early and stay late.

"I brought the people on my staff up from the line. I was a tool-maker and a union steward so I have a great sensitivity to the line. Some of the smartest people in the world are on the line. In order to 'walk the walk,' one has to understand the line.

"For example, my corporate controller is only 29 years old. He was a college student when he came to us as a line worker. He expressed an interest in getting somewhere and, in relatively short time, we moved him to the accounting department because he had a 'thing' for numbers. He grew in knowledge and experience and now, as a corporate controller handles $40 million for the business. He is extremely bright and does an outstanding job.

"Many talented women work at 80/20. They know how to get things done. They are great motivators. I remember hearing Margaret Thatcher speak after the United States bombed Muammar al-Qaddafi. The Prime Minister had give U.S. air space immediately, but the French never did. The interviewer asked Mrs. Thatcher why she was so decisive on air space. Her response—'I learned long ago that if you want something talked to death, you give it to a bunch of men. If you want something done, you give it to a woman.' She was absolutely right.

"Our plant is in the middle of a cornfield in Northeast Indiana, not in a city. Many of our employees are farmers and they were born with a work ethic that fits well with 80/20's philosophy.

"If you want to win the series, you have to have the best players. My major role is consistently finding the best players, and they are right here in my own backyard. 80/20 is an extraordinary company made up of extraordinary people."

Monitor for Growth

"We tell our new people that if you think this is a place to show up to get a paycheck so you can go shopping, they are in the wrong place. This is where they can grow. If you don't want to grow, then don't waste their time. We insist on growth, and we monitor our employees for their growth. If they are not growing, they will be told about it. That statement often elicits a look of surprise.

"We have a periodic review to monitor for growth. Each supervisor is advised to know your people. Don't take anything for granted. Everyone has his or her own hopes, fears, ambitions, and desires and they want to be recognized. They want someone to care, someone who will help them do their best. Each review is done keeping that attitude in mind.

"The local high school has a work/study program that places students in jobs in the community where they work half a day and attend school the other half. I love working with those young minds. They are like sponges. We let them know that this is a growth opportunity, and many still work here after they graduate from school. Some have gone to other places to work, but many come back to us. When asked why they wanted to return to our company, they tell us that there is no other place like 80/20."

In Charge of Our Own Happiness

"The current U.S. economy is in the doldrums. Manufacturing has been the hardest hit by the downturn because we make the stuff that people buy. If they don't buy it, we don't make it, which means we have less business.

"Right now the greatest challenge is in explaining where we are economically. People are mystified. Look at the stock market. In short, it has confused people, and the terrorist attacks of September 11 confused everyone even more. Yet, I think we are still recovering from that event. The employment rate in Indiana has been pretty tough; we are at a 6 percent unemployment rate in our area.

"To help our employees understand our situation, I have said that 'we can control what is here, but we cannot control what's out there. Most of all, our attitude can't be influenced by what's out there. We are in charge of our own happiness.'

"Charles Swindoll, the chancellor of Dallas Theological Seminary, says every day one has a choice of how that day is going to go. That is my own personal philosophy and I attempt to instill it in our employees.

"This is where vision comes into the equation. One knows what the current situation is and also what you would like it to be. I encourage employees to think about this on a daily basis. Positive attitude makes the difference between no expectations and the realization of vision."

What's Right, Not Who's Right

"We have the word 'Attitude' on the back of all of our business cards. We also have an Attitude pin, a gold one, and we advertise it in our product catalog. That item is a best seller.

"When you wear 'Attitude' on your lapel, it influences the person to whom you are talking. It has a subliminal adjustment to the dialogue. It adjusts the tenor of the relationship and the persons involved in the conversation are not even aware of what is happening.

"I am a great believer that anything that starts out wrong is going to end up wrong. One has a mission to start everything right, fully expecting it to end up right. Acknowledging that individuals have paradigms that differ from others, an attitude of open mindedness is necessary. I happen to be a visionary and I know what's right. I see it. I have to deal with what's right, not who's right, and that is how I practice leadership. When our staff meets, we don't deal with who's right. We begin by asking these questions: Where are we going with this thing? What's your attitude? Why are we going there?

"We begin with the end in mind, then the floor is open for discussion. All attitudes are open at that point. There is no time to self-promote. Instead, the results of that which we are seeking are promoted.

"My method works well. I started this company only 12 years ago and, with the help and dedication of our employees, took it to almost $40 million in sales the first 10 years. The market was untapped. In fact, there was no identifiable market. We had all new technology, and opened many doors in the market. We did it with a 'what's right for results' attitude."

Find Your Ah-Hah!

"I'm a journeyman toolmaker by training. I was determined to be the best and I was. My determination was a real big part of the equation. I know my limitations and back off when I know that I am not suited for a particular challenge. For example, I am not an NBA star at five feet eight inches tall. I realized it was okay to let that dream go, because I knew I could do other things well.

"As one ages, one goes through the process of elimination. You have tried many things, and then go through a discernment process that allows you to recognize what works and does not work for you. You recognize your limits, your talents, and your ability to do what you want to do.

"My turning point was at the age 50. Up to that time, I was listening to the story that others had written. At 50, I began to write my own story. It was an Ah-hah moment for me. All of a sudden, the lights went on, the bells started ringing, and I knew. This was the way to go! Ah-hah is a positive attitude energy word."

Keith's Attitude Check

A gentleman rushed up to me after a motivation speech I gave for the company where he worked, and he said, "You've got to connect with this guy I know. 'Attitude is Everything' is engraved on a rock outside his company." When Don Wood and I talked, we had a super-fantastic conversation about attitude and how attitude is everything.

Attitude is the reason behind the name of his company 80/20, Inc. It's named after the Pareto Principle that states that 80 percent of your results come from 20 percent of your efforts.

The company philosophy comes from a Chinese proverb: "There is a man in the world who will never be turned down. He is the man who delivers the goods." A customer-service attitude is the mantra of every employee. Company business cards reflect the team effort 80/20 puts toward customer sevice. No titles are listed behind the employees names.

Don Wood has instilled vision and a "whatever it takes" attitude to motivate employees to deliver goods in such a way that the company leads the pack in the T-slotted aluminum assembly industry. The company Web site sums up the company attitude toward continued success: "We can't predict the future—we're too busy creating it!"

Like other leaders, Don focuses his attitude for leadership daily on the word WIN—What's Important Now, and what's important to Don is his team of people. He is a licensed facilitator of Stephen Covey's, *The Seven Habits of Highly Effective People*, and often teaches the course in a one-on-one fashion. By teaching the course, Woods helps people in his organization who are eager to learn do the right things for themselves. Don's CAPSIZING attitude (Cultivate an Atmosphere of Productivity by Sensing an Individual's Zeal for Involvement and Nurturing it for Growth) helps his employees find their ah-hah without having to spend 50 years of trial and error. Don' company, 80/20, Inc. benefits from the positive energy as well.

Insight is required to identify or discover the potential in people. If leaders do not know how to discern their own potential and limitations, they will find it difficult to discern the same in their people. Identifying weaknesses will be the focus, rather than developing strengths. Don Wood is able to develop the strengths of his employees, because he operates in self-awareness of his own limitations and potential. He treats his employees as protégés, rather than personnel projects.

Don Wood is dedicated to positioning people where they excel, where their gifts are. He feels so strongly about positioning people correctly that he is willing to go beyond the needs of 80/20 to help people succeed, and in doing so, he demonstrates that a leader's attitude cannot be selfish with people's abilities. Don's passion and vision attitude toward promotion is unique when compared to the conventional paper-and-votes attitude. His ability to go beyond credentials and promote based on passion and a can-do attitude has been beneficial to the company and its progress.

You Gotta Have Heart

A colleague of mine shared an occasion where she felt credentials and numbers were weighed too heavily in a hiring decision, and the results were not productive in the long run. "Our plant was in need of an electrical engineer. The company policy, however, ruled out anyone with less than a 3.0 grade point average. A candidate submitted a resume with strong engineering and other work experience. We found out that he was married with children and working full time while securing his engineering degree. He finished with a 2.5 GPA. A few of us lobbied on his behalf, noting that he had 'real life' skills and obviously showed potential to balance multiple projects and still do well. Our lobbying did not prevail.

"The engineering manager hired a fresh-out-of-school 4.0 GPA graduate with limited 'real life' skills, despite the red flags in character and maturity highlighted during non-interview interactions. The candidate answered the interview questions in such a way that the evaluation system indicated he was hirable. It wasn't long before the maintenance department targeted him for playing jokes on others and giving people unpleasant nicknames. He was transferred to another facility in less than two years, and was no longer with the company in less than three years. Sometimes the numbers just don't add up to the attitude of the heart."

Meet the Challenge

Sometimes being a leader means challenging and allowing your people to grow. Sometimes leadership is not always about leading others, but about leading yourself. Personal leadership can be difficult. We all need friends, mentors, or leaders to challenge us, whether we are working for Fortune 500 companies, are self-employed, or are single parents.

Three years after I started my business as a professional speaker and trainer, a colleague of mine, Larry Winget, challenged me to write a book. I remember being at the National Speakers Association Annual Conference in a writing workshop with Larry. I walked out after the session and commented, "Boy, that was a great workshop. Lots of valuable information, but I can't write a book." To be totally honest, I thought my inability to write was my biggest weakness. That leadership skill was the one I thought I did not possess.

Larry responded to my comment with, "You will never write a book, if you say you can't." He followed up with a personal invitation to fly to his Oklahoma office. He guaranteed me if I would change my attitude and be willing to pay the price, he could coach me and help me write a book.

Larry was correct. I would never write a book if I kept saying I couldn't. Today I am a published author, because of the grace of God, a solid support team, and my mentor, Larry Winget.

ATTITUDE ACTION PLAN

- Do you know your limitations and potential? Have you discovered your epiphany?

- If not, what are you waiting for? What are you afraid of?

- If so, have you shared intimately with your teams about your experiences?

- What systems do you have in place to help identify the potential in people? Have you perhaps overlooked potential leaders because of academic or social credentials? What methods do you use to identify, grow, and position up-and-coming leaders in your organization?

(continued)

Continued

▪ How do you maintain an attitude toward what's right versus who's right, when working toward results?

▪ How does your organization respond to outside influences on productivity and morale? Does the rumor mill conjure up fears of downsizing and distrust, or does the innovation wheel crank out enterprising ways to increase efficiency?

Brief Biography

Founded in 1989, **Don Wood** and two of his sons began to build a company that by design, was unprecedented. Their goal was to offer a new product to the industrial marketplace and a novel way of doing business . . . the customer is and always will be . . . the boss.

The Wood family had a clear vision of what opportunities that could be created by their revolutionary concept. They understood the value of interdependent relationships between manufacturer, sales, personnel, and the customer. 80/20's rapid growth is a testimonial to this understanding. Always reinvesting in our people, technology, and product development, 80/20 continues to set a standard, which other companies can only hope to achieve.

Look for the Seed of Advantage

Joe Louis Dudley Sr., President and CEO
Dudley Products

Joe Louis Dudley knows that fear does not have to thwart a person or keep him from excelling. He learned to face his fears, meet his challenges, and look for the hidden advantages. As a result, he overcame many difficulties that would have hindered lesser people. He could have given up at an early age and believed he was too mentally challenged to amount to anything. Instead, through strength, determination, and faith in himself and God, he outstripped all expectations that others had for him and eventually established his own empire in the hair-care and beauty-products industry.

"When the school counselor told my mother I was retarded, she came home and told me, 'That's all right, son; I believe slow people can rule the world, if they only have patience, because when slow ones get it, they got it for good.'

"Later, when other people told my mother that her boy Joe would never amount to much, she'd whisper in my ear, 'You go ahead and fool 'em.'

"Those positive statements were the first of many lessons my mother imparted to me. She often said, 'In every disadvantage, there is the seed of an advantage.'

"It's a seed, so you have to grow it, to overcome the disadvantage you face. I learned that while some thought I was 'slow,' I could use that

93

misconception to my advantage, to focus seriously on things. For example, I learned to read very well, because I took my time, and I read things over and over. To this day, I'll read a book four or five times, and I enjoy it and learn more, each and every time. I taught myself to look for the advantage in all circumstances, even those that other people considered to be disadvantageous. There is an advantage to be found in being young, old, short, tall, black, or white. In every situation or circumstance, there is an advantage, and you can act on it, rather than worrying about the disadvantages.

"I also believe that if you don't act on it, someone will step in and act against you. Others may say, 'Well, you are black, and that's a minority;' or they'll say, 'You have a speech impediment, so you must be slow-minded.' I prefer to find advantages to everything I have and to act on those advantages. The system has worked well for me.

"Money doesn't give me confidence. I have confidence in myself, not in my money. If I lose my money, I know there is plenty more money out there, and I can get it. I started out with no money, and I acquired it, so I have no fear that I couldn't acquire it again. When you've got confidence in yourself and believe God is on your side, no one can defeat you. If you believe in those solid principles, you can work through anything."

Negative Experiences Trigger Positive Action

"When I was 17, my girlfriend was a beautiful woman, and I was in love with her. One day she came to me and said, 'Joe, I want to get married.' I was excited about her statement, until she said, 'But I want smart kids, and you are retarded.'

"Some guys might have jumped off a bridge or become a monk after getting slapped down like that, but I didn't get depressed; I got motivated. That was the incident that changed my life. I decided then and there that I was going to develop my mind and acquire knowledge that nobody could ever take away from me.

"Up to that point, I hadn't put much energy into school, because I'd accepted the labels the teachers had put on me. They told me I was slow, so I'd lived down to their expectations. After my girlfriend told me I wasn't smart enough for her, though, I decided I was going to make up for lost time. I gathered my schoolbooks all the way back to first grade, and I started my own self-study program. I read what I should have been reading when I was out playing around. I was determined to improve my mind and show people I was not slow-minded. Catching up on my education wasn't easy. While other guys played sports, I stayed in and read and studied. Every time I got tired of studying and trying to improve myself, I would think about what my ex-girlfriend had said, and the memory gave me inspiration. I was motivated to go for greatness, to do more with my life. That drive has never gone away. I still always strive to be more and do more.

"One of the most important things that ever happened in my life was that I was able to take the negative situation with my girlfriend and turn it into a very powerful force for positive change. Looking back, sometimes I don't understand how I thought to do what I did, because like any other person, my first thought was to get in a big fight with her. Instead, I calmed down and did something good with it. I don't know how I managed to follow through with my plan, but I'm very glad I did, because the benefits still come to me today.

"Courage is the power to do something in spite of the difficulties and challenges. I started selling products house to house, and people said to me, 'You can't make it.' You have to have the courage to believe you can make it, in spite of whatever problems you have. I used to knock on doors and people would show sympathy for me and teach me how to pronounce the words I mispronounced. It didn't bother me. I knew I didn't know that day, but the next day, I would know. That's how I got started. It was hard. On my first day out, I sold $2.60 worth of products. I made about $1.20. My feet were tired; my hands, my shoulders, and my legs were worn out, too, but not my spirit. I decided I wanted to be somebody, and I was at the turning point. I kept walking and knocking and selling and reading, and I finally finished college. I was 26 years old before I finished. I stayed in sales, and I've been in sales ever since. I learned that while you may be afraid of certain things, you have to have the courage to go into it."

The Image of God

"The secret is really knowing God and understanding and knowing yourself, too. Like I tell people, 'We could have been dogs or cats or rats or roaches, but we're made in the highest form of life, the image of God.' We have to recognize that we are the highest form of life, the image of God, and accept it. I understand it. At least, I work toward understanding it. God is good. He said if you ask, he will give it to you. If you seek, ye shall find.

"When I went to work for Fuller Products, I found that my faith and belief in self-determination were perfectly matched to the corporate philosophy, which encouraged positive thinking and rewarded initiative. My wife and I built the most successful Fuller distributorship in the nation. When we had difficulty getting Fuller products, we made our own, which led to the establishment of our own company. In 1976, S. B. Fuller, the founder of Fuller Products and my mentor, was having health problems. He asked me to come to Chicago and run his company for him, which I did for eight years. During that period, Fuller taught me many lessons in entrepreneurial leadership.

"In many ways, my mentor and I were alike. He was reared in poverty in Louisiana and had only a sixth grade education, but he possessed an innate intelligence and drive. He started as a door-to-door salesman and built one of the first African-American multimillion-dollar conglomerates.

"Mr. Fuller eventually owned or controlled nine corporations, including the Courier newspaper chain with papers in Pittsburgh, Chicago, New York, and Detroit; a Chicago department store; and a New York real estate trust. He was a champion of black self-determination through business, which made him the focus of attacks by white racists. Oddly, Mr. Fuller also had enemies among his own people. Some blacks called him an 'Uncle Tom,' because he stated that blacks could achieve success and prosperity if they pursued educations and developed businesses instead of relying on government handouts and demanding their civil rights.

"While some African Americans misunderstood Fuller's calls for self-determination, which echoed those of Booker T. Washington and many of today's black leaders, I understood my mentor's belief that once blacks had economic power, they could claim a full share of the American dream.

"I credit my mother and my wife with the success of our family business empire, which began in 1957 when I invested $10 in a sales kit and became a Fuller Brush man. I sold Fuller beauty products door-to-door part-time while studying business at North Carolina A&T State University. I continued to sell door-to-door in Brooklyn, New York, during summer vacations and later when I became a protégé of S. B. Fuller, the pioneering African-American entrepreneur and founder of the Fuller Products Company in Chicago."

Direct Sales Equals Direct Leadership

"The thing I liked about direct sales was that it developed my attitude and leadership qualities and rewarded them. Nobody stood over me every day telling me what to do. Whether or not I made money on any given day was up to me. If I hit the streets and made sales, I was rewarded. If I stayed home, I didn't make a dime. I saw immediate rewards for being industrious and for working hard. I reaped the benefits of learning more about my products and my customers.

"I liked being self-reliant. When I met other people selling Fuller products, I was also impressed at their initiative. They were like me. They were hard workers who didn't look for handouts anywhere. And they were successful. They had cars and houses, and they were confident, successful people. Their success impressed me and inspired me."

Four Qualities of Leadership Plus One

"When I think of the characteristics of leadership, I think of courage, initiative, integrity, and loyalty. You don't have to be born with those qualities. You can acquire them as I did, and once you have done that, God will give you the fifth gift of leadership, which is insight or wisdom. Together, those qualities give you the creativity to accomplish great things.

"I look for people who work because they want to create something. I'm not interested in people who work to acquire things or to make money. If you are working somewhere just to buy things or pay the bills, that's okay for the short-term, but you've got a problem for the long-term. Money is a by-product of work. It shouldn't be a goal. I tell people they should work to create accomplishment and a successful life. The money will follow.

"I've always believed that part of being a leader was helping other people, so as my business grew, I tried to do that. I hired others and helped them grow. I've always encouraged my employees to save and invest and do everything they could to build their economic bases. In fact,

I made it a requirement that everyone who worked for me save money to buy a house, because a house is one of the best investments you can have.

"Sometimes, though, you have to put a little salt in the water to make people thirsty. You give them a taste, so they develop an appetite. I'd let people stay in my guesthouse, so they could see for themselves the benefits of saving money and buying a home. Believe me, my little tactic worked."

Help Others

"I went to a predominantly black high school to give a speech, one time, and I discovered only three or four kids were on the honor roll. I didn't like those statistics, so I decided to do something. It was important to the kids to have hope for a better future through education, so I made a promise. I guaranteed them that I would make sure that every one of those kids who finished high school would also get to college.

"My staff and I figured the cost of such a program would be about $250,000. I wanted to make the project something that more people could get involved in, so I told my employees I wanted each of them to give six dollars a week to the fund for the high school students. We had about 200 employees, then. Some of them said they'd like to help, but they couldn't afford it. I said, 'If you could afford it, would you do it?' They said they would, so I gave them all eight-dollar-a-week pay raises to cover the taxes and the six dollars. I didn't want their money. I wanted their spirit. I wanted them to be a part of helping these kids. It's been a great thing for all of us. Some of the kids we helped have become doctors. We took some of them to the White House to receive their awards. Not long ago I ran into two of our graduates in one day. I was at the airport, when one of them came up and told me he was preparing to become a doctor. It was heartwarming. If you asked me what leadership is all about, I'd say leadership is what makes the world change. True leaders step up and do what needs to be done. If they are leaders, they won't have to worry about followers. If you are a true leader, people will follow you."

Keith's Attitude Check

Joe Dudley was born the fifth of 11 children. He grew up in a three-room farmhouse in rural North Carolina. Joe was held back in the first grade and labeled mentally retarded, because he stuttered badly. Fortunately, he had a loving mother who never stopped believing in him. With her support, he overcame the incorrect assessment of his mental abilities and became one of the nation's leading African-American businessmen.

Think back in your life to when your mother, father, family member, or friend might have said something encouraging to you and how those words have made a positive mark on your life. One of my signature stories is about running home the first day of kindergarten. My teacher asked all the kids to stand up and to individually say their name out loud, when it was my turn, I stuttered so much I couldn't get my name out and the other kids laughed so loud that even today, I can still hear the giggles. I lived about two miles away from the school and I remember running as fast as I could. I saw a movie a few years ago that kind of reminded me of that day, it was *Forest Gump*. Seems like everywhere that little kid went, he ran. The main theme of that movie in my opinion was the love of a parent inspiring a child. Forest had obstacles to overcome, Joe had obstacles to overcome and starting that day knowing I didn't talk like other kids, I had a slight speech impediment, I had obstacles to overcome. I remember running up on the porch and my mom coming out of the house and giving me a big hug. When I tried to explain what had happened, she said she already knew, having just spoken to my teacher. I can't recall the exact words but my mom said something to this effect, "Honey, I know this hurts, this is what we call a challenge. We are not going to worry, we are going to work hard. Mommy's going to get you some help. Because mommy can already see it and you have to start seeing it, start seeing that one day you are going to stand tall and one day you are going to say your name as loud and as well as all the other boys and girls." My mom was right, if you want to overcome anything today as a leader you have to work hard.

Challenge Offers Opportunity

Quoting directly from his own life experiences, Joe Dudley says that in every challenge lies an opportunity.

When others pinned degrading labels on Joe and told him his future was limited, his mother stepped up and became his champion. Her voice became the only one he heeded, and it has guided him to a lifetime of achievement as one of the country's leading entrepreneurs.

My grandmother used to say that what they say to you doesn't have to live through you. In my speeches, I tell my audiences to set up a "no toxic zone" around themselves. I believe in life there are two kinds of people, those that pull you up and those that try to pull you down. Let's face it. Some people are toxic, their attitudes are so bad, sometimes they don't have to say anything to you, just their presence and nonverbal communication can affect your attitude. Setting up a no toxic zone means that you have an imaginary positive shield around what you hear, around what you see, and around what other people try to do to you. Therefore, no negative force can penetrate. Every leader needs to master setting up a no toxic zone.

Many great leaders bring to their lives the same optimistic attitude that drove Joe Dudley to succeed. His life is proof that every new challenge is accompanied by a fresh opportunity, and for every door that closes, another opens. "The greatest challenge you face is to be ready to enter these doors of opportunity," said the Reverend Martin Luther King Jr.

I'm not talking about some Pollyannaish rose-colored-glasses approach to life. No one succeeds in business without being realistic. Instead, Joe's attitude reflects his deep belief in his own power to determine the course of his life. He looked for and seized on every advantage he could. He even found the seed of an advantage in being born to a poor black family. As he notes, once you've proven that you can rise from such humble beginnings, you have nothing to fear. The worst that can happen is that you go back to the poverty you were born with, and you've already shown you can overcome that.

Turning Points to Learning Points

One of the benefits of Joe's proactive approach to life is that he learned to turn bad experiences into positive motivation.

I call this shifting your turning points (which are your negative challenges and setbacks in life) to learning points. Most leaders realize that life is nothing more than a series of lessons and, if you don't learn the lesson, life will serve it to you again, and again, and again. Let's face it, we are born into this world, no one receives a life certificate that reads hassle free, adversity eliminated, problems/setbacks null and void. As a leader today, you can't hold onto your past, making excuses for why you are where you are. No excuses, turn your bad experiences into a force for positive motivation, remember your past may be impacting your present but it doesn't dictate your future.

Booker T. Washington said, "Few are too young and none are too old to make the attempt to learn." Joe Dudley has spent a lifetime proving the value of a positive attitude, a courageous heart, a self-disciplined mind, and energetic human initiative. He keeps learning, as a leader Joe never stops growing. He was inspired by his mother's readings of the Bible, particularly the scripture, "Seek and ye shall find. Knock and the door shall be opened."

What are you seeking, what are you going after, what do you really want to accomplish? Are you knocking, which means are you making an effort, an announcement that you are prepared to step up and step into those things or areas in your life you are pursuing? Do you have an optimistic attitude, are you confident now that you have knocked at the door of opportunity?

This young man who was labeled "retarded" graduated from college with a business degree and has lived a life of success as an entrepreneur, business leader, philanthropist, and inspiration to people everywhere.

In his frequent speeches to students around the country, Joe tells young people, "There is a champion in you that's struggling to come out. Let the champ out." He also tells them, "When life gives you a lemon, run for the sugar. Tough times don't last, but tough people do." Those familiar phrases carry an unusual amount of power when delivered by someone who is living proof of the power of positive thinking.

By the way, Joe Dudley tells me he has read Norman Vincent Peale's classic book, *The Power of Positive Thinking*, at least 300 times. As a leader, you are what you read. Repetition of the right information is the master key. You can't stop learning. If you think you are ripe and know it all as a leader, it will not be long before you rot. Joe definitely has a positive attitude about life—one that has propelled him to great heights from humble beginnings.

Courageous Leadership

Joe's depth of character served him well when he was young and continues to do so. Even after he had proven the agility of his mind and the strength of his spirit, Joe still had to enter the working world and prove himself in the marketplace. Think of the courage this man needed to become a door-to-door salesman! His speech impediment was so severe that his teachers had thought him to be mentally deficient. It turns out he was mentally efficient; he turned their dark declarations into a bright future for himself and for others.

The leader in you should always strive to maintain the highest level of character. You should always remind yourself that you are only an attitude away from success. Who you are and what you are will always be the blueprint of your destiny. What level of courage do you need to embrace? Every leader is a salesperson. What is your product and what benefits do I receive by following you? Like Joe Dudley, you must be able to handle criticism, the false reports, the negative things others will say. Remember, garbage in, garbage stays. I remember when I was dating a very nice looking young lady who just out of the blue dumped me. I know she didn't dump me because she didn't think I was intelligent, in my personal opinion she got rid of me because I didn't have enough to offer her. She was a few years younger than me, she had other men knocking at her door who were able to offer her more. Looking back, I can't blame her, who wouldn't want to travel, go to major sporting events, be wined and dined and hang out with celebrities. That situation had a profound effect on me. It inspired me to set higher goals for myself, motivated me to take a closer look at myself and to challenge myself to improve in every area in my life. Her dumping me, just like Joe's girlfriend dumping him, turned out to be a blessing in disguise.

Joe did not mention one final leadership quality he also possesses and models every day, so I'm going to add it for him. He also has an attitude of gratitude and generosity. The final mark of a true leader is someone who achieves success and then does everything possible to spread it around. Joe Dudley has built many bridges back across the economic divide and has escorted scores of people to the side of success.

Joe Dudley's philanthropy extends beyond his employees. Several years ago, he received a Points of Light Award from the foundation established by former President George Bush. Joe received this honor for providing scholarships to the entire student body at Dudley High School.

ATTITUDE ACTION PLAN

- Have you made a list of your challenges?

- Have you examined those challenges to find the hidden advantages in them?

- What negative trait, label, or challenge would you like to overcome first?

- Have you created a plan that will keep you focused on overcoming your challenge?

- Do you challenge your employees to give back to the community?

- How do you encourage your employees to save for the future and invest wisely?

- Do you build bridges and give opportunities to others less fortunate than you?

- What have you accomplished that others thought was impossible? How did you feel when you've faced the challenge and overcame it? Savor the feeling and let it drive you toward staring down and winning over all challenges and obstacles in the future.

Brief Biography

Joe Louis Dudley Sr., president and chief executive officer of Dudley Products, Inc., is one of the world's largest manufacturers and distributors of hair care and beauty products and is a provider of basic and advanced training for cosmetologists.

He received his bachelor of science degree in business administration from North Carolina A&T University in Greensboro.

By 1975, Dudley had launched Dudley Products Company with a salesforce of more than 400, owned a beauty school, a chain of beauty supply stores throughout the southeastern region of the United States, and was an entrepreneurial success.

Joe L. Dudley Sr. is much more than just a successful entrepreneur. He is known nationally and internationally as an inspirational speaker and humanitarian who spends much of his time identifying needs and giving back to the community and mankind.

He is married to the former Eunice Mosley and is the father of three children, all of whom are very active in the business. Mrs. Eunice M. Dudley is Chief Financial Officer and Executive Director of The Dudley Beauty School System. Son Joe Jr., holds undergraduate and MBA degrees from Northwestern University and is vice president of finance. Daughter Ursula, a graduate of Harvard University, is director of Dudley Cosmetics, General Counsel for Dudley Products, Inc. and vice president of Marketing. Youngest daughter, Genea, a recent graduate of Duke University's MBA Program is brand manager in the marketing division. Mr. Dudley has one grandson, Mark Oglesby Jr.

Who Are Your Bellwethers?

General Lance Lord
U.S. Air Force

Sheep growers learned centuries ago that one lamb usually stands out as the leader, the smartest of the flock, the one who finds the best path. If the shepherd puts a bell around the neck of that natural leader, the rest of the animals follow, and the herd travels together wherever it is supposed to go. The lead sheep, the bell wearer, became known as the bellwether. Business leaders of today know to locate the natural leaders, the bellwethers, the smart ones within their organizations, and allow those people to blaze trails. Others will follow the bellwethers, and the organizations benefit. General Lance Lord understands the bellwether concept and lives by it.

"As our Chief of Staff likes to say, 'We have 0 percent chance of being 100 percent right.' That's why it's important to have a bellwether committee we can turn to when we're facing daunting decisions. Bellwethers are individuals with different areas of expertise, people we trust implicitly, who help us 'think broad' and see all sides of an issue. You test out your proposed course of action on them and can count on hearing balanced feedback on why it will or won't work. When advisors play devil's advocate, they draw out our thinking and increase the likelihood that we'll move forward with the best possible solution.

"The perception is false that the military is a total autocracy and only rank has its privileges. Yes, there is a chain of command that we honor; however, the smartest leaders, military and nonmilitary, have always been participative managers who seek out the opinions of others. Rank may have its privileges, but leaders who actively involve their people are better able to get the job done."

Visit the Field

"There's no substitute for face-to-face communication. Taking the time to talk with your staff members one-on-one makes a statement. It says, 'I want to know what you think. I care what you think. What you think has value.'

"If I ever get overwhelmed by the bureaucratic red tape of a government job, I make it a point to get out of my office and visit the field. As soon as I start talking with the people on the frontline who are actually doing the work, I get excited all over again about our mission. These are the people designing, flying, and tracking the satellites. It gets me out of my administrative head and into the 'hands' of our organization. I get to see the tangible results of our work, and it reminds me of our credo, 'If you're not in space, you're not in the race.'"

Having Fun Yet?

"What do I do to get away from it all? I jump on my Harley-Davidson and take off. It's thrilling, because it demands complete, total concentration. Sometimes I ride solo, and sometimes I ride with a group. I've even gone on a 1,000-mile bike run for a charity fund-raiser. I think it's important for leaders to have a hobby that gives them an opportunity to do the opposite of what they do at work. That way, they truly get a break and come back refreshed and ready to go.

"Phil Jackson, the coach of the Los Angeles Lakers and the former coach of the Chicago Bulls, wrote a great book called *Sacred Hoops*. In that book, he talks about immersing yourself in what you do, and that's what happens when I'm on that Harley. The only thing that exists is the wind in my face and the freedom of being on the road."

What's Integrity to You?

"One of the keys to leadership is behaving in a way that engenders trust. What makes people trust us? They trust us if they perceive we are acting with integrity. What causes them to think we're acting with integrity? If we do things right and don't cut corners.

"Integrity is understanding that cutting corners is not an option. There is a cumulative effect from cutting corners that is like radioactivity—it can kill you. It can kill your reputation. It can kill your mission. It can kill your organization. In our business, it can even kill people. That is simply not an option."

The Evolution of a Leader

"In the beginning of my career, I was ambitious like many others, I'm sure. Quite honestly, I was in it for myself. My goal was to move up the ranks as quickly as possible. After a while, my priorities changed, and my primary commitment was to accomplish the mission. Now what drives me, what satisfies me the most, is seeing the people who work for and with me succeed. I think true leadership is not about self-achievement; it's about empowering and motivating your staff to achieve."

Keith's Attitude Check

Do you have a bellwether committee? Do you have trusted colleagues you turn to for advice, because they, too, are natural leaders? One of the reasons I've been fortunate to do well in my career is that, from the beginning, I sought out the best and learned from the best.

When you surround yourself with people who have areas of expertise to offer you, you multiply your knowledge, your abilities, and your effectiveness. Interestingly, the bellwether effect often turns into a two-way street, where your experts turn to you for your opinions and knowledge in your area of expertise, as well. The give-and-take of good bellwether associations creates an ever-growing network of experts, exponentially increasing your efficacy.

Have You Lost Touch?

Do you find yourself getting caught up in all the logistical requirements of your job? As leaders, it's easy to lose touch with the frontline impact of what we do. We may spend so much time handling the big-picture aspects of our job that we feel removed from the hands-on part of our work. A friend who started his own rafting company became disillusioned with being an entrepreneur, because he spent all his time in the office running the business instead of being out on the river running rapids, as he'd visualized. He needed to surround himself with experts in his office, and then leave them, let them do their job, and take in some "time in the field," enjoying the sport he supported. If he took time to enjoy his sport again, he would be energized to keep going with his business, and he would be more helpful to his clients, as well, because he would constantly be increasing his firsthand knowledge of rafting.

General Lord's practice of visiting the field is a wonderful way to reconnect with the team members who are experiencing and producing the real-world results of our work.

I remember one particularly busy time I returned home exhausted from a two-week speaking tour. I had flown from one end of the country to the other, and back again. Because it was winter, I experienced many flight delays due to bad weather and often had to rush to hotels and meeting halls. All in all, I was beat, and I dragged myself to my desk to take care of some paperwork that had piled up while I was gone. Donna, my office manager, does a wonderful job handling my business; however, when I get back, a number of items still need my attention.

While I was in the middle of trying to drum up the energy to tackle my paperwork, the phone rang. I picked it up and a friend I hadn't heard from in a long time said, "I just had to call and tell you the good news."

She told me her son, who had been having some hard times, had broken through. My friend had endured a difficult divorce, and she and her two sons moved to a part of the country where they didn't know anyone. She said, "It seemed like I was the only single mom in that area, and it was really hard on my sons not to have their father or a father figure looking out for them. Although my youngest son has always been a good student, his new school put him at the bottom of his sixth grade class. He wanted me to go to the principal's office and fight for him to get switched, but I told him he already knew what it was like to start on the top and stay on the top; now it was time for him to learn how to start at the bottom and work his way to the top.

"As you can imagine," she said, "he wasn't very happy about it, but I told him he needed to learn that life is unfair. Those first few months were tough on him. He almost committed suicide. You sent one of your 'Attitude Is Everything' audiotapes, though, and he listened to it. It was a turning point for him.

"Your tape motivated him to stop complaining and to understand he had a choice. He could gripe about how unfair things were and that he did not deserve to be treated that way, or he could start doing something to changes things."

My friend pronounced proudly, "Not only did he graduate from eighth grade with straight As, he got one of five awards for the whole district given to students who were deemed Most Respectful to Teachers and Peers. Plus, on the last day of school, he told me, 'Mom, please drive me over to the high school. I hear they have a track team that practices at seven in the morning, and I want to be there to run with them.'

"When I asked if he had any friends he was going to meet there, he said, 'No, I don't know anyone there, but I've learned a lesson from the past two years. It's a whole lot more fun being on the top than being on the bottom. When you're on the top, people respect you. They want to know you and be around you. When you're on the bottom, no one cares. From now on, I'm going to make sure I'm on the top.'

"He has confidence now. He's one of the best runners on his high school track team. He's done a 180-degree turnaround, because of his attitude about the 'Big MO.' He learned from your tape that action triggers momentum, and that when you're down and out, if you can take just one action, it triggers momentum that leads to more action, and before you know it, it's a spark that explodes.

"He's planning to go into the Air Force, and he's looking into a program at MIT that interests him. Your ideas on attitude helped him get out of his funk and start taking the first steps that led to all these wonderful things in his life. I wanted to call and thank you for creating the 'Big MO' in my son."

In Need of Some "Big MO?"

All of a sudden, I wasn't tired anymore, and that pile of paperwork didn't look as daunting. My friend's thoughtful phone call reminded me of—and recommitted me to—my mission of sharing my belief that Attitude Is Everything.

We've all heard the term MBWA, Management By Walking Around. How long has it been since you've gotten out from behind your desk and checked in with people on the frontlines? How long has it been since you've called your customers, visited your factories, or walked through the warehouse? Like it did for General Lord, and like it did for me, it will probably remind you of why you do what you do. It will make your work worthwhile, all over again. One action can trigger the momentum, the flow of energy that recharges your leadership batteries.

Fun Is Not Frivolous

Do you have a hobby that gets you away from it all? I once heard that the purpose of a vacation is to provide contrast. If you're around people all the time, you probably want to go to an island retreat where you have peace and quiet. If you're sedentary, you're probably interested in doing something adventurous. If you work in a busy office where you make decisions all day, you might want to take a cruise where the biggest decision you have to make is whether to have lunch at the buffet or on the pool deck.

I've taken up golf, and although it can be frustrating, it can also be fun. I admit to playing Army golf (left, right, left, right); however, it's thrilling to hit a drive that sails 250 yards straight down the fairway. I don't do that very often, but when I do it sure feels good. So much of my life is spent in hotels, convention centers, airports, and concrete cities, that it's a joy to get out in the middle of a natural setting where trees, lagoons, and colorfully landscaped grounds surround me. A few hours on the course, and I'm ready to hit the road again, refreshed and full of energy.

What reenergizes you? We can't be effective leaders if we're running on empty. What makes your soul sing? What do you do that you're good at, that you enjoy, and that makes you feel like a kid again? Having fun is not something to do only after our work is done. It's something to do so we can get more high-quality work done.

Cut the Temptation to Cut Corners

As leaders, our responsibility is to set an example of excellence and establish and enforce a standard for excellence. Good enough is not good enough. There is no shortcut to success.

A friend who operates a printing business says her biggest challenge, as a business owner, is to impart the attitude of excellence. "When I interview potential employees, I tell them up front that part of their responsibility is doing everything with excellence. When they ask what that means, I tell them, 'It means every project that goes out our doors is something we're proud of. It means that if the counter is cluttered with trash a customer left behind, we clean it up. It means if the ink runs low and copies are coming out fuzzy, we replace the ink then, instead of thinking we'll take care of it later.'

"In the beginning, I have to hold new hires accountable for little things like that. I don't know if people are lazy or if they're simply accustomed to producing shoddy work, but it seems many employees try to get by with only a halfhearted effort. I don't let them slide, though. I'm not unkind about it; I just let them know I mean what I say. If a task isn't up to standard, they need to redo it until it is.

"I've noticed that people start taking pride in their work to the degree that they're held accountable for the quality of that work. If they're allowed to do sloppy work, they will. If they're held accountable for excellent work, they'll rise to the challenge and eventually do it voluntarily, because people want to be proud of what they do."

Turn Me into We

I was impressed with General Lord's honest confession of his ambition early in his career. I think it's natural for us to be "in it for ourselves" when we start out. When we're young, we're eager to prove ourselves. Climbing the corporate ladder is what life is all about.

Usually, though, our goal of individual achievement morphs and matures into wanting organizational achievement. As we assume leadership responsibilities, our focus switches off ourselves and on to helping others achieve their potential.

I feel blessed when I get a phone call or an e-mail from a program participant who is thoughtful enough to get in touch to tell me how my ideas have influenced him or her. Just the other day at the airport, a woman who walked by stopped in her tracks, turned back toward me, and said, "Keith Harrell?"

She came over, threw her arms around me, and gave me a big hug. She said, "I thought that was you! I bought your book for my husband a few months ago. He had been with a company for 14 years, when a huge conglomerate bought it out. He was let go the next week, just like that. He was angry and bitter. He moped around the house for weeks and wouldn't even look for another job, because he was upset. No matter what I said, he just got moodier and moodier.

"I saw your book in the bookstore and thought maybe it could help. I bought it and left it out for him on the kitchen table. The next thing I know, he was quoting you! He talked about your Little League coach, Sarge, and how you weren't very good at baseball, because you were so tall, and that your first year you didn't even get a uniform, just a baseball cap. He talked about how your coach would hit those high fly balls to you in the outfield and tell you, 'Get on your horse and go get it.' My husband said you made the team that year, not because of your talent, but because of your hustle and your attitude.

"I guess your story helped him realize that sitting home moaning and groaning about what had happened to him wasn't going to change things, and it was time for him to get on his horse and get out there and hustle for a job. He got involved with the Chamber of Commerce, and by the next month, found a job through a contact he'd made there. I'm so glad I get to thank you in person for what you've done for us!"

I told her, "No, thank you."

ATTITUDE ACTION PLAN

- Who is the bellwether advisor you turn to for advice? If you don't have one or more, what plans do you have for finding wise people when you need counsel?

- Do you find yourself getting stuck behind your desk? What do you do to get out and stay in touch with your employees, customers, and vendors?

- What is your hobby?

- How often do you take time off from work to change your environment, refresh your attitude, decompress, or learn something new?

- How would you define integrity?

- Who is someone you know who models integrity?

- Can you think of a time you cut corners on a project or in your dealings with someone?

- How do you get the message across to your employees that cutting corners is not an option?

- How do you hold them accountable and reward them for high-quality work?

- Think back to the beginning of your career. Were you ambitious or in it for yourself? Do you still feel that way?
- If you have matured since then, what drives you in your career today?
- Have you had the satisfying experience of having someone tell you how you've influenced him or her?

Brief Biography

General Lance Lord is commander, Air Force Space Command, Peterson Air Force Base, Colorado. He is responsible for the development, acquisition, and operation of the Air Force's space and missile systems. General Lord oversees a global network of satellite command and control, communications, missile warning and launch facilities, and ensures the combat readiness of America's intercontinental ballistic missile force. He leads more than 39,700 space professionals who provide combat forces and capabilities to North American Aerospace Defense Command and U.S. Strategic Command.

General Lord entered the Air Force in 1969 as a graduate of the Otterbein College ROTC program. He completed a series of Air Staff and Department of Defense-level assignments in strategic missiles after serving four years of Minuteman II ICBM alert duty. He directed the Ground-Launched Cruise Missile Program Management Office in Europe. He was a military assistant to the director of Net Assessment with the Office of the Secretary of Defense and represented the Air Force as a research associate in international security affairs at Ohio State University.

General Lord commanded two ICBM wings in Wyoming and North Dakota. In California, he commanded a space wing responsible for satellite launch and ballistic missile test launch operations. He served as director of Plans and as vice commander for Headquarters Air Force Space Command. The general led Air Force education and training as commandant of Squadron Officer School, commander of 2nd Air Force, commander of Air University, and director of Education for Air Education and Training Command. Prior to assuming his current position, General Lord was the assistant vice chief of staff for Headquarters U.S. Air Force.

Leading the Cheers

David J. Serlo, President and CEO
PSCU Financial Services

The leadership philosophy of PSCU president David Serlo permeates his every conversation and everything he does. His personal motto is "Make your own breaks." His attitude of personal responsibility and proactive living has carried him to a life of achievement, even though a high school counselor once said he wasn't college material. It also permeates his philosophy of leadership. He does not wait for something good to happen for his company. He works to make things happen.

"I grew up in Jeannette, a blue-collar industrial town outside of Pittsburgh, Pennsylvania, where I learned early on that nothing would be handed to me. My dad worked in a factory, and my mother worked as a cashier in a grocery store. They taught me from the very beginning what it meant to give somebody a good workday, and for my parents, a good workday was not eight to five. It was 10 hours. The work ethic was baked into my life's lesson plan, and so was the value of a good education. I don't think a day goes by that I don't think back to the experience that made me dedicated to getting a good education.

"Dad worked nights at the factory to make a few extra bucks, and one night, I took his lunch in to him. It was the first time I had walked into the factory area. I felt the dampness and the cold of the lunchroom and saw it was rat infested, too. It was a defining moment for me. I thought that if my dad was willing to put in long hours in that kind of environment so that he could pay for the education of my younger brother and me, then I was going to make the most out of every dime he spent. My parents often talked about the fact that once a person obtained a good education, no one could ever take it away. Education was something that would provide benefits for the rest of my life.

"I was so struck by how hard he had to work that I decided I needed to make a significant commitment to repay him and my mother by giving a 110 percent effort to my schoolwork. Those two concepts—the need to work as hard as I possibly could and the desire to get the best education possible to repay my parents—have stayed with me to this day."

The Right Attitude Creates Opportunity

"When I was in high school, I took a college aptitude exam in my freshman year, and I did poorly. My counselor encouraged me not to follow the college preparatory curriculum, but instead to take a business curriculum. He said I probably would not get into a four-year college, based on how I had tested. In my junior year, I met a professor from a nearby college, Indiana University of Pennsylvania (IUP), a small school with very high academic standards. The professor came to our high school to evaluate the student teachers in my business classes. He spent a great deal of time sitting in my classes that year, and when he returned during my senior year, he asked me about my plans after high school. I told him what my counselor had told me, that I could probably only get into a two-year business school somewhere and get an associate degree there. The professor said he believed I was college material, in spite of what my counselor had said.

"That professor wrote a letter of recommendation for me to IUP, and based on that, I was accepted as a probationary student because I hadn't been allowed to take college prep courses in high school. He told me I was going to have to work incredibly hard to keep up with most of the other students who had been much better prepared for college. I hadn't taken any advanced science, math, or language classes in high school, so I had a lot of catching up to do. For me, my hard work wasn't about getting ahead. It was about getting to the level of the others in my class. The professor told me I wasn't going to be able to have the sort of social life that most of my classmates had, because I was so far behind. I accepted that fact. I sensed it was my opportunity to pay back my parents by working as hard as they had."

A Sense of Urgency

"One of the most important things I do as the president of PSCU-FS is provide a process to help create a common vision or mission in the company. After that, my job is to keep our people, our systems and structures, and our financial resources aligned with that mission. One aspect of that alignment is recruiting with our strategic goals in mind. I work to help our recruiters identify the kind of people we need, to fulfill the company's strategic plan. Another way I help keep us aligned is by supporting the training for our people who either need new skills or must learn how to adjust and deal with change.

"I see my responsibility in the company as aligning the right people at the right time in the right position as the strategic plan is developed. Envision a triangle. The left side of the triangle is the strategic plan, and the right side is the financial plan. The base of the triangle is our greatest asset—our people. If you are in the service business, I really don't know how you can be successful without spending a significant amount of time making sure the right people are in the right jobs delivering those services."

Fan and Cheerleader

"When I've done my job building the strategic and financial plans and a strong base of people, then my role is to be the our employees biggest fan and cheerleader. They answer all of the phones and the letters and deal with all of the problems. They bring in significant technical skills, and we rely on them day in and day out. In many ways, they are far more important than I am. Without them, the day-to-day victories would not happen. It's important that I let our employees know that I value what they do. One of the ways we show appreciation at PSCU-FS is to recognize employees. The walls of our offices are not lined with photographs of the board of directors and me. Instead, we hang pictures of our most accomplished employees.

"I think most employees really do want to make a contribution to the company's success. If you create the right culture within the company and give people the opportunity to use their knowledge, their creativity, and their experience, you don't have to think up artificial ways to motivate them. I see my job—and that of my management team—as finding ways to empower our people to make more and more decisions.

We need to think about empowering them all the time, because giving power to your employees creates motivation and excitement.

"I was the first employee of this company, and as the leader I consider it my duty to let our people know they are our most important assets. One of the ways I demonstrate that principle is to be one of the first to welcome new employees to the company. Whether they are entry-level employees in the mailroom or senior executives, I meet them face-to-face and spend an hour or so talking about the mission statement and our company values. I let them know where their company is positioned, where it is going, and where they fit into that picture. Later, their direct supervisors talk to them in more detail regarding the ABCs of their specific jobs. We also have regular employee meetings every four months, where I update them on company matters, and we recognize their achievements. I think it is their right to know what is going on and where we stand. We also update them more frequently in the company newsletter and in e-mail exchanges in which people can ask me direct questions. We also have Lunch-and-Learn sessions during which I present information.

"Aside from my communicating with employees frequently, we also support family events such as our Children's Day, where the sons and daughters of employees shadow their parents for a day. We also have company picnics, and we get involved in community service functions supported by our employees. We make it easy for them to be involved in things like Junior Achievement or the American Cancer Society or local school fund-raisers. Given my background, I'm especially interested in supporting our people financially, when they are willing to seek out additional educational opportunities. Those efforts pay huge dividends, because people stay with us longer, and the longer they stay, the smarter they get."

Building Trust

"I'd advise any business leader to put a high priority on building trust with employees. You do that by showing respect for them, giving them your trust by allowing them to make things happen, and by delivering on your commitments. Our company went through a difficult time in the late 1980s. We had to make a change to keep growing. Change is always threatening, and our strategy was controversial. It was a difficult time, yet it led not only to survival, but also to greater success.

One reason it worked was because we didn't abandon our existing customers. We looked after their needs and, in many cases, we exceeded their expectations.

"Our ability to uphold the commitments to the customer who stayed with us was one of the cornerstones in helping the company be successful. Our satisfied customers gave us a loyal base, and they actually helped sell our services to others in the marketplace.

"In 2000 we developed a new strategic plan. The new strategy included a realignment of our employees, which in many cases is a sugar-coated term for cutting costs by firing people. We didn't do that. We created a new strategic plan, but we adjusted our resources in alignment with it. We consolidated six offices into two. When we made that business decision, I knew it might adversely affect many people who would have to relocate or leave the company based on their family needs. I didn't want them to hear the news through the gossip mill or read it in the newspapers. I told them straight up that we had to do it, and I explained why we had to do it. I also let them know we would do everything we could to help them, whether they decided to stay with us or to seek other opportunities.

"Once I explained the logic behind the move—that it was about growth, not downsizing—I told them I would do all I could to keep as many of them as possible. In the offices that closed, we paid for each employee and spouse to visit both new locations, so they could decide whether to move with us. We gave them more than a year's notice to begin the process, so they weren't under pressure to make quick decisions. We took the long-term view, knowing what was going to be in the best interest of the company and our customers, to keep as many employees as possible. I told employees that my goal was to retain all of them, because we needed their experience. In the end, we kept 67 percent. Those employees represented collectively more than 400 years of experience, and that intellectual capital makes our company successful in delivering our services at high levels."

Keith's Attitude Check

David Serlo does not wait for something good to happen for his company. He works to make things happen. His attitude of personal responsibility for the success of his company and his focus on keeping the people of PSCU-FS aligned with the corporate mission has paid off well.

He builds trust and a sense of unity among his staff members that has resulted in one of the lowest employee turnover rates in the industry. This business leader has risen from humble beginnings to the top of his industry by sheer force of will and a sound work ethic.

David's commitment and appreciation for his parents' support drove David to excel in school, and it propelled him to his level of business achievement. His success is a great testimony to the power of attitude, because he had to work for everything he achieved, even the right to go to college. You will notice that his attitude of personal responsibility and being proactive carries over into his philosophy business leadership. He joined a company as its first employee, a company that outsourced every aspect, and within a few years, it had 800 employees!

When faced with negatives, some people get angry. Others get even. Successful people develop an "I'll show you" attitude, rather than getting angry. They channel their highly charged emotions into positive forces in their lives. That's what David Serlo did with the guidance counselor who wasn't wise enough to see his potential. He used his anger to drive himself to exceed the counselor's expectations. Once he established his attitude of overachievement—and what a great attitude that is—he kept right on going.

David also identified the things that he most enjoyed doing, and he built his career around them, which is another example of his proactive approach.

Personal values and attitudes are reflected in an individual's philosophy of leadership. The way David has led his life—always striving for greater accomplishment and always taking responsibility for his own success—is mirrored in his approach to leading his company.

ATTITUDE ACTION PLAN

- What do you do to make your own breaks?
- How do you repay those who supported you in the past, financially or emotionally?
- Do you constantly check to be sure your corporate decisions align with the company's strategic plan?
- Do you check to be sure your personal decisions align with your personal strategic plans?

- Do you hire employees with the company plan in mind?

- Do you strive to give power to the employees, to keep them motivated?

- What systems will you implement to motivate your employees even more?

- Do you have an attitude of overachievement, or are you satisfied to quit after a job is done well enough?

- How do you continue to educate yourself, now that your formal education may be completed?

- Do you educate and inform employees, so they will feel trustful and comfortable in their environment?

- What can you add to your current communication method? Have you considered newsletters, meetings, posters, fliers, e-mails, and other methods of communication?

- If change is imminent in your organization, do you give employees as much advance notice as possible? Do you give them options, or do you merely inform them that their jobs are about to change or end?

- Do you look for ways to keep your trained and faithful employees, even if you have to move them or retrain them?

- Have you recognized your strongest assets? What are you doing to help them align with your vision?

- What motives are effective in rewarding and motivating your strongest assets—your people?

- Are you a cheerleader? Is your enthusiasm contagious?

- Seventy percent of your attitude is nonverbal. What does your body language communicate?

- What ways do you display, communicate, and express your feelings and compassion for your people?

Brief Biography

David J. Serlo is the president and CEO of PSCU Financial Services headquartered in St. Petersburg, Florida. The company's 850 employees operate out of St. Petersburg as well as Phoenix, Arizona. PSCU Financial Services, a cooperative, exclusively services the credit union industry. Its product lines include credit cards, debit cards, electronic services, and call center support. The products are used by over 6.5 million consumers, who are members of 500 credit unions that own the company. Annual revenues total $200 million.

Dave is a graduate of Indiana University of Pennsylvania where he received his BS degree in Business Education in 1968 and his master's degree in 1970 from the same University, also in Business Education. In 1978, Dave earned his executive MBA from Loyola College in Maryland.

On graduation from college in 1968, Dave taught business subjects at Latrobe High School while attending graduate school. In 1970, after receiving his first masters degree, he began a 13-year career with the National Credit Union Administration (NCUA), an agency of the federal government that regulates and insures deposits in credit unions. He started as an examiner near his hometown in Pennsylvania, and quickly moved up the ranks to an executive level before his departure in 1983 at NCUA's headquarter office in Washington, D.C. Dave arrived at PSCU Financial Services as its first full-time employee in 1983 and now serves as its president and CEO. He has spent the past 33 years serving the credit union industry.

Dave grew up in Jeannette, Pennsylvania, a small glass factory community near Pittsburgh. His father, a local football star in high school and World War II veteran, worked at one of the glass factories until his retirement. Dave's mother worked long hours at a grocery store. Dave attributes his strong work ethic and Christian principles to his parents.

Dave and his wife, Tina, have been married for 33 years and have three children—Adam, Mark, and Katie. Tina and Dave met while in college and still have strong family ties in the Pittsburgh area. Dave attributes much of his success to having a very supportive wife who is a wonderful mother to their children.

13

Cage, Confine, but Do Not Define People

Dr. Lloyd Vincent Hackley, Chairman Emeritus
Character Counts Coalition

In my travels, I've seen many examples of powerful people whose attitudes have carried them above and beyond the circumstances that befell them. True leaders are never cowered by circumstances. They use challenges as steppingstones to opportunity. They determine the course of their own lives. They recognize the power of attitude wherever they encounter it. Dr. Lloyd "Vic" Hackley is that kind of influential leader.

Dr. Hackley told me that one of his most formative experiences occurred when he was still a boy in Roanoke, Virginia. He asked his father a question that brought tears to the man's eyes. The teenager never expected to see such a reaction from his father, and what happened next taught the child the lesson of a lifetime.

"I loved my father dearly, but I was terrified of him, because he was so big in my eyes. I was 13 years old before I had the audacity to confront him about anything. I was working with him cleaning up an apartment building. He worked part-time as a janitor to supplement the family income, because there were eight of us in need of shelter, food, and clothing. My father was highly respected on the black side of town. He'd been a four-sport star in high school, and he was known as one of the finest athletes ever to come out of the state of Virginia. He was a leader in the black community, but that day we were on the other side of the tracks. For the first time, I was witness to whites mistreating a black man. They were brutal to him verbally as we walked down the street, and he just ignored them. When the white people were talking badly to him, his face remained passive.

"I couldn't understand why he was such a different person on the white side of town. He never would have tolerated such treatment in our own neighborhood, so I confronted him when the two of us were alone. I asked him why he had let the white men talk to him that way. His face showed something I'd never seen in him. He seemed close to tears. What he said stayed with me from that day on: 'Those people don't define me, and you shouldn't let them define you.'

"He told me he was the same person, no matter what was said to him or about him. He told me he was working for the white people and tolerating indignities, so that I wouldn't have to. I commented that I'd never be able to take that kind of treatment from anyone, and he said I should never say what I would do or what I wouldn't do, until I was responsible for somebody other than myself, particularly children.

"He added that I should not go away from that spot with a chip on my shoulder, that if I had to get even for the indignities he had suffered, then I should go and be as successful as I could be.

"That day marked a turning point in my life. I realized that if he could tolerate those indignities for me, then I could never dare to do less than my best."

Leaders Define Themselves

"I didn't grasp the full weight of my father's teachings until I visited the Senegalese coast of Africa and the infamous Goree Island in the harbor of Dakar. The small island is home to the *Maison des Esclaves*, or House of Slaves. Historians are uncertain exactly how many enslaved Africans passed through the 'door of no return' before being shipped to the United States and other countries in the early 1800s. Some say it was as many as 40 million. Whatever the number, the island has become a major destination for African Americans and other visitors seeking insights into one of the cruelest undertakings in human history.

"I listened to the curator of the House of Slaves talk about how slaves in poor health, or those who were too rebellious to control, were thrown to the sharks that prowled the shoreline. I was moved by seeing where so many Africans were kidnapped from their native continent and sold into slavery, but when our group stepped inside the slave warehouse filled with cells—cages that were only eight square feet—my father's words came back with a much deeper resonance.

"The slave cages were so small we couldn't stand up straight. I couldn't lean to the left or the right. I couldn't sit down. I couldn't lie down. I had to crouch. Many of us got very emotional. Some fainted. Some cried. I did not react that way. Instead, my father's words and his experience as a black man in rural Virginia came back to me. All of a sudden, I understood where my father got the power to take the racial taunts and not respond to them with his son at his side. I understood, too, what he passed on to me. Instead of being sad inside that slave cage, I felt pride.

"I was extremely proud of the men and women—my ancestors among them—who had survived that treatment, the middle passage, and the brutality of slavery in the United States. I was proud to be the product of my father and mother and so many other strong-willed people who had persevered and endured. Because of them and their sacrifices and strength, I have been able to define myself in this world."

Self-Definition Leads to Self-Determination

"I managed to complete all three of my levels of education with academic scholarships, and it was as a consequence of being willing to work as hard as necessary to be the first in the class, to get the highest grades. When I stood in that cage, I remembered how I was driven by what my father had said, that it was my responsibility to be the best that I could be. While I was at Michigan State, my classmates were going to football and basketball games and going out and drinking beer and raising hell and having parties, but I spent my time in the library and in the lab. As a result, I graduated with a high grade-point average, and then I obtained my master's and my doctorate on scholarships.

"After college, I volunteered for duty in Vietnam with the Air Force. While I was there, my father died. Several years later, I returned to Roanoke at the invitation of city fathers to give a speech. I used that occasion to honor the man who prepared me for success by telling me it was up to me alone to define myself.

"I was the keynote speaker for a big event in the community. In my speech, I pointed out some of the buildings where my father had worked as a janitor. I said that in one generation our family had progressed from a person who cleaned up the town to a person who had a key to the city. I don't think that quick a progression can happen any place else but in America."

If It's Going to Happen, It's Up to You!

"After I signed up for coaching the track team and picked up the numbers for the meet, I looked around for my runners. I couldn't find them at first. Then I saw them. They were down on their knees in a circle, joining hands in the center. I waited for them to finish praying, and then I asked, 'Okay, what were you guys doing?' 'We were praying, Coach,' they responded. I told them prayer was fine, but once they were done with their prayers, they still were going to have to stand up and run real fast, or they would lose.

"'If you pray and run slow, you will lose,' I told them. 'God will not do anything for you that you can do for yourself.'

"I wanted them to understand, because people can do a whole lot more than they thought they could if they decide it's totally up to them to get it done. I always make the point, 'If it's going to happen, it's up to you!'"

Leadership Begins Within

"I am mission driven. Missions are more than words on a piece of paper. Your mission should be built upon things like morality and ethics and decency. It should be related to a vision of a better organization, a better America, and a better world.

"That adage sounds wonderful, of course, but the mark of true leaders is how their stated missions are applied in the real world. It is one thing to espouse personal responsibility in a mission statement; living it is an entirely different matter. In 1992, I became president of the University of Arkansas at Pine Bluff, a historically black institution. Around the time I arrived, the school came under fire, because students in the education department were not performing well in national testing for teacher certification. As a man on a mission of self-determination, I took responsibility for improving the performance of the underachieving students at my school.

"I announced that I was not satisfied with the scores, and the students were not intellectually inferior; they had simply been undereducated in high school. I told the state that the students were the product of its public schools. A law in Arkansas says all students who graduate from high school have the right to go to a state college. Unfortunately, many students who were unprepared for college studies were enrolling in the state's historically black institution.

"These students had been told that they were college material, but they hadn't been given the tools they needed to succeed at that level. I felt the state had an obligation to remedy the situation. I told state officials, 'You made these students believe they were capable of going to college and succeeding, so you have an obligation to help them.'

"I devised a formula that would allow additional state funds to address gaps in the education for the freshmen and sophomores. I created a University College that eased the course requirements for students who were not performing up to standards. I hired additional teachers from the high school level to offer remedial courses in English and math at the university. Within a short period, the underachieving education-department students had nearly doubled their average test scores. The improvement was so dramatic that I was inspired to take an even bolder move."

Guaranteed Performance

"We became the first black institution in the country to give a warranty with all our education department graduates. It said that if anything were found to be wrong with these teachers, our institution would be responsible for making it right. I was determined that the students they taught would not suffer because we had put out a product that couldn't do the job. Instead, they would benefit from having good teachers.

"Because the university took responsibility for the performance of its graduates, they were soon in demand by school systems around the country. I kept thinking if we sent out teachers who couldn't teach, then the generation coming up behind them would suffer, too.

"Young people were being undereducated from kindergarten through the twelfth grade, and somebody had to take responsibility. It was not fair to anyone. We worked on students' cognitive improvement in their first two years of college, and by their junior years, the students were on track. They not only passed their teacher certification tests, they went on to become great teachers in the classroom.

"I became a champion of school reform throughout the Arkansas public school system. I played a leading role in what was widely recognized as a very successful rejuvenation of education in that state. While I have reaped the rewards and accolades, the people who benefited from my leadership have garnered even more.

"The greatest reward I could ever receive comes when I'm traveling here and even overseas and run into people who remember something I said to encourage them when I was visiting their classrooms."

Keith's Attitude Check

Dr. Lloyd Vincent Hackley demonstrated another side of leadership when he followed in his father's footsteps and refused to let others define him, any more than his father did. He heeded his father's words and strived to be the best he could be. As a result, he has led thousands of students to be the best they can be. His influence has spread exponentially, because he not only has ensured the solid education of many teachers, but also because he made sure those teachers passed along good educations to their students. Who has any idea of how many students have benefited from his determination to make a good education available at the universities where he has served? I am certain the numbers are incalculable.

Does he stop? No. Even in retirement, Dr. Hackley continues his quest to support education through the National CHARACTER COUNTS! Coalition. The purpose of the coalition, which has been adopted by 600 communities nationwide, is to fortify the lives of America's young people with ethical values called the Six Pillars of Character: trustworthiness, respect, responsibility, fairness, caring, and citizenship.

If the Label Doesn't Fit, Don't Let It Stick

Not all educators have the character or the enlightenment of Dr. Hackley. A friend of mine told me of a grammar-school teacher of hers, way back in the 1950s, who thought she was could teach a student to be neater by embarrassing him. She made him write the note "I am a slob" on a large piece of paper, and she hung it from the front of his desk. Did he straighten his desk and keep his papers and person neat after the sign was hung? No, day after day, he came to school looking sloppier and sloppier. His desk overflowed with crumbled papers, broken pencils, gum wrappers, and erasers. His clothes grew even more rumpled, and he appeared to care less than ever before. Eventually the teacher ripped the sign off his desk and declared, "I give up on you! You will always be a slob."

Psychologists today would shudder in horror at such a story. Today, we know that labels, such as the one the teacher put on that student, often stick with children for the rest of their lives. That boy, if he allowed his teacher to define him, was going to be a slob the rest of his natural life. My friend doesn't know if that small boy broke out of his cage and decided to define himself and ignore the words of his ill-informed teacher, but my friend never forgot the incident. As a result, when she reared her son, she always said, "You're so neat! You're so smart! You did a perfect job! You can do anything!" Those were the labels, the definitions her son heard, and so it is no surprise that from an early age, he believed he could be anything. He excelled in everything he tried, from playing soccer to playing a violin, bass, or drums. He ran for office in school and won every election. He made the Dean's List as an undergraduate and eventually chose to become a veterinarian, even though entry into veterinary school was limited and difficult. He practices in the suburbs of Washington, DC, today.

Good Person or Good Persona?

Abraham Lincoln said that there is no such thing as a private person and a public person among leaders; they are both the same thing. Dr. Hackley's public persona as a man of high character and integrity reflects his private beliefs and actions. His father gave him a great gift when he told him that while he might not have power over what happened to him in life, he did have the power to choose his attitude and how he responded. His father served as a role model by refusing to let racist remarks embitter him, enslave him, or define him.

George Bernard Shaw said, "People are always blaming their circumstances for what they are. I don't believe in circumstances. The people who get on in this world are the people who get up and look for the circumstances they want and, if they can't find them, make them." Dr. Hackley's father had an attitude that elevated him above the cruelty and injustice of racism. By his very attitude, he also elevated the life of his son, so that his son got up and looked for the circumstances he wanted. If you've ever doubted the power of attitude, consider that the son of a janitor, Dr. Hackley, helped thousands of students at the universities he served and now elevates the lives of millions of young people through the National CHARACTER COUNTS! Coalition.

From a memorable experience with his father, a young boy developed an attitude of self-reliance and responsibility for his own success. It worked wonders for Dr. Hackley's life, providing him with access to an education, a career, and to the opportunity for public service. Now, he has extended his reach by taking responsibility for developing the characters of millions of school children across the country.

Dr. Hackley was the only black student at Northwestern Michigan College in the 1960s where he graduated with honors. He earned his master's and doctorate in international relations at Michigan State University. He served in the U.S. Air Force in Vietnam and later was an intelligence specialist before moving to the U.S. Air Force Academy, where he taught and coached.

In talking to Dr. Hackley, I was reminded again of how a true leader's powerful attitude has the same rippling effect of a rock thrown into a pond. Its force moves from the center out, expanding the impact in ever-growing ripples, well beyond the point of origin. In his case, the ripples have spanned an ocean, because Dr. Hackley has had an impact on many lives in many situations.

I love the story he tells about instructing his Air Force Academy Cross Country Team runners to pray, but then to get up and run. The tale is a simple but important lesson on personal responsibility and self-determination.

As an educator and motivator, Dr. Hackley has certainly become a major force for positive change in the world around him and, as he noted, it all began within him. Inspired by his father, he became determined to rise above his circumstances, and that passion grew into a mission to help others do the same.

ATTITUDE ACTION PLAN

- Do you feel that something in your past has put you in a cage, has limited you? If you could replace those labels with more positive ones, what would they be?

- What steps will you take, starting today, to change your personal image, so that you can reach your full potential?

- What labels do you put on your associates, family members, and friends? Do they limit them or allow them to be free to be themselves?

- If you had absolutely no limits, if you could do absolutely anything at all, what would it be? What can you do, starting today, that will lead you closer to being a person with no limits?

- Have you shared your knowledge with others today? Are you writing a book, planning a lecture, giving a course, or simply mentoring a younger person?

- If you are teaching others, have you asked your students and protégés to pass along their knowledge to others when the time is right?

Brief Biography

Lloyd Vincent Hackley is chairman emeritus and a full-time volunteer as a nationally certified ethics and character development instructor for the National Character Counts Coalition and a member of the board of governors of the Josephson Institute Ethics.

Since January 1997, Dr. Hackley has taught in or conducted more than 2,700 seminars, workshops, and lectures in ethics and character development throughout America and overseas for parents, teachers, children, and others who work with children, as well as for businesses, universities, various governmental agencies, and other organizations.

Although officially retired, Dr. Hackley continues to serve numerous constituencies and communities. His various board affiliations include the National Commission on Civic Renewal, the NC Methodist Home for Children (chair), the Advisory Board of the Duke University/Kenan Ethics Program, the North Carolina Supreme Court Commission on Professionalism (legal ethics), the North Carolina State Bar Council, and the Southern Poverty Law Center.

He was president of the North Carolina Community College System, chancellor and tenured professor of both Fayetteville State University and the University of Arkansas at Pine Bluff, and associate professor of political science, as well as coach of track and cross-country at the U.S. Air Force Academy. He was chair of the North Carolina Child Advocacy Institute, chair of the Arkansas Civil Rights Commission, and chair of the President's Advisory Board of Historically Black Colleges and Universities. Dr. Hackley was also a faculty member in the Government Executive Institute at the

UNC-Chapel Hill School of Business and vice president in the University of North Carolina system.

A Phi Beta Kappa scholar, he is a graduate of Michigan State (BA) and the University of North Carolina at Chapel Hill (PhD). A retired Air Force Officer, he earned numerous military decorations, including the Bronze Star for Valor, the Meritorious Service Medal, and the Vietnam Cross for Gallantry. Included among his hundreds of other awards and honors are keys to cities, honorary doctorates, man-of-the-year awards, public service awards from the Michigan and Florida state community college systems, and a day named in his honor in North Carolina.

Recently he was presented the North Carolina PTA's highest award for service to children for the second time, and the North Carolina Methodist Home for Children's Guardian Angel Award. He serves on four corporate boards: Branch Banking and Trust Company; Tyson Foods, Inc.; AAA-Carolinas; and Blue Cross/Blue Shield—North Carolina.

Strong Leadership Builds Strong Teams

Maria A. McIntyre, Executive Vice President and COO
Council of Logistics Management

All great leaders understand the importance of people in the success equation. Without people to lead, we would have no leaders. Maria McIntyre embraces the elements of people and personal interactions as the keys to her leadership style.

Leaders Build for the Future

"In a work environment, leaders cannot overestimate the value of one-on-one interactions, both to the organization and to their employees' personal development. People need to feel listened to and valued, if they are to excel. It is part of my leadership foundation to help my staff members understand the rationale behind decisions and invite them to be involved. I would rather not answer questions with a simple 'yes' or a 'no.' I also give them an explanation, a rationale behind the decision. It is important to me that employees understand why conclusions were made the way they were.

"When I was growing up, my father was a foreman in a manufacturing plant. Every once in a while, he took me into the plant and showed me how the machinery worked. He talked to me about his management practices and the proper ways to hire and fire people. He discussed basic management skills with me. My father always had patience in answering my questions and spent time talking to me about some of the challenges he faced and how he approached the challenges. Through my father's sharing, I was first exposed to the intricacies of good leadership and the need to do every job right.

"My father was in corrugated paper manufacturing, and here I am in logistics, paper packaging, that whole process. I didn't plan the course of my life to follow my father's, but it's funny how it worked out.

"Sometimes when I finished my homework, I was tired and ready to go to bed, but he'd look at me and say, 'Listen, now, you got it right, but it's messy, so you need to go back and clean it up.'

"As a result, although I'm not fanatical, I do like things neat. I like things done well and done right, and being neat is part of that, too. I am the oldest of six children, and I was fortunate my father spent so much time with me. He really shaped me.

"I had a professor in college who also spent time with me. We would sit in his office and talk. We discussed books we'd read, along with business theory and principles. Business was always something that was of great interest to me.

"As I began my career in the association industry, I was fortunate enough to work for a boss who strongly believed in mentoring his employees. He took the time to help me understand the business. He was an executive director who cared about the organization and the people working with him. He had a passion for what he was doing and knew the organization could go only as far as his people could take it. Although he taught me specific skills in developing processes and procedures, he also encouraged me to do my own things and put my imprint on what I was managing. His impact was instrumental in my development as a professional and, in the end, it was the stimulus for my growth in the work environment.

"Real leaders cultivate people. I encourage an open-door policy that welcomes the people I work with to discuss questions, concerns, or ideas with me without hesitation. By allowing my employees to come in, query me, and bounce ideas off me, I empower them to make good decisions and, with my approval of the idea, the individual builds confidence and develops a sense of contribution to the organization.

"When you allow people to come and and talk with you, you're empowering them to make good decisions. Weekly, we sit down for an hour, walk through things, and share things. We make group decisions, at least from a management perspective, because everyone has an idea of what's going on. Even if an individual isn't the resident expert of that particular department, he or she can understand what's going on and therefore work better with others. We don't have an agenda, but everyone knows if they need to discuss something as a group, they can bring things up. We go around the table that way. I have a parking lot system, so as things come up, if it's not quite time to discuss an item, we can park it in the parking lot so we don't lose the idea and then go back to it later."

Individuals Toward a Common Goal

"Exercising patience in a team environment can be difficult, but it is essential to producing high quality work. A leader cannot force the team concept; it has to happen on its own. We all have good plans, goals, and focus, but you can't do everything yourself. You need people to be on board with you, and that's where leaders need to concentrate their attention, focusing the team on a common goal and empowering them to achieve that goal. Each team member may have a distinct task, but all tasks should point toward the same end. Each team member should understand that end.

"When I was promoted from a member of a team to the position of supervisor of that team, the new change was slightly awkward for the group to embrace. For the first couple of meetings, I sensed an obvious strain in our working relationship. I needed to recognize and acknowledge the situation and find a way to move the group toward cohesion. I understood that the relationship could not be repaired overnight, but I needed to find a way to create a healthy new beginning for our team. One of the best decisions I made was to acknowledge that the issue existed. I told them that I knew the situation was going to be awkward at first, but we all had common goals within the organization. I said, 'Let's see what we can do to make this work.'

"I thought one thing that we might be able to do together was take on a project. As peers, away from our boss, we talked about some things we would do if we had control. I took one of those things and said, 'We've been talking for years about what we would do, if only we could change this. Let's take this particular project and do something with it.' The project I suggested spoke to the conversations we had together as peers. It connected the new reality with our previous existence and showed the group I was committed to listening to them and supported their ideas. Each member of the group was responsible for a different element of the project, but we all worked together to execute the plan. In the end, we implemented the changes successfully and pulled together as a team. It was a big win for me, and a larger win for the team in moving forward.

"The team continued to implement new ideas and find great successes in working together. In listening to individual ideas and making a concentrated effort to act on appropriate leads, I was able to gain everyone's trust and, in turn, improve the performance of the organization."

Change for Growth

"As a manager, you are often faced with the task of implementing change. Change is necessary, to continue the growth of your business, but many individuals find change difficult to embrace. In fact, many managers believe 'If it ain't broke, don't fix it.' I, on the other hand, hold the philosophy, 'Maybe we need to break it once in a while, to make it interesting.'

"When I was promoted to executive vice president at the Council of Logistics Management, the organization was deeply locked into doing things the way they always had, occasionally at the expense of ignoring requests from members. When I assumed my position, we decided to address some of the suggestions our members had presented.

"We began by implementing value-added programs where association members have the opportunity to attend in-depth sessions on topical issues. The sessions were designed with the member in mind and were very different from what the association had offered in the past. We changed the length of individual speaking times to give members the opportunity to learn more intensely about each topic, and we improved our standards for speakers, to give clients the information they desired, rather than the agenda the speaker wanted to present.

"We also eliminated our annual banquet. Although a nice event, our feedback indicated sitting down with a small group to have a meal was not the most important thing. People much preferred an environment that was conducive to networking and meeting many people. In the banquet's absence, we offered a reception. As opposed to each individual being seated at a table with a limited number of other guests, the reception was conducted in a manner that allowed attendees to mingle with any number of the 4,000 guests in attendance.

"Our changes to date have been well received, both within the organization and by our members. It was important to me during the process to keep the needs of our members in mind, while encouraging each member of my team to contribute to the projects individually."

People in the Leadership Equation

"People can make or break a business. You can't do it alone. It is a manager's responsibility to cultivate employees, to grow a team that consistently produces high quality outcomes and builds a community that actively reflects the greater goals of the organization.

"Individuals believe in an organization based on what it stands for and what it does. As a leader, you are responsible for forming relationships with the people you work with and exhibiting a passion for the work that keeps others energized. There are two ways to lead. You can come in every morning with a smile and empower individuals to work with you to achieve goals or you can start each day with a frown and demand the work be done your way and in your time frame. The manager who uses a smile and recognizes employees as individuals with individual thought processes will achieve much more than a manager who does not respect employees. In the end, you are managing human beings, and you have to take a humanistic approach to management, to achieve the best possible results.

"My goal, when I retire, is that people will feel that I improved the organization and made it an even better place than it was before I took over the leadership role.

"Success requires effective processes and procedures, and if an infrastructure is in place and the team works together, we can move anything. The details can be changed, but the infrastructure is intact. My intent is to build a team of capable people, so that I can walk out that door when I retire and know the footprints have been set to take the organization into the future."

Keith's Attitude Check

A company can have a good product or service, but without the proper people in place, the company will struggle to survive. Managers must realize the importance of building and creating positive relationships in the workplace. Strong leaders use their influence to create a culture based on people. Such a basis not only helps leaders build better relationships with individual staff members, but also helps each staff member build better working relationships with fellow employees.

If a tree falls in the forest and nobody is there to hear it, does it make a sound? If a person tries to lead and nobody is there to listen, does the business grow? Maria McIntyre brings up one of the most important attitudes of leadership, and that is leading for the future, not just the future of your business, but also the future of the people working for you, who become the future of your business. It is not enough to believe in the future. You must actively build for it, and doing so requires giving of yourself to your staff as a mentor, leader, and guide.

Have you ever had this thought? "I could never take that vacation or be out of the office for that long. The organization would fall apart without me." If you harbored such thoughts, then you haven't been mentoring anyone below you to help move the organization forward. As a leader, you are in a position to prepare those working under you to take on more responsibility. If you are stuck in performing all of the day-to-day tasks, you are not concentrating on developing the overall strategies to grow your business. Good leaders recognize the need to nurture and mentor the next generation of leaders and groom them to take over leadership positions at the appropriate time. In this way, you can freely advance again or retire, leaving behind a healthy legacy.

As the leader of my own company, I know how important it is to be able to rely on your staff to accomplish things that are bigger than yourself. I pride myself on leading my team with trust and respect, and I hope I am giving them the tools they need to grow and succeed, just as the business does. I have to empower my staff to do more in their roles, so our business can grow. Although I make many of the bigger decisions, I try to provide them with enough guidance and leadership to perform their roles independently with the goals of the organization in mind. Without an empowered staff, our company would have to shut down every time I am on the road, which is almost 60 percent of the time.

Maria actively listens to her staff members and works with them to support not only her visions, but also *their* visions. Her positive leadership style, based on personal interactions, trust, and respect, opened the doors for ongoing dialogue with her team, allowing everybody to contribute and take a vested interest in the success of the business.

Everyone in your company is there to work toward the same goals. Everybody wants to be successful; everybody wants to be a part of the winning team. Identify the projects and visions that will get you there. Communicate that information to your team, and work together with that goal in mind. As with Maria's team, you'll be surprised at what you can accomplish.

ATTITUDE ACTION PLAN

- You and your staff must believe in today while working for tomorrow. Do you think today's new assistant wants to retire as an assistant?

- Shouldn't today's manager be working to become tomorrow's director?

- Put your company on the shoulders of those capable of moving it forward, and arm them with the tools they will need to advance to higher levels in their career. What have you done toward that goal today?

- Can you think of where you would be right now if someone hadn't helped you advance? Isn't the best legacy to leave behind one that will continue to grow with time?

- How open is your door? Can employees discuss any business-related question or concern with you? What do you do to encourage such communication?

- Does your staff work as a team, or are they working as individuals? Can you put them on a project where they will build into a team that works together?

Brief Biography

Maria McIntyre is the executive vice president and chief operating officer of the Council of Logistics Management, a not-for-profit professional association consisting of 10,000 businesspeople around the world who are interested in logistics and distribution-management skills. As the EVP/COO working in concert with the executive committee, she is responsible for strategic direction of the organization and oversees the tactical operations to ensure the organization functions efficiently and effectively in serving its members and the logistics profession.

Maria is a graduate of Chicago State University, Chicago, Illinois. She received her bachelor of science degree in business administration in 1986. She also received a certificate from the University of Tennessee in its Executive Development Program in 1987.

Maria grew up in the section of Chicago known as Little Italy, the oldest of six children. Her father was in the paper packaging industry, so she learned at an early age about the role of packaging in the overall logistics profession. After several interruptions to finishing her formal education, she finally achieved her bachelor's degree while working full time, after her two daughters were born, and with the support of her husband. Maria had several business mentors over the years, which is why she is such a strong supporter of mentoring programs to help others achieve their career goals.

Maria and her husband Don, an educator by profession, reside in Homewood, Illinois, a south suburb of Chicago. Their two daughters are in education and association management.

Are You a Long-Term Leader?

Robert Shoptaw, CEO
Blue Cross and Blue Shield of Arkansas

Robert Shoptaw makes a distinction between episodic leaders and long-term leaders. Episodic leaders are those who are brought in for a particular purpose (such as turn-around specialists), or those who are only effective in certain conditions (such as a military officer who is a brilliant battle commander but not a good peace-time leader).

Long-term leaders are rare because they possess a comprehensive collection of qualities that make them effective in a variety of circumstances over the long term. I think you'll agree with me after reading this interview that Bob is the latter.

Looking for the Larger Picture

"I was basically reared in two geographies, central Kentucky and Arkansas. My family had pretty much the standard Protestant Puritanical attitude that hard work pays off, and there is nothing you can't do if you are willing to make some sacrifices and invest your personal capital. I was always interested in what motivates people to do what they do and why they don't do what they really should.

"For whatever reason, instead of focusing on the football game and Friday night dance, I was always trying to figure out where I fit into the broader scheme of things. I seemed to have an ability to set goals and generate the self-discipline, focus, and tenacity to achieve them. I was always looking for ways to innovate, and really enjoyed testing limits and moving things forward in a progression."

Learning Enables Us to Be on the Leading Edge

"It became evident to me that education was the common denominator that enables people to fulfill their potential. I studied for my MBA taking night courses while I was working, and then I had a chance to participate in the Advanced Management Program at Harvard Business School. I believe our perspectives are shaped by how actively we invite new stimuli into our life, so I welcomed this opportunity to learn how things blend together in terms of interactive functionality. In fact, I enjoy learning so much, I would have gladly been a professional student all my life, if given the opportunity.

"In retrospect, one of the best things that happened was that I had been in the business world for almost 10 years before I went back for my MBA. That meant I had real-life experiences to apply to the theories taught there so it wasn't just a paper-chase proposition."

Kudos to Deming's Continuous Quality Improvement

"While at Harvard's executive education program, we studied Edward Deming's approach to Total Quality Management (TQM). His suggestions dovetailed with my own job observations about the importance of inviting employees to get involved. Frankly, I think TQM is one of the fundamental reasons American businesses such as Wal-Mart have been so successful over the years.

"When I became CEO, I sat down and worked with staff at the local team level to customize Deming's template of continuous quality improvement within our organization. At least a couple of times a year, we assemble our employees in small groups of 12 to 20. We give them a personal briefing about what's going on in the company. We then address their issues in an interactive Q and A and have meaningful discussions on how we can be proactive in improving everything we do.

"We have 2,200 employees, and about 1,350 of them have been with us for more than 10 years. As you can imagine, switching from a traditional 'I say Jump' and you say 'How high?' management style to this 'What do you think?' approach required quite a paradigm shift.

"Realistically, we're not going to be able to convert everyone, however I believe once you get 50 to 60 percent of an organization buying in to the kind of culture you're trying to create, it exerts a positive peer pressure on those who are neutral or even negative. That's what causes an organization to mature, when the philosophy becomes integral to how everyone operates. It's analogous to parents who do their best to instill values in their children, and know it's working when the kids start practicing those values of their own accord."

Internal and External Benchmarking

"I was extremely fortunate to be on Dr. George K. Mitchell's staff. Dr. Mitchell, who subsequently became CEO of Blue Cross and Blue Shield of Arkansas in 1975 was one of those leaders who practiced participative management before it had that label on it. He was a firm believer in investing in people and giving them opportunities to excel. In large measure, going to school under his mentorship was the best education I received.

"I never saw Dr. Mitchell compromise fairness or honest dealings when it came to dealing with people or business situations. No one ever had to look over their shoulder and second-guess his actions because he could be trusted to act with integrity. He had an uncanny ability to make employee-based decisions that may have been tough in the short run, but invariably turned out to be the right thing to do in the long term.

"I think he was able to exhibit the traits I call a 'long-term leader' because he benchmarked in two directions when he was dealing with challenging situations. He benchmarked internally by reflecting on his life experiences when faced with an equally difficult or even worse predicament. He would then relate to the actions that had helped him successfully deal with that situation and thus establish a growing set of reference points over time.

"He would then externally benchmark by seeking objective advice from external resources and by studying competitors or other organizations' best practices. He would compare those findings to what was happening in the health care industry in general so he had a broader, over-arching context in which to chart the company's course.

"I consciously use both internal and external benchmarking when I'm facing daunting circumstances because it helps me maintain a balanced perspective. It reduces the stress of the situation and keeps me from getting swept up in the negativity of what's happening. It also gives me a decision matrix that helps me move forward with the confidence that I'm proceeding on the wisest path."

Good Leaders Don't Rest on Their Laurels

"When something goes wrong at the corporate level, if, for example, we lose a major account, it acts as a wake-up call for our top management to sit down and do a case study to assess what went wrong and determine how we can use this as a learning opportunity. We try not to point fingers or generate blame, we just want to understand how it happened, why it happened, and how we can generate a better outcome in the future.

"I think one of the worst things a leader can do is put things in neutral and allow them to move sideways when times are good. My ingrained philosophy is that when things are going smoothly we need to be most innovative and invest attention to details. We may not be putting out fires, but that doesn't mean we can rest on our laurels and grow lax. Those good times are when we have the capital and the human resources to keep our shoulder to the wheel, practice preventative maintenance, and chart a clear-headed, strategic approach to the future.

"One of the ways we try to stay sharp is to practice the SWOT analysis:

S = Strengths
W = Weaknesses
O = Opportunities
T = Threats

"We constantly remind our employees that the only reason we exist as an organization is to fulfill a community need on a customer-to-customer basis. If we don't do that, if we aren't constantly striving to do a better job for our customers, then the good times we're enjoying won't exist for long. Maybe it's the economist in me (my first love is the study and real-world application of economics), but I'm constantly trying to figure out how we can capitalize on our strengths, improve our weaknesses, accentuate our opportunities, and best minimize the threats to our organization."

Strategic Direction Is the Capstone

"With all that said, I believe the most important responsibility of a leader is to provide strategic direction to the enterprise. It's important to operate as a visionary on behalf of your organization instead of getting so engaged in the day-to-day administration that you lose clarity about the big picture of where the organization needs to be next year or in five years.

"I try to do this in three different pieces. One, and I'm never as good at this as I'd like to be, I try delegating as much as possible those activities that staff members can do as well, if not better, than I can. This is absolutely imperative given the complexity of our industry and today's business community in general.

"The second piece is visiting with customers and looking at customer survey results to see what their preferences and expectations really are. My goal is to identify how customer needs and expectations are changing so our organization can anticipate, meet, and hopefully, exceed them.

"The third piece is spending quality time with staff and board members so everyone has a clearly defined understanding and hopefully buy in to our business model. I want everyone to understand where we are today and what we are trying to achieve so we can do a gap analysis in terms of what initiatives we need to set in place to move from our current position to where we want to be five years from now."

I Need Somebody, Not Just Anybody

"I believe the key to freeing yourself up to do what only you, the CEO, can do is to (1) surround yourself with the very best people you can find, and then (2) give them the authority to do what needs to be done.

"A great example of this is Sharon Allen, our President and COO, Sharon began as a claims processor in 1966 and has grown over the years to be the lynchpin in terms of our operational execution. She has 100 percent credibility with everyone who works with her because she's been in the trenches. She may not have a PhD or a MBA diploma on her wall, but she has more common sense in her little finger than most of us have in our entire body.

"There is simply no substitute for her acquired knowledge and her incredible ability to pull everything together and suggest a course of action that makes sense to everyone involved. She has the ability to sit down with a doctor or hospital administrator who's upset about something and work things through so everyone can accept the outcome. She is particularly gifted in that regard.

"Sharon is always looking for the win-win resolution. She makes sure everyone has a chance to share his or her perceptions. Even if they can't reach a resolution, she's able to achieve a 'let's agree to disagree' outcome where people still respect her."

Character Is King

"Sharon displays the temperament of a long-term leader in that she has a set of core principles that don't waiver under pressure. Her character is noncircumstantial.

"Episodic leaders, like some politicians I won't name, put their finger in the wind everyday to see what the public opinion polls are saying. They're mostly concerned with their image, popularity, and giving people what they want.

"On the other hand, long-term leaders get more of a thrill from seeing their employees excel. Long-term leaders care less about having their name associated with achievement and more about seeing their team fulfill their potential.

"Long-term leaders have the rare ability to work at both ends of the continuum. They have enough confidence to take charge when they see a situation that demands strong leadership—and they have the humility to know when it's time to back off and let other people take the lead and receive the credit. Their integrity stays constant but they have the flexibility to lead in whatever style gets the best results for the organization. Simply said, long-term leaders love seeing their people succeed, and they take responsibility for creating a culture that enables that to happen."

Keith's Attitude Check

Long-term leaders have constant character balanced with an ability to lead in a style that works best for their organization. You can almost tell after an hour of watching how employees act toward and around their boss whether that leader is genuinely respected or if he or she simply has "position power."

Have you worked for an authoritarian "my way or the highway" leader? Was that person's "do it because I said so" style appropriate for the situation or did you chafe under that tight control? Did you appreciate the clear directions or did you dislike being ordered around?

Have you worked for a participative leader who solicited your input and valued your suggestions? What was that like? Did you find yourself blossoming under the type of management where your involvement was encouraged and appreciated?

Four Most Important Words in an Organization

A professor in college once asked our class if we knew what the four most important words in a business were. One student guessed it was, "Here is your paycheck," and another wondered if it was, "Take the day off." After we had jokingly contributed our suggestions, our professor supplied the answer. It was "What do you think?"

When was the last time your supervisor asked your opinion? Did you feel flattered or honored? Sincerely soliciting someone's input is a way of saying, "I value you." It's a way of telling you that your observations matter and your opinion counts.

When was the last time you asked your employees for their point of view? When was a time you sought their input, listened to their suggestions, and implemented one of their recommendations?

Turn Commands into Requests for Cooperation

Another way to show respect for employees is to reduce the use of the phrases "You'll have to" and "You'll need to." Imagine yourself at the receiving end of these commands. "You'll have to clean this up before you leave today." "You need to call that vendor and find out why they haven't delivered that merchandise." "You'll have to bring that up at the staff meeting. We don't have time to discuss it now."

Hear how those phrases "You'll have to" and "You need to" grate on your nerves? As adults, we don't appreciate being ordered around like children. You may be thinking, "But I'm their leader. It's my job to give them directions." That's true, and the good news is, you can give directions without showing your employees a lack of respect. Here's how. Change "You'll have to" and "You need to" to "Could you please?" "Could you please clean this up before you leave today?" "Could you please call that vendor and find out what we haven't received our merchandise yet."

"Could you please bring that up at the staff meeting? We'll have more time to discuss it then." Do you hear how these instructions are couched in courtesy? The other person will feel he or she is being treated with respect and will be motivated to cooperate willingly instead of complying reluctantly because they have to.

You Can Be Respectful without Being Soft

Are you thinking, "But that's too soft. What if they really have to clean their work area before they leave?" Then, explain the urgency or reason behind your request so they understand its importance. "Could you please make sure your work area is clean before you leave today? It's really important because the safety inspector is scheduled to come by for their monthly visit tomorrow morning."

Communicating with employees in a respectful way motivates them to respond in kind. Instead of harboring resentment, they are likely to voluntarily do a quality job because they want to.

Think about it. Do you like to be ordered around? Neither does anyone else. Next time you give a "to do" list to an assistant, don't just list the tasks that need to be done. Take the few extra seconds to put "Could you please . . ." at the top and then bullet the list of tasks to be done. That little extra effort on your part can go a long way in setting the precedent for a mutually rewarding relationship.

There's No Shortcut to Character

Growing up, my dad used to tell me, "You have to pay a price for it. If you try to find a shortcut or try to cheat somebody, in the long run you are only cheating yourself." My dad had another quote, "What goes on in the dark, will come out in the light." I agree with Bob that we can't compromise our honest dealings with others. As he pointed out, one of the reasons everyone respects Sharon Allen is that she acts with integrity.

Have you worked for or around someone who did not act with integrity? What did this person do that caused you not to trust him or her? A friend used to joke when he tried something that didn't work out, "I didn't fail. I succeeded in setting a bad example." How can you use that person's bad example as a lesson in how not to lead?

Bob talks about using mistakes or failures as wake-up calls. Thinking back over your professional career, was there a mistake you made that taught you a valuable lesson? Did you try something that didn't work out as planned, however you rebounded and learned from the experience? What was that?

Next time you make a mistake, could you look the other person in the eye, raise your eyebrows and say, "I was wrong, sorry." Try it and see what happens. Obviously, there are caveats to this. If this is a complex issue or a culturally sensitive negotiation, this response may seem flip or inappropriate. So use your judgment, however, there may be some situations in which a "I'm wrong, sorry" may be just what's needed to wipe the slate clean and move forward with a fresh start.

Do You Have a SWOT Team?

Bob talked about internal and external benchmarks. Have you taken the time to identify your own Strengths, Weaknesses, Opportunities, and Threats? Do you have an annual personal performance appraisal where you hold yourself accountable for taking one tangible step to improve each of those areas?

Do you sit down with your employees to assess your organizational SWOT's as they pertain to customer service? What are your company's strengths when it comes to customer service? What are your company's weaknesses? How are you capitalizing on your company's customer service opportunities? Are you utilizing your talents to manage the threats to your organization to the optimal degree?

As to external benchmarking, do you compare yourself to other leaders in your industry? Are you falling behind your peers? As Bob said, continuing education is the common denominator in whether we fulfill our potential. Could you improve your effectiveness by enrolling in an executive education program?

Are You and Your Company on the Leading Edge?

How does your company compare to its competitors? When was the last time you analyzed your competitors' Strengths, Weaknesses, Opportunities, and Threats? Have you identified what is working for them and what is not? Have you applied those insights to your own organization so you're taking specific steps to improve your customer service?

As Bob pointed out, a business can't continue to exist unless it continues to give the quality of service that makes every customer want to be a repeat customer. How are you providing the strategic direction to make sure your company is doing that?

ATTITUDE ACTION PLAN

- What role has education played in your success? Have you been able to apply what you learned in school to your work life? How so?

- Identify a personal Strength, Weakness, Opportunity, and Threat.

- Identify a professional Strength, Weakness, Attribute, and Talent.

- What's your motivation for wanting to become a leader? What do you hope to achieve with your leadership opportunities?

- Think back to a personal/professional benchmark—a tough time. What were the qualities/decisions that helped you handle that situation successfully?

- Are you familiar with Deming's TQM approach? What do you think about it? Do you apply it in your organization? Why or why not?

- How do you provide strategic direction for your enterprise?

- Do you have a way of immediately turning mistakes into a wake-up call and a learning opportunity? What do you do?

Brief Biography

Robert Shoptaw is chief executive officer of Arkansas Blue Cross and Blue Shield (ABCBS) which serves approximately 40 percent of the state's population through a combination of private health insurance offerings and government programs contracting. ABCBS has revenues of $1.3 billion annually and more than 2,200 employees. Robert also serves on the national Blue Cross and Blue Shield Association (BCBSA) board which is composed of the 42 CEOs of the various Blue Cross and Blue Shield Plans across the country. BCBSA has a combined policyholder base of 85 million people. In November 2002, Robert was elected to serve as chairman of the national Blue Cross and Blue Shield Association board for 2003.

Robert is a graduate of Arkansas Tech University with an undergraduate degree in economics. He received his MBA from Webster University (St. Louis,

Missouri) in 1983 with a dual concentration in business administration and health services management. In 1992, he completed the Advanced Management Program at Harvard Business School.

Robert is a native of Richmond, Kentucky, and divided his formative years between Kentucky and Arkansas. At age 9, his family permanently relocated to Central Arkansas where he completed his secondary education and subsequently attended college. Robert lives in Little Rock, Arkansas, with his wife, Lisa. He has three children.

16

Clarity, Communication, Compassion

Ken D'Arcy, President and CEO
Corsman Acquisition Corporation

Ken D'Arcy discovered by accident that spending a little time each day mentally relaxing brought him clarity and insights unmatched by harried executives who think they don't have time to slow down, sit down, and calm down. He allows his subconscious mind to tackle issues and help him make decisions, even as his conscious mind handles other matters. As a result, he has ferreted out many options and solutions he might not otherwise have considered, had he not spent time focusing on specifics.

D'Arcy's trust that anything is possible has resulted in corporate turnarounds that no one thought could happen.

"I'm a great believer that you can do most things you want to do in life. Time and time again, I see that the two most important things are attitude and a willingness to work. My daughter is a competitive figure skater. She started competing much later in life than other athletes, but she loves it, she's got a great attitude, and she works and works and works. She gets better every day. I might never be an award-winning concert pianist, but if I wanted to play the piano, I could probably learn to play reasonably well, if I had the right attitude and worked at learning and improving my skills.

"The same skills are important at work. If you have four people with the right attitude and the willingness to work and you add a fifth who doesn't have the right attitude or willingness, before long, that new person will realize he or she had better shape up or leave. In a way, work ethics and attitudes are infectious among coworkers.

"I learned from my father the importance of a work ethic. I saw him going to work at 5 o'clock in the morning and coming home at 7 or 8 o'clock at night, and he worked weekends, too. I learned from him that work is really important.

"You have to love what you're doing, though; I don't care what it is. Loving your work helps you maintain the right attitude and willingness to work hard. The need to love my work has certainly shaped my career choices. When I was about 24, my father was the president of a large oil company, and I was just starting out in the workforce. I opted not to go to college, which was a huge thing to my father, who was highly educated. He was a geologist, a geophysicist, and an attorney, but he confided in me that he hated his job.

"I said, 'Dad, how could you hate your job?' He didn't have an answer, so I asked the next logical question: 'If you could do anything, what would you do?'

"He said, 'I'd open a bookstore.'

"I told him that's what he should do, but he answered that he couldn't. He said, 'I can't change now; I've got too many commitments.'

"It stuck with me for the rest of my life that I would never have a job I didn't like, and I never have. In my career choices, I've worked with things that were the kinds of challenges I wanted.

"Before I take a new assignment, I typically look at what the company has done. I look into the management, to see if it is good, and check out the employees, to see what they are like. I figure out if the company has been around a while, if my particular type of management would make a contribution."

Walk Around

"I manage by walking around. I am a jack-of-all-trades. I spend almost my entire day overseeing what people are doing. For example, when I began with this company, it had a new plant with about 450 to 500 employees. Someone asked me if I would spend time in the factory. I said that within two months, I would probably know at least 80 percent of the people who worked there. The executives rolled their eyes, as if they'd believe it only when they saw it.

"I spent three or four days a week walking through the plant, and within the first few months, I could say hello to most of the people by name. When people never know when the boss is going show up, they always keep on top of what they're doing, in case he shows up at any time. That's the first thing. Also, managing by walking around gives me an understanding of everything that's going on in the company. I don't get an in-depth understanding, because I don't really want that, but I do want to know the critical things, the highlights, where they are going, and how they are going.

"A public relations person once told me that people like nothing more than to hear their own name. Let's say you're a $7-an-hour night-shift worker in a factory, and the CEO says, 'Hi, Ed, how are you today?' That person thinks, 'Oh, boy, he really does care about me.' The caring part, though, has to be genuine. I do care about the people. That's integral to the way I do my job. People are important parts of our business, and because I care, I should try to get to know a little bit about whom they are.

"Sometimes companies get so big that executives think they can't spend a little bit of time learning what their employees do or think. They don't have time to listen to their grievances, until the petty complaints grow into large problems and have to be approached in a formal setting. In some places you might even have the union after you. I'm not brilliant, but I have good common sense, and to me, it's good common sense to get to know your employees a little bit and listen to what they have to say.

"Like my father did, I usually arrive early. I'm in my office by 5 or 6 o'clock in the morning, and I spend the first few hours catching up on paperwork. I spend the balance of the day touring, until sometime between 4 and 6, when I take time to think, clean up the details of the day, and later, leave."

Happy Employees Make Good Employees

"I think the employees are amazed and pleased as punch at my methods. I put a bonus plan in place, and each employee is striving to meet our goal. They are all looking for ways for improvement.

"Any time a company of any size has employees looking for ways to improve the operation, the company will be a great success. If the managers are the only ones who look for improvement, the company may never be a success.

"Whenever I walk around, I ask all the time, 'Is this working?' 'Can we improve it?' 'Do we need to do anything differently?' 'Can we get something better?' 'Can we do something better?'

"I get answers—hundreds of them—daily.

"It's good that I'm right there, on the floor with the workers, so they can be candid and ask me anything, too. One of the questions they ask me is, 'What is a CEO?' I've told them a CEO is somebody who makes sure they have the tools to accomplish what they need to accomplish, without any roadblocks. I tell that if a roadblock comes up, I want to know about it, because I'll unblock it.

"When I ask them questions, I let them know they should always evaluate ways to be better, more efficient, and more competitive. That's part of their job. Some senior managers think they need to complicate things, to make themselves look more intelligent and industrious than they actually are. I prefer to keep it simple. Employees know their jobs best, so they know best how to improve them. Good leaders realize they have two ears and one mouth, so they can listen twice as much as they talk. Listening is very important, because it doesn't matter who the person is, what the corporate environment is, or what the environment is in general—everybody has a good idea about something, and if you listen, you can pick up on some good things."

Turnaround without Fallout

"It's very interesting that when I was brought on board for some companies, they were doing poorly, and we've been able to effect a complete turnaround in profitability and efficiency by listening to the people. To the additional amazement of others, we did it without massive layoffs. We had to let only one or two people go. Most people fear wholesale dismissals in such a changeover, but if leaders listen to the people in the trenches, they can quickly get an idea of any inadequate handling in the past and also get solid suggestions on how to improve things. I listen, watch, ask, walk around, and surround myself with good people willing to give me good information. It always works for me.

"I lived in Germany, Austria, and France for some time, and I enjoyed learning other languages. The Germans have a fabulous saying: 'The fish stinks from the head first.' I use that saying often, because it is so true. I've seen some companies where the CEO becomes so greedy that he doesn't care about the company. If I were the kind of CEO who showed up at work at 10 o'clock in the morning and went home at 3 o'clock in the afternoon, right after I came in off the golf course, my greatest concern might be how my options were doing. That would be the example I set. Everyone would think, 'He's looking after number one, so I'd better look out for myself and forget about everything else and everyone else.'

"The example we set determines whether we will succeed as a group or fail. Morale is everything. If you're only looking out for yourself, you're not looking for improvement in your work, and you're not looking out for the company. No one will look out for you, either.

"Communication is a huge part of morale. If communication is poor, morale will suffer. Interpersonal communications courses are important, if communication skills are lacking.

"I want people to figure out what needs to be done in their areas and then go out and fix it. Things get done, that way, instead of just being discussed at upper levels.

"Here's another interesting thing about the few people we do let go, when we undergo change. After those people leave, the rise in morale is immediate, as if fellow workers had for a long time been wondering why that person was still there. They've been uncomfortable, but unable to do anything about it. Finally, someone came and said, 'You're not pulling your weight; your attitude is bad; it's affecting everybody around you, and you can't stay.' All the employees go, 'Holy cow! Someone finally demanded accountability.'"

Name It and Frame It

"One of the things I do, too, is that I tell my staff, whether it's a floor worker or senior management, if something needs to be done, they have to come up with a time frame in which it could be done. Sometimes it's not critical that something be done by Monday at 10 o'clock; it may be next month. Whatever it is, I allow the person to set a time frame on it. God help you, though, if the project is not done by whatever time frame you set. If I set an unreasonable time, then shame on me, but if you set a time you can't live with, then shame on you.

"Setting a time frame ensures the project will be completed. It gives people a goal. People have to feel they have control of their life, whether it's a corporate employee or my own children. They have to feel they have value, and that they are contributing. They have to feel good about what they contribute."

Peer into the Future

"One of the primary responsibilities of a CEO is to look into the future and decide where the company is going. The CEO should determine what strategies the company needs, to get where it's going. The employees don't have the luxury of forward thinking; they have to improve their immediate jobs daily. A CEO, though, should look into the future and decide what the company needs. A CEO has to think, 'Where is our future? Will diversification be the way to go? Should we make acquisitions? Should we be looking at other companies for possible mergers?' That's the job of a CEO.

"I set aside an hour of time every day, when I close my door and put up my feet. That's my hour to reflect and relax, think about anything that comes into my head, look into the future, or go over the day.

"The first company where I was named president, I was just darned tired around 3 o'clock in the afternoon, so I'd close my door and have a little rest.

"Afterward, I was energized and could again attack my job with enthusiasm and clarity. I was 32 years old, and from that time on, I have set aside time, from about 3 until 4 o'clock every day, to sit quietly and reflect. I put notes up on a white board, notes about anything I have to ponder, and I sit and look at them. I think about them. 'What do I need to do?' 'How am I going to do this?' If I have a challenge to overcome, I look at the note every day, in my quiet time. Eventually, the answer comes to me, because I've allowed my subconscious to formulate the answer over a period of days.

"I spent a lot of years practicing martial arts, and one of the things I learned from that discipline is that you can have tremendous focus when you need to have tremendous focus. Often subliminal things in the background eventually come out to strike you as a solution.

"That one-hour time period gives me a chance to have a clear vision about things. I go over and over issues, thinking about any number of topics, including what to do a year, two years, three years, and five years down the road."

Clarity and Compartmentalization

"Perhaps because I spend that time clearing my mind and solving challenges, I am able to compartmentalize almost everything I've done. At the end of the day, when I go home, my workday is finished. I don't even think about work any longer. I spend 80 hours a week at work, but when I'm home, my family deserves all of me.

"My wife says I'm observant. Others call it clarity. Some of the people who know me well say I have no gray areas of my life; everything is black or white. I can probably be the most focused person anybody has ever seen.

"I used to have to sit, clear my mind, and do breathing exercises. Part of my breathing exercises involved bringing one particular item into focus. It has become second nature to me, now. I can eliminate everything else and focus on one thing."

Decisions, Decisions

"Somewhere along the line, I learned there is no such thing as a bad decision. You can do some things better than others, but if someone is committed enough, they will make a reasonably good decision, even if you, I, or others think it's not a good choice. There are a bunch of different decisions you can make, and whichever one you make is the right one, if you're committed to it. I'm precise, but I also don't waste time questioning or second guessing resolutions. I say, 'Let's make a decision and move forward.'"

The Human Touch

"Just as I like to know my employees' names and have open channels of communication with them, I also like to communicate with others on a more personal level than with e-mail. With e-mail, you can't hear the inflection. Meanings can get confused, lost, or misinterpreted.

"People buy things from people. Companies should never forget that. What sets any company apart from others is how that company deals with people. When I came into this company, I cut e-mail way back, because people were firing e-mails back and forth, when their offices were just across the hall from each other. Employees were doing the same with customers, e-mailing instead of calling or visiting. I explained that customers may not interpret e-mails the way they were meant. We made it part of our culture, now: We spend much more time speaking to people than we do sending e-mails, and the human touch has worked much better.

"At first, some people may not appreciate my 'human touch,' but they will, in the long run. I was president of a company and turned it around in three years, to become the number one organization of its kind. We were given retail dealers' awards two years in a row. We had one salesperson who had potential, and I drove him and drove him. I never let up. I saw a spark in him. He showed that he was a committed person who really wanted to learn, so I wouldn't give him any slack. He grumbled and didn't like the way I singled him out and pushed him. I left the company and didn't see him for a long time, but two or three years ago, I saw him at a show. He came up, shook my hand, and said, 'My wife and I talk about you at least two or three times a year.' He thanked me for everything I did for him. He said, 'If you hadn't done what you did, I wouldn't be where I am today.' He is president of that same organization."

Keith's Attitude Check

Ken D'Arcy learned the value of making others accountable, and he has seen it succeed in several companies where he has taken leadership roles. He listens to his employees, then he hands responsibility over to them, because they know their jobs best.

Rene Champagne, CEO and chairman of ITT Educational Services, Inc. gives his own perspective of what happens when leaders hand responsibility to others. For him, leadership responsibility arrived sooner and more arduously than he expected. In the 1960s, two days after he was graduated from college, Champagne received his draft notice. He did not want to serve as an enlisted man, so he quickly enrolled in the Naval Officer Candidate School in Newport, Rhode Island. When he finally arrived on his assigned ship, he was handed a number of assignments that boggled his mind.

As a 23-year-old, newly minted officer, he was stunned to realize the Navy was empowering him without knowing who he was. He had the power to make major decisions on the ship. He quickly realized that he could either step up and do everything he was assigned, or the officers would find out very quickly that he was not capable. He did not want to be labeled a leadership failure, so he rose to the challenge.

He toughened his resolve and worked extra hard to complete all the projects assigned to him. He also learned he had to rely on other people to help. "I couldn't do all the work myself." Encouraging others to work with him was not just a means of spreading the workload. He had to win people over to his ways of doing things, because the sailors were there to stay, either helping him along the way or standing in his way.

"I had very little hire or fire authority over anyone on these projects, and there was simply no way of doing the work alone, so I had to come up with leadership skills that would motivate the others to help me complete those projects."

Empowerment Multiplies

Like D'Arcy, Champagne soon discovered the power of using other people to get the job done. Just as he found himself empowered by his superiors, he had to empower his coworkers to find ways to do their jobs better and better.

Most great leaders today do not work in a vacuum. They do not work alone. They have a staff; they have underlings and associates and clients and vendors, all of whom can help accomplish more, by constantly looking for ways to improve. Each time you deal with someone, you have the opportunity to get feedback and suggestions that could improve your relationship. Unfortunately, when most people think of communication, they think it refers to methods of speaking to others or imparting information to them. To be effective, though, communication must be a two-way street, preferably with two lanes coming in and only one lane going out. Listen twice as much as you talk. Ask questions. Probe for answers. Reflect those answers back, to be sure you heard correctly.

For example, if your office manager says, "I am having trouble balancing the schedule for next week," you have the opportunity to listen and learn. The harried executive thinks he's empowering his employee if he says, "I know you'll figure it out." The compassionate, communicative executive draws out more information by repeating what the person said. The assertive listener, the effective communicator, might say, "Having trouble?" Or "Having what kind of trouble?"

You may be surprised at all you learn by effectively listening through questioning. Your power will be multiplied, as others feel they can give suggestions, report challenges, and share in the successes.

D'Arcy also told us how successful he has been by taking one hour out of each day to focus on challenges by relaxing and letting his subconscious refresh itself and ruminate. Mystics and gurus have long touted the power of meditation and visualization. D'Arcy brings it out of the occult and into a day-to-day easy-to-understand way to take time out from the hectic work world and let the power of the mind work its magic.

Leadership Comes with a Price

The leader in you will be empowered when you discover your purpose and vision for your life. I had the opportunity last summer to go back to the beautiful Bahamas in the Virgin Islands. It was 10 years ago that I attended a worldwide leadership conference put on by Bahama Faith Ministry International. I had met Dr. Miles Monroe, one of the top leaders in the world, on a plane earlier that week and he encouraged me to attend. I was only able to make it to the final day of the conference and the only speaker I was able to hear speak was Dr. Monroe. For two hours, he spoke on leadership and his words of wisdom have never left me. One thing in particular he said was, "When a leader has tasted possibilities, it is very difficult to settle for impossibilities," and that there is a price, a cost you must be willing to pay to be an effective leader. There will be countless challenges, tests, and adversities that a leader must endure. In essence, the job of a leader is not just a walk in the park. So let me remind you, if you are facing some serious challenges or adversity, hang in, you are simply paying your dues, you are paying the cost for what it takes to be an effective leader.

ATTITUDE ACTION PLAN

- What tactics do you use to get to know your employees? Do you know their names?

- Do you ask for suggestions? Do you listen and write them down? Do you tell employees to implement them? Do you make them set time frames for implementation?

- How do you schedule your day? Is it spent shuffling papers, attending meetings, and 'putting out fires,' or do you create a quiet time to sit and ponder the future and reflect on new ways to avoid or resolve challenges?

- What image do you project to your employees? Do you show your enthusiasm and willingness to work by putting in long hours, or do you celebrate your success (and demonstrate a loss of enthusiasm) by arriving late and leaving early?

- Do you sit in your office all day, or do you get up and see what others are doing?

- Do employees know your schedule, or do you drop in unexpectedly, so they are always on their toes?

- When employees complain, do you shrug off their grumbles, or do you ask them questions and draw out the essence of their grievances? Do you ask them if they have a solution? Do you tell them to implement the solution?

Brief Biography

Ken D'Arcy, born and raised in Calgary, Alberta, Canada, is a 35-year veteran of the sporting goods industry. His varied background includes working as a roustabout on Canadian oil rigs, ski racing and coaching, and tenure with several international companies in the consumer products industry. D'Arcy is best known as a turnaround specialist, having successfully contributed to the dramatic growth at AMF Canada, Blizzard North America, Bollé International, and, most recently, at Corsman Corporation. In each case, his energetic, inclusive management style and his belief that people's "can-do" attitude made the difference, were the keys to his success.

People: The Ultimate Measure

Bill Pollard, Former Chairman and CEO
ServiceMaster, Inc.

Time and time again, we hear leaders say they cannot get the job done alone. Some leaders live by the principle that people are the most important ingredient in the business pie. Bill Pollard, who has served as a leader at ServiceMaster for more than 25 years, takes the concept even further and treats coworkers as family.

"At ServiceMaster," Bill says, "We try to operate in a family atmosphere. We reach out, not only to employees, but also to their families. Employee motivation can be handled in a variety of ways, but it starts with trying to understand who they are and why they work, not just what they do and how they do it."

I have had more than one opportunity to listen to and learn from Bill Pollard on the subject of leadership. He has a lot to say, much of it coming from his personal experiences at ServiceMaster. Continuing with the "people" theme, he recently told me, "Personally, I think that to be a good leader you have to love people. My definition of a leader is someone who has followers. Those followers are obviously people. So people are the key ingredient. Leaders can't get the job done alone. It takes people."

Bill continued, "It's important for a leader not to be concerned only with *what* people do and *how* they do it. The deeper question for the leader is to be thinking about *why* people do their work and *who* they are becoming in the process. When you think you respond to these questions, you begin to understand that a person is a whole person, not just a pair of hands.

"Henry Ford once said, 'Why do I always get a whole person, when I only want a pair of hands?' Sometimes that's the way we look at people; we just want them to produce. It's so easy to look at people in that simplistic way. But people don't come as just a pair of hands. They come as whole people, with an intellectual side, a rational side, a physical side, a spiritual side, and an emotional side.

"Leaders have to understand the fundamental truth that people are individuals. You can try to categorize people into groups, but when you finish working with them, you understand that each one is a unique individual.

"Now that doesn't mean that there aren't certain common characteristics and common skills among people. For example, market research lumps people together in certain classifications. That still doesn't change the fact, however, that each person who participated in that research is different from every other participant."

Working for a Cause

While people are central to the subject of leadership in Bill's mind, there are certainly more elements of leadership that must be considered. Bill explains: "Several factors have to be considered when leaders are growing a business or making decisions. It starts with having a common mission or purpose with which people can identify.

"One of Peter Drucker's sayings is that 'people work for a cause, not just for a living.' He means that people are motivated by the mission and purpose of the organization. For that reason, I think it's extremely important for an organization to have a well-defined mission and purpose.

"At ServiceMaster, we have four objectives: To honor God in all we do; To help people develop; To pursue excellence; and To grow profitably. These four objectives did not come easily or quickly. Employees developed them as concepts over the years. Committees worked to refine them. The actual listing of objectives started in the mid-1970s, and our objectives have been the same since then. But they require constant reinterpretation as we apply them to any decision or business direction.

"Our first two objectives are end goals. The second two objectives are means goals. In seeking to honor God in all we do, we recognize that there are absolutes, right and wrong, in running a business. We also recognize that the development of people in the work environment is an essential part of reflecting their dignity and worth as individuals created in the image of God. But our means objectives also are important. If we do not perform our services to the customer with excellence, we won't have a business. We are in business because we serve and do so in a way that benefits the customers and generates a profit.

"These objectives are values that move a person to say, 'You know, there is *meaning* in this.' This goes back to the issue of the individual. People not only act as individuals, they learn as individuals, too. That concept is sometimes hard to integrate in the training process. But it means that, even in classroom or group training, we have to be able to relate to each person.

"As part of our training and development, we encourage people not only to be skillful in their work, but also to read about who they are and to read the classics. We expand reading opportunities and teaching opportunities for people. We have courses at ServiceMaster that go all the way from sweeping a floor to the equivalent of an MBA."

Transparency Yields Trust

Leadership is not a perfect science. But that is what makes it such an opportunity. Bill recounts his thoughts on the fallibility of leadership. "I've made my share of mistakes in the way I've treated people," he says. "We are all human. We won't all do just the right thing all the time in our relationships with each other. I have found that, especially in a stressful situation or a difficult time, it's easy to be disrespectful to someone. When that happens, a leader should recognize it, apologize, and ask forgiveness. That shows the true strength of leadership. It has been my experience that this quality resonates with strength. That's all part of trust and being real or transparent, qualities that are very important for a leader. Transparency and openness are increasingly important standards. I have found that leaders sometimes try to segment their lives. They say, 'This is my public life; this is what's expected of me. But my private life, that's not your business.' True leaders cannot conduct their lives that way. If you cannot be trusted in your private life, there should be a serious question as to whether or not you can be trusted in your public life."

Get Out and Do Things

But leadership is certainly not just telling others what to do. It requires action. Bill Pollard describes it like this: "During most of my leadership time at ServiceMaster, our company was doubling in size every three years. The organization grew from a little more than $200 million in size to over $6 billion. Vigorous activity was going on, and my decisions affected many people.

"As you make decisions that affect people's lives and responsibilities, you should continually ask yourself and think through whether you are asking people to do things you are not willing to do yourself. For me, it was also praying things through. When we made the decisions of moving into new markets and going into a partnership forum of organization, some of us had to assume as our personal liabilities the debts of the business. It became more than merely taking a risk on behalf of others. We had to take the risk for ourselves. So one of the core elements of leadership in my judgment is the ability to serve those that you lead. I make sure I never ask anyone to do something I am not willing to do myself.

"To test yourself, to see if you have the right attitude in this area, you have to relate to the people where they are doing the job. For most of the time I was CEO, I spent 70 percent of my time out of the office, among the people of ServiceMaster. I looked at what they were doing. I listened to what they were saying about their jobs and their responsibilities or while interacting with customers.

"The administrative side of the job can be managed and handled in such a way that it shouldn't require a great deal of desk time. I believe that desk time for a leader of people should be a limited portion of the total work time."

Never Stand Still

But how does a leader get things done and still move the organization forward? Can a leader be concerned for the people and the organization at the same time? Bill seems to have found the answer. He relates, "There was a time in my leadership at ServiceMaster, in the three and a half years after I had become CEO, when the growth of our main business was slowing and our stock value wasn't moving much. We ended up setting a strategy and building a whole new side of our business. In addition to commercial services, we decided to provide consumer services, which has become the basis of ServiceMaster today. As we made that change, we also made a major acquisition and converted from a corporation form of organization to a partnership.

"During this time period, a great many things were happening. It was an intense time. We were taking big risks. It was all part of transforming the company to be a whole different company and a new direction for growth. As I look back at it, I say to myself, 'Boy, I don't know how I ever took those risks and led the company to get all that done.' During that period of major change, quite a few people retired.

"Realistically, we understood that if the company did not shift, it would not survive. We were a public company; consequently, the public measured us every day by the price of our stock. I had people buying or selling, voting on my leadership every day.

"In a business environment, you never stand still. You are either growing or shrinking. As a leader in business, the question is 'How am I going to maintain a pattern of growth?' If something doesn't happen in a direction with respect to creating value, then your job as a leader is over.

"It turned out that we made the right decision, and it allowed us to move forward. A change was happening in society. With the increase in two-wage-earner households, the need for services in and around the home increased. A market was out there for us to tap. We saw the opportunity and grabbed it."

Basic Questions

In his discussion of leadership, Bill Pollard keys heavily on the critical importance of being a good listener. He says it this way: "It's important for a leader to listen. As I reflect on my own experience, I'm not sure I disciplined myself enough to be a good enough listener. Sometimes I made mistakes by jumping into the middle of a discussion, trying to get resolution before all the information was on the table. I'm the type of person who is always striving for a result or a solution, not just identifying the problem. But if I would have listened more, someone else's additional thought might have been a much better direction or solution to the problem.

"When taking on a new responsibility of leadership, it is very important at the front end to listen and not to be afraid to ask questions. Soon enough you will be expected to know the answers. But in the first couple of months, you don't have to know all the answers. You had better know the questions, though.

"Whether you are leading a business, a nonprofit organization, a church, a hospital, or a government office, step back and ask the Peter Drucker questions:

- What is your business?
- Who is your customer?
- What value are you bringing to your customer?

"The answers to those three basic analytical questions are important to keep in front of you. Asking those questions in a meaningful way—and listening to the answers—results in a thorough examination of the organization. This step is important for the organization to continue to be viable. Leaders ought to be asking those questions all the time, as they look at the function and effectiveness of the organization they are leading."

The Ultimate Measure

So, after all this, what is the bottom line? Bill Pollard sums it up by explaining, "Leadership is both an art and a science. I have no artistic talents when it comes to painting or playing music. But I know that, to become a fine musician or fine artist, I also have to train diligently in addition to having a unique ability or gift. Similarly, leadership represents a special gift, but also many aspects of leadership can be analyzed, studied, learned, and understood.

"There are different types of leaders. Leadership occurs in various environments and at all levels of an organization. Leadership at Service-Master is occurring everyday in our field of organization, where our people are serving the customer and then sharing the experience with colleagues and inspiring them to do likewise. These leaders may not have some of the same skills and gifts or qualifications I have, but, conversely, I may not have some of the same skills and gifts or qualifications they have.

"Often those who have a big title or a corner office are singled out as leadership examples. But the principle of leadership affects each of us in our relationships with others. Whenever a particular task involves a group of people, leadership is in the middle of that pursuit. Leadership is expressed in a variety of ways and in many different circumstances.

"When we study examples of leadership, we can examine positive characteristics as well as problems in someone's leadership. It's not all perfect. Some leaders lead people in the wrong direction. Some leaders make mistakes. But we can learn from all of them—the good as well as the bad.

"For almost 25 years, leading ServiceMaster was my primary responsibility. We have recently chosen a new CEO who is doing a fine job, so I'm stepping back from the responsibilities in ServiceMaster for now. That's another important element of leadership about which I feel very strongly. I think a leader should hold his position until his successor has been identified and is ready, *and not one day longer*. If a leader holds his or her position too long, he or she may no longer be leading, but just holding on to a position as a liability, not an asset, for the organization. That's part of a leader's responsibility—developing people to take over our job. Leadership is not something you own and keep for yourself. It is a responsibility you are entrusted with for a period of time, and it is a duty you fulfill. There is an obligation to leadership, but it is not something you can hang onto indefinitely.

"Leadership makes a difference. I can share example after example of business units that weren't doing well. But we changed the leadership and, even though the markets were the same and the people were the same, the business unit perked up and started producing. Nothing else changed except the leadership. That's how I know that leadership definitely makes a difference.

"Having said all this, I come back to the original concept of people. The ultimate measure of leadership is in the changed lives of people. If lives are being changed, then hosts of people are able to accomplish more. They also feel better about themselves and how they relate to others, especially their families, as a result of someone inspiring them through leadership. The value of my leadership shall be measured in the changed lives of others. Changing and improving others: This was my ultimate goal as a leader."

Keith's Attitude Check

Bill Pollard lives and breathes leadership through his attitude toward others, always wanting to help others. A perfect match for him, then, was ServiceMaster, with its corporate objectives as outlined above: To honor God in all we do; To help people develop; To pursue excellence; and To grow profitably. These objectives provide the company with a foundation and a reference point for making decisions and taking action, and it draws people to the company who abide by the same principles.

Pollard calls the objectives "a living set of principles" that helps him and other leaders overcome challenges. He also feels that when a company's mission becomes its organizing principle, the organization becomes a community of people caring for each other and for those they serve.

What is truly impressive about the ServiceMaster objectives is that they really do serve as the guidepost for the company from the highest level of management to the people treating lawns, cleaning carpets, and repairing broken furniture. Adhering to those objectives has also led to long-term success for one of the most respected companies in the world.

James L. Heskett, professor emeritus at the Harvard Business School, described ServiceMaster as a firm "that has broken the cycle of failure and has basically reengineered jobs, provided training to people, and attempted to deliver a level of self-esteem that many workers have never had in the past."

Service to employees and to customers comes in many more forms than mere training and respect. As Pollard said, it also involves listening; and in Pollard's case, it meant stepping up when needed and stepping down at the right time.

He points out that anyone can be a leader, sometimes by being thrust into the role. Likewise, not everyone has to be a leader to contribute to the bottom line, the finished project, or the success of a company. Dr. Blenda Wilson, president and CEO of the Nellie Mae Education Foundation, says it well, too. "It's hard to avoid getting locked into the notion that only people with a PhD know certain things and only people with certain responsibilities can contribute to certain decisions. Our world was organized in a bureaucratic and hierarchical sense, and it doesn't frequently take advantage of the knowledge that is learned from experience."

Pollard made his point clearly when he said that even the pest-control technician has information to contribute to a company, something that can aid in the overall success of the division or corporation.

Most of the successful organizations I have had the pleasure of working with all have some type of suggestion program or open lines of communication to be able to communicate with the leaders within that organization. Some of these organizations pay substantial bonuses depending on how that idea helps reduce expenses or improves productivity. As a leader, how can you encourage those around you to willingly contribute their ideas, insights, and wisdom?

Changing lives starts first with changing yourself. Identifying areas of improvement is often one-sided when leaders evaluate their goals versus actual accomplishments. I suggest that the ultimate measure is a 360-degree measurement. It requires an inward and outward examination of character, growth, and impact. The latter will require feedback from others. How others measure your leadership in the community, at home, and in the business gives you a complete image of your effectiveness. John Maxwell says, *"The first person you should lead is you, because if you wouldn't want to follow yourself, why would anyone else?"*

Being a leader doesn't mean you can't be coached. About a year ago, I spoke at the Masters Sales Convention for Prudential, Fox and Roch Realtors—the fifth largest realtor in the United States. The president and CEO, Larry Flick, also made a presentation. Afterward, I told him how much I enjoyed his presentation, and then he did something that really impressed me. He asked me for feedback, because he was working on improving his communication and presentation skills. I gave him a couple of pointers and he shared some improvement ideas with me as well.

Months later, I was asked to speak to the Administrative Support Team, and Larry spoke as well. Again, we took the opportunity to seek coaching and feedback from one another. Iron sharpens iron. Leaders can learn from peers and mentors. Those who participate in a 360-degree measurement and seek to improve do so for one purpose: to help change lives.

Change: The Difference Maker

The ultimate measure Bill Pollard uses to evaluate the effectiveness of his leadership is changed lives.

Bill changed my life when he approached me after hearing me speak to a group of his franchisees at a meeting in Memphis, Tennessee. What he said that day had a profound affect on me. "Keith, I enjoyed your message. I can tell you are a believer, a Christian. Next time you get the opportunity to speak to any one of my companies, and are led by the Holy Spirit to say something, well, feel free to share your testimony."

ATTITUDE ACTION PLAN

- Do you treat your employees as you would family, with pride and trust?

- Bill suggests 70 percent of a leader's time be spent checking the pulse of the organization. How much time do you spend with customers and employees serving and listening? Are you guilty of asking others to do what you wouldn't do yourself?

- Do you acknowledge some form of leadership in everyone, no matter the level of education or position?

- What programs do you have in place to reward those who take initiative or show leadership?

- When you make a mistake in handling someone, how do you handle it? Are you willing and able to apologize, admit your mistake, and do something to repair the damage?

- Have you set up an environment that allows employees to embrace changes as they come along and to aid each other through the transition?

- Are you coachable? If so, take time to conduct a 360-degree measure of your leadership. So listen to feedback of people you trust to be honest and want to help you succeed.

Brief Biography

C. William Pollard served as chief executive officer of the ServiceMaster Company from 1983 to 1993 and from October 1999 to February 2001. He served as chairman of the board since 1990 until his recent retirement. During Pollard's first tenure as CEO, he led the company's entry into consumer services through the acquisitions of Terminix, TruGreen, ChemLawn, American Home Shield, and Merry Maids.

Prior to joining ServiceMaster, Pollard was a faculty member and a vice president at Wheaton College from 1972 to 1977. From 1963 to 1972, he practiced law, specializing in corporate finance and tax. Pollard received his bachelor of arts degree from Wheaton College and his law degree from Northwestern University School of Law. Bill and his wife Judy have been married for over 40 years. They have four children and 12 grandchildren.

In addition to his work at ServiceMaster, Pollard serves as a director of Herman Miller, Inc. and UnumProvident Corporation. He is also a director of a number of education, religious, and not-for-profit organizations, including Wheaton College, The Leader to Leader Institute (formerly The Drucker Foundation), and The Billy Graham Evangelistic Association, and he is actively involved in teaching and speaking on subjects related to management and ethics. Pollard is the author of the best selling book *The Soul of the Firm*.

Are You Using Your
Self-Correcting Mechanism?

Bruce Camacho, President and CEO
Assurant Group

When asked if he had a mentor, Bruce Camacho, president and CEO of Assurant Group, did not hesitate. "Otis Maxfield," he answered immediately. "One mentor is an organizational psychologist who is an energetic 75 years old. This man, who has worked with General Colin Powell and many other great military leaders, taught me how to use power correctly so it doesn't become abuse of power."

When asked to explain that concept, Bruce elaborated, "When Admiral Rickover was selecting the commander for the first nuclear submarine, he was faced with an enormous responsibility. Nuclear submarines can make their own energy, supply their own water, travel worldwide, and they carry weapons capable of terrible destruction. The leader in charge of this vessel needed to be absolutely trustworthy and beyond reproach. Otis Maxfield proposed to Rickover that the quality that was vital for such an important position was a *Self-Correcting Mechanism (SCM)*.

"As human beings, we all make mistakes. If we have a Self-Correcting Mechanism, we constantly monitor our behavior to see if we're operating effectively. If something's gone wrong, we have the security to admit it and the courage to face it—instead of trying to deny,

177

defend, or hide it. We have the motivation to correct it because we are committed to acting with integrity, and that means being honest about our actions.

"Leaders without SCMs often lose touch with what's going on in their organization because when complaints are brought to their attention, they kill the messenger instead of trying to resolve the issue. As a result, those problems can 'bring down the ship' because they go unaddressed. Leaders without SCMs can't be trusted because they don't hold themselves accountable. They're always looking for scapegoats because they don't want to accept fault. They don't have the discipline or awareness to stop unhealthy habits because they refuse to look at themselves honestly.

"On the other hand, leaders who role model a healthy SCM can be quite demanding because employees know they're only being held responsible for the same standards their leader has already demonstrated him/herself."

It's Clear: Don't Coast

"My father, a former World War II Royal Air Force veteran, taught me a lesson about humility and hard work that has stayed with me throughout my life. I was only 9 years old at the time. My father was actually talking to my brother who was 10 years older.

"My father didn't want any of his sons to think we were indispensable so he filled a glass with water and told my brother, 'Picture that a company is like that glass of water. Now, put your finger in the water. That's you in the company. Now, pull your finger out. Do you see a hole in the water? Do you see a hole in the company if you're not there?'

"My father was trying to drive home the message that we have to earn our pay and position every single day. He wanted us to have a combination of humility (understanding we're not indispensable) and responsibility (understanding we have an obligation to contribute). He said, 'Every single night you should ask yourself, Did I do a day's work for a day's pay? Everyone has low periods, but you better be aware of where you stand because, especially in this economy, there are no guaranteed positions.'"

"If you're hoping to build a career, ask yourself regularly if anyone in senior management perceives that you're coasting. If you can honestly say to yourself, 'No, I think they would all say I'm a hard worker,' you're probably okay. The day you realize your reputation is for taking it easy, is probably a few days before you get fired. I believe nothing is owed to us, that we have to earn whatever we get. And that means working hard instead of hardly working."

Are You Giving Your Extreme Effort?

"This lesson was reinforced when I went to a very strict boarding school in England. There were two brothers at this military kind of Irish Christian Brothers school, Brother Keegan and Brother Coleman, who felt that effort was first and foremost. Whether it was sports or studies, they simply would not let you give up, ever.

"When we were practicing for rugby or cricket, Brother Keegan would push us to the brink of collapse. We would be totally exhausted, almost in pain; and we hated him at the time for driving us so hard, but it strengthened us tremendously from a physical standpoint.

"The same was true of Brother Coleman. We would stay up studying until two in the morning for chemistry and biology. He would check in on us, and if we were falling asleep, he would use his 18-inch wood ruler (use your imagination) to waken us and get us back to the books. He wanted to make sure we were applying our full brain power, our full endeavor.

"My wife has a similar love of discipline. She believes in 'working your weakness.' She feels that, as parents, we know the strengths and weaknesses of our children. We can usually see at an early age what they're naturally good at and what they're not.

"Her philosophy was that if you identify their weaknesses, you can then instill habits to help control and counteract them. You can't remove weaknesses because we all have them; but you can overcome them with character strength attained through healthy habits."

Work Your Weakness

"I try to 'work weaknesses' as an individual with myself, as a leader with my employees, and as a parent with my children. One of my sons is a natural loner who's comfortable being on his own. My wife and I have actually forced him to interact with others. He's the one in our family assigned to answer the door so he gets opportunities to greet people and gain more social skills.

"We think it's important for him to understand that it's fine to sit by himself sometimes, as long as he also has the ability to join a group of people and fit in easily and graciously. By identifying and then working on the areas where we don't have natural gifts; we can at times often turn weaknesses into strengths. But often, we can certainly build strengths/good habits around our weaknesses."

Are You Keeping Your Nose In or Your Hands On?

"Someone once told me, 'There's a big difference between keeping your nose in and keeping your hands on.' A leader should always keep his nose in so he is aware of what is going on and so employees know he is monitoring the company's activities; but you shouldn't have your fingers in everything.

"The people you hire are the do'ers. You are there to give advice and help them do their jobs, not to do their jobs for them. That's a real challenge for most leaders who've risen to the top as do'ers themselves. The very same 'take charge and fix it' qualities that made them successful as they rose through the ranks now make it difficult for them to pull back as an executive. They end up being the person driving the car instead of the traffic cop giving directions."

No Leader Should Be an Island

"I've also seen leaders who go to the other extreme. I've watched business leaders of high integrity, great intellect, and phenomenal vision become ineffective because they lost that all-important connection to their people. They didn't want to 'meddle' so they made the mistake of withdrawing and staying in their offices too much.

"These leaders missed the distinction between delegating and advocating. They reached the top position, and in an effort to remain above the day-to-day operation of the company, they went too far and isolated themselves. They abdicated their leadership role by delegating all the responsibilities of their position. Colin Powell talks about the traits of leadership and he notes that the day your troops stop talking to you is the day you are no longer their leader. I think he's absolutely right on."

Talk to Me

"Some of my direct reports have become upset when people down the chain of command blow by them and come directly to me. I tell my direct reports that they should only get upset if I blow by them in taking action. I want people to feel free to talk directly to me because I want to stay in touch with what is going on. I don't want things filtered. I don't want gatekeepers controlling the flow of information that comes to me. I keep the chain of command intact by discussing the information I receive and my response to it with my direct reports so they stay involved and in charge of their areas of responsibility. I tell them not to be upset if someone comes to me because if that person is that concerned and motivated, I want to hear what he or she has to say.

"I like to 'round robin' issues with my staff. My communication style is almost 'in-your-face' because I believe we should all be big enough people to talk about our opinions freely. When we're problem solving, we need to look at issues from all sides and we can't do that if people are holding back what they really think and hiding what they really feel. I want us to be able to brainstorm out loud and get our thoughts out on the table. It doesn't do anyone any good to cow-tow to the leader and say, 'Well, he's the boss and that's what he thinks, so that's what goes.'"

From a Distance . . . Doesn't Work

"Sometimes it may seem easier to stay removed from your employees. If you have to make a tough decision that is going to negatively impact peoples' lives, it is tempting to distance yourself. But when you do that as a CEO, you hurt yourself and the company. By cutting yourself off from your people, you lose empathy for them.

"That's a problem, because more and more, I've come to recognize that empathy is the key to effective leadership. Having empathy is important because it's one thing to think you understand how people feel, but it is much more important to feel what people are feeling. Empathy is what enables leaders to be in touch with the heads and the hearts of our employees.

"There are some leaders who don't have empathy, of course, but all things being equal, I believe those with the ability to relate to their people are better leaders. There is a difference between leadership and management. Leadership is the ability to get people to perform above what they are capable of performing. Management is just holding people accountable and being accountable."

Are You Pushing or Pulling?

"How do we motivate people to perform above what they are capable of performing? I think we accomplish that by role-modeling what we want. I was privileged to work with some leaders at Price-Waterhouse who never mentioned working hard, they just went about their jobs doing it. Their quick walking, speed of communication, energy, and all-out commitment to doing a quality job just kind of pulled us along.

"It's like a boat. When a boat is moving quickly through the water, it's easier for you to get behind it and move faster yourself. You're not having to buck the current or generate all your own momentum; you can feed off of and follow theirs.

"I've also worked around hypocritical leaders who talked, talked, talked about work ethic and all the while they were leaving work early. They would push you to do things they themselves never did. It actually demotivates you. How can you keep going fast if your leaders are going slow or not going at all? I kept putting in extra effort because of my personal work ethic, but it was like swimming upstream.

"One of the responsibilities of 'pull' leadership is demonstrating your passion and urgency every single day. When you do that, you look around and see that other people are moving with the same sense of passion and urgency; which means you attract other people who want to work with passion and urgency. It becomes self-perpetuating."

Straight Talk or No Talk

"Sales trainers talk about the four barriers to making a sale: (1) no trust, (2) no need, (3) no help, and (4) no satisfaction. I believe trust is the most important aspect of any business relationship, and any personal relationship, too. You don't buy from someone you don't trust. You don't want to work for someone you don't trust, and you certainly don't follow a leader you don't trust.

"Want to know one of the keys to trust? Straight talk or no talk. There are times something is going on in the company, and I'm not at liberty to discuss it. If one of my employees starts hinting around the subject, I simply apologize and let him know I'm not free to discuss the issue right now. That is so much better than spinning some story and getting caught up in a web you've woven that's untrue. If you tell half-truths, people start second-guessing you and looking for hidden agendas. If you want employees to trust you, talk straight or don't say anything at all."

Keith's Attitude Check

You've probably heard the analogy of the plane that never flies straight to its destination. Planes are constantly buffeted by winds and other weather conditions so they're frequently "off-course." The key to arriving at the desired destination is for pilots to be alert to when their plane starts heading in the wrong direction so they can quickly make an adjustment and get back on course as soon as possible. These adjustments are called *course-corrections*.

As Bruce pointed out, leaders need to make course-corrections for themselves as individuals and for their organizations. By catching ourselves doing something wrong and correcting it as soon as possible, we keep ourselves on track. Furthermore, we are setting an example of accountability so employees are more comfortable admitting when they're wrong and more committed to making it right. As John F. Kennedy said, "Our task is not to fix the blame for the past, it's to fix the course for the future."

Are You Finding Fault or Finding Solutions?

People don't expect us to be perfect. They expect us to be honest. Have you ever been part of a staff meeting that deteriorated into finger-pointing and fault-finding? Not pleasant, is it? As leaders, it's our job to move people from a critical "Who did it?" frame of mind to a constructive "What can we do about it?" frame of mind. Instead of wasting precious time on fixing blame, we can invest that time searching for a solution.

Has something gone wrong recently in your organization? Is a project overdue? A bid proposal rejected? A product not up to standard? Are employees busy passing the buck because no one wants to accept blame? Could you hold a meeting and refuse to allow the discussion to focus on who dropped the ball? Could you instead insist that all discussion concentrate on brainstorming exactly how this program, proposal, and product can get back on track?

Pearl S. Buck said, "Every great mistake has a halfway moment, a split second when it can be recalled and perhaps remedied." Role-model a Self-Correcting Mechanism in action by recalling and remedying this problem, and hopefully, next time a mistake is made, employees will be more likely to make an adjustment than an excuse.

Are Your Habits Helping You or Hurting You?

What's your weakness? A fellow entrepreneur claimed to be a non-techie. She was a brilliant speaker, but she was also the type of person who, when asked what type of computer she had would reply, "Beige." She forced herself to sign up for computer classes at a local community center. This high-powered individual was very good at what she did, but she realized she was compromising her overall effectiveness by allowing her lack of knowledge about all things electronic to undermine her.

She said there were many nights that the last thing she wanted to do after a hard day's work was to go to that three-hour seminar from 6:30 to 9:30 P.M. However, at the end of the six-week course, she felt proud that she disciplined herself to do what needed to be done.

Dostoyevsky said, "It seems, in fact, as though the second half of a man's life is made up of nothing but the habits he acquired during the first half." Are your habits serving you or sabotaging you? What's one specific action you can do today to start counteracting or correcting a weakness? Like my friend who is now a whiz at computers, you won't be sorry you acted, you'll only be sorry if you don't.

Do You Encourage Straight Talk?

Bruce brought up a good point about wanting all employees, not just his direct reports, to have access to him. He wanted everyone to feel they could freely share their concerns instead of only being able to communicate with the manager who was one step higher in the hierarchy. Do you have an open-door policy in which you encourage employees to talk directly to you? Do you ever have brainstorm sessions where you "round robin" problems and tackle them from all angles?

As a leader, maintaining open access accomplishes several things. By hearing what's on our employees' minds, we are more empathetic to what it's like for everyone on the front lines. Getting perspectives from the "trenches" gives us insights that might not have occurred to us otherwise. Furthermore, it's a statement that straight talk on all levels is promoted, not punished. Perhaps most importantly, as Bruce pointed out, a reputation for straight talk sets up trust.

I'll always remember the time I came back to my hotel after a long day on the road making sales calls for IBM. It'd been an exhausting day and I was past ready for bed. There, resting on my pillow, was a simple card from the hotel with this quote from Shakespeare, "To sleep, perchance to dream." My mind immediately responded with, "To trust, perhaps to buy." When it comes to leaders, we can change that to, "To trust, perhaps to follow."

Lead People Like You Lead a Horse

When Bruce was talking about "push-pull" leadership, I immediately thought of my friend who's been riding horses ever since she was 5 years old. Her first horse was a big black draft horse named Elko. Elko weighed almost 2,000 pounds, and my friend, at the time, weighed about 50 pounds. That first day at the stable, she was so excited she could hardly wait to ride him. However, her dad put a halter on Elko and told her she first had to lead him to the barn where they kept the brushes so she could clean him up before saddling him.

She faced Elko and tugged on the rope. He just looked at her. She tugged harder. Elko didn't budge. She really leaned into it this time and yanked on the rope. Elko leaned back and set his feet, determined not to move. She couldn't get behind and push him. A 50-pound girl wasn't going to move a 2,000-pound animal who didn't want to move.

She looked at her dad, puzzled and exasperated. He gently said, "If you want him to follow you, you've got to lead the way. Just turn toward the barn and start walking." She did, and guess what happened? Elko started quietly walking behind her.

My friend told me she's used this valuable lesson ever since. We can't push, prod, or drag people into doing what we want them to do. It's better to use what's called a "loose lead." Just walk the way you want to go, and people are likely to follow of their own accord. Remember what Bruce said about the leaders at Price-Waterhouse who worked and walked with such energy, you were intrinsically motivated to do the same? Leading the way shows the way. When you show the way, people often choose to walk that way, too. That's "pull leadership."

ATTITUDE ACTION PLAN

- Do you have a Self-Correcting Mechanism? Describe a time you got off track and made a course correction. What happened as a result?

- Do you 'fess up when you mess up?

- Do staff members have open access to you? Why or why not?

- Describe a time an employee came to you with a problem or concern. What action did you take and how did you honor the chain of command?

- What is a weakness you have? How have you tried to counteract or correct it?

- Talk about the delicate balance between helping and doing, keeping your nose in versus keeping your fingers in.

- Do you hold brainstorming meetings? Why or why not?

- What is a specific way you encourage straight talk?

- Have you ever worked for a "push" leader, someone who prodded others to work but didn't himself? What was that like?

- Have you ever worked for a "pull" leader who "showed the way" by leading the way? What was that like?

- What's one specific way you do your best to practice "pull" leadership?

Brief Biography

Bruce Camacho is president and chief executive officer of Assurant Group. He was appointed president in August 2000 and promoted to chief executive officer on January 1, 2003. Assurant Group was created in August 1999 after Fortis, Inc., acquired American Bankers Insurance Group, Miami, Florida, and merged it with the operations of American Security Group, Atlanta, Georgia. He previously served as Assurant's executive vice president for sales and marketing.

Bruce joined American Bankers in 1990 as vice president of information systems. At the time of the American Bankers' acquisition, he was executive vice president of investor relations, with additional responsibility for legal and regulatory affairs, marketing services, licensing, state filings, and client administration.

A certified public accountant, Bruce is a graduate of Prior Park College, Bath, England, and Florida State University, where he received a bachelor's degree in accounting. Before joining American Bankers, he was accountant with Price-Waterhouse, specializing in insurance in the United States, United Kingdom, and the Caribbean.

Bruce, his wife Amy, and their six children live in Cumming, Georgia, north of Atlanta.

Headquartered in Atlanta, Assurant is the largest Fortis company in the United States. Assurant provides specialty risk management for financial institutions, retailers, and auto and manufactured housing dealers through insurance, extended service contracts, and membership programs. Assurant leads the financial services industry in credit insurance, third-party administration of debt deferment programs, hazard insurance tracking, lender-placed hazard insurance, and insurance for manufactured housing. The company has more than 5,600 employees and maintains operations in 11 states in the United States, Canada, Argentina, Brazil, Denmark, Ireland, Puerto Rico, and the United Kingdom.

Assurant is part of Fortis, an international financial services provider active in the fields of insurance, banking, and investment. At year-end 2002, Fortis had total assets of more than $400 billion. Fortis is listed on the Amsterdam (FORA), Brussels (FORB), and Luxembourg (FOR LX) stock exchanges and has a sponsored ADR program (FORSY) in the United States.

When Synergy Creates Energy

Jeffery A. Joerres, Chairman, CEO, and President
Manpower, Inc.

Jeff Joerres is one of the world's leading bankers of "human capital." His company, Manpower, Inc., employs more than 2.7 million people worldwide annually. I find it fascinating that someone whose business is workforce management has a strategy of welcoming conflict within the company. He considers disagreement to be healthy debate and an opportunity for growth.

In talking with Jeff, I learned that his strategy of welcoming conflict is a part of his overall focus in creating a diverse culture built on trust, loyalty, and open communication. As any marriage counselor or expert in human relationships will tell you, the healthiest relationships are those in which mistakes are allowed and conflicts are openly discussed, so that individuals can grow together. The same holds true in organizational relationships, according to this CEO.

"When you suppress any kind of confrontation, it becomes much more of a draining organization than an exciting one. At Manpower, Inc., I work very hard to put together teams—whether it's senior teams or ad hoc global teams—that consist of individuals from diverse backgrounds with diverse ideas and diverse methods for expressing their passion and energy. I think diversity makes for a great company.

"In a diverse corporate culture, it is important to welcome conflict as a healthy opportunity. There are *destructive* forms of conflict based on selfishness, and that sort of conflict is bad. It's an exciting thing when conflict leads to healthy debate, though. That's the sort of conflict I encourage, because when issues are debated passionately and intellectually, you discover solutions that move a company forward. I try to create that kind of healthy debate in the company, whether through global videoconferences, meetings of top people from around the world, or one-on-one meetings with customers. I also encourage people on my management team to recognize areas of conflict and discuss issues openly, so they get resolved and things move forward.

"Seventy-five percent of our sales come from outside the United States. My senior management team is not located in our Milwaukee headquarters. Our top people are scattered around the world in France, London, Singapore, Toronto, and elsewhere. Despite—and because of—the fact that we aren't under the same roof physically, it is essential that we have open communication and candid dialogue.

"Just recently, one of my senior managers contacted me concerning a project and reported that it was not going well, because of a conflict between this person and another manager. It was believed that the project was suffering because the managers did not understand each other and had communication problems.

"During our conversation concerning the situation, I said to that individual, 'Hold on for a second, because I'm going to call the other person, and we're going to conference him in to solve this right now.'

"The first person backed away, probably in fear of having a conflict on the telephone in my presence, but I insisted that because there was an issue, we should work it out together. I put the senior manager on hold and called the other person, who was in another part of the world, and conferenced everyone in. I used that call as an opportunity to resolve the issue immediately, so we could move forward. I just said, 'Look, there seems to be a communication problem here. We have a great opportunity on this project, but I have two of my senior team members who really aren't communicating on this, so let's resolve the issue.'

"The first five minutes of the conversation were a little uncomfortable, which I expected, because I'm their manager. They probably were concerned about my discovery about how much they have *not* worked things out together. They also know I have set up an environment where I don't write things down in a secret folder and hold them against anyone. They know my motivation is to move the project and the company forward by resolving the conflict through honest dialogue.

"After the first five minutes, there was a kind of catharsis, in which the two sides accepted responsibility for the conflict and then they began solving the problem. Within 15 minutes, the conflict was put to rest to the point where I could hang up and let the two of them work things out. The two managers eventually met in person and strengthened their working relationship. Since then, I have never heard another thing about a conflict between those two senior managers."

The Door's Open

"It's my job to set the pace by saying it's okay to have those kinds of conversations in which the motivation is to resolve problems and move on. Progress requires cutting to the chase and getting to the heart of the matter. Again, it's all about finding a solution so we can move the company forward.

"As far as I am concerned, being solution orientated is a big part of being a leader; it's a tremendous leadership quality. A true solution-oriented leader says, 'Here's an issue. Let's face it and not run from it. Let's not dance around the issue; instead, let's talk about it.' Usually, within a short period of time, the issue gets resolved.

"It is also important that no one be destroyed in the process of conflict resolution. If someone is in constant negative conflict with other members of the team, you must adjust your approach in dealing with the problem.

"It takes hard work to build teamwork and trust, because of the negative forces that work against conflict resolution. Every company has employees who tend to speak their minds, not during meetings, but during 'watercooler' conversations. My goal is at least to minimize those secret meetings until they are eliminated. Of course, when you are a part of a multicultural organization, a truly global organization such as Manpower, those situations are often harder to resolve. It is important to realize that you probably won't solve these types of issues in a couple of meetings, but rather over time.

"Developing positive conflict resolution is vital, especially when you spend most of your time working with people by telephone or in person to move projects, concepts, and strategies forward. It means cajoling the people involved and injecting energy into the project. It also means making the right decisions and helping to keep others focused on what we're trying to accomplish.

"I easily spend 75 percent of my time on people issues. That is why I am all for promoting healthy dialogue, building positive attitudes, and encouraging constructive relationships.

"I consider my role to be a coordinator of talent, behavior, and organizational culture. A key part of that role is fostering a culture in which people feel free to express themselves, even in the midst of negative conflict. I don't want them to feel uncomfortable when it comes to openly discussing problems, especially when the problem affects the company's momentum. I want our people to be able to express their business needs freely and inform me of what things would make things flow easier for them and, ultimately, the company.

"I believe in straight language, not pomp and circumstance. I want to be straightforward with everyone, because people trust openness. It creates a better working environment. Along with being honest with others, I make it a point to be accessible as well. Because I am the CEO, there will always be a certain degree of separation, but I want people to be able to have a conversation with me. I don't want them to have the feeling that I am so far up the ranks that I am not approachable.

"I receive plenty of e-mail from people around the world who offer suggestions and ideas and share their complaints and feedback. A few people around me want to shield me from people issues, but I don't believe in being shielded, especially when it comes to helping people become better.

"Anyone at Manpower can come to my door without an appointment and with a soft knock have a sit-down with me. In some cases, having an open-door policy can be disruptive; however, I have discovered that most people don't abuse it.

"Some efficiency experts might say this is not the best use of my time. As far as I am concerned, it is important to listen to people. People have real issues that require time to iron out, to find real solutions. Whenever I am able to talk to someone, regardless of his or her dilemma, I get to send a message that I am approachable.

"I think it's dangerous for the CEO to be shielded from people. It's the personal, one-on-one meetings that make all the difference, when it comes to making good decisions. You learn facts and can weed out personal opinions that hinder the progress of a project.

"Impromptu, open-door meetings energize me and give me the opportunity to build my information bank. What I learn during these meetings is often stored away for future use, whenever I am faced with making tough decisions. Sometimes I have to make difficult, unpopular decisions; however, I would rather stay connected to my people at all times and avoid greater problems in the future."

Don't Forget the Human Element

"Most of the issues I deal with regularly are people- and talent-related. Even when my decisions about a project are geared toward moving business forward, I always try to focus more on the people involved and less on the elements of the business. I try never to get so bogged down in the process of business that I neglect the human element. Although my job requires communicating with shareholders; interacting with board members; and dealing with some of the operational intricacies of 63 countries, including gross margins, operating profits, and so on, I don't enjoy those things as much as I like working with people.

"In the end, what will matter most is your attitude. My daily attitude about work is that I am here to move things forward and to build the great brand of Manpower. My strategy involves developing a great bunch of people who are excited about promoting Manpower's vision.

"As you read through our most recent annual report, you will discover the Manpower heartbeat, which is, 'It's more than work. It's more than a routine. It's more than moving paper. It's more than the passage of time. It's about life! It's about being regarded for our efforts. It's about learning something new every day. It's about being on a team where team members truly care for one another. It's about setting good examples for others. It's about pride. It's about knowing you made a difference. It's about Manpower!' This kind of attitude makes us a successful organization."

Heart Issue

"If you start a business, you can create the culture; you can influence the environment. I did not establish Manpower; it began 54 years ago. Therefore, I inherited this business culture. As CEO, I am responsible for understanding this culture, so I can do my part to maximize it.

"In my years at Manpower, I have discovered that people here respond positively to open discussion. Those who are not as comfortable with candid dialogue eventually discover this may not be the best working environment for them.

"My heartfelt desire is to see people succeed. One of my faults may be that I am too loyal to people, but I would rather err on the side of giving people the opportunity to succeed, rather than giving them the chance to fail. If someone does not buy into our culture, I certainly don't take it lightly and ignore it.

"Like any company, we deal with politics and all sorts of scenarios and individuals, such as poor performers who attempt to stop our progress. Despite the obstacles, the main issue is how we deal with those situations and individuals, and how committed we are to moving forward. If someone on the team is not committed to progress, but rather works against it, we move the person out, so he or she won't create a destructive environment. You have to do that sort of thing for the sake of the company.

"When we have a first-line or second-line manager who doesn't buy into what we are trying to do, we have a problem on our hands. For this reason, we coach individuals and give them every opportunity to understand and actively support the company's vision.

"Our job is to train people to succeed. We specialize in taking people out of their home and introducing them into the workforce. We take people who have been released from one job and train them in another area, so they can thrive in the workforce. That concept excites me!

"Manpower provides a service that develops not only the minds, but also the hearts of the people who use our services. If this were just a pure intellectual kind of company—like an accounting firm—and someone made a serious mistake on a financial transaction, the person would have to leave, because we could not tolerate mistakes that adversely affected the company's progress. In our case, however, being a company that develops human capital, we encourage people who make mistakes to learn from their mistakes. Our executives and managers are skilled enough to act as coaches, and people work through their conflicts and mistakes."

Keith's Attitude Check

In the game of basketball, when a player is competitive and plays the game exceptionally well, others are quick to say, "He's got game!" He knows how to score the last-second game-winning shot. He also knows when to pass the ball to make good assists. Most importantly, a successful player is a team player. Team players win games. Team players make good leaders in the lineup. They don't take credit for the success of the team. Instead, their attitude is, "As a squad, we do whatever it takes to win!"

Jeff Joerres, the CEO and chairman of the board of Manpower, Inc. is a team player with a positive attitude. Jeff's attitude of leadership helps Manpower, Inc. be the forerunner in the world of staffing services.

I met Jeff on February 11, 2002, at one of my speaking engagements in Scottsdale, Arizona. I was the keynote speaker for about 800 managers and key salespeople from around the world.

What impressed me about Jeff was his level of confidence, including his passion and enthusiasm for what he does. There's something about meeting people with steely determination and a love for what they do. It encourages you.

In my brief encounter with Jeff, he made me feel I was a part of his team at Manpower. His confidence rubbed off on me. I felt I was a part of making the meeting a huge success. Because of his influence that day, I personally started to focus on the word *win*—What's Important Now.

During that meeting, I realized what was important was that I clearly understood that my job as the keynote speaker was to reinforce everyone's value to the company. Jeff did not want anyone to leave that meeting not knowing they play a vital role in making things happen. He wanted them to know that without their talents and contributions, Manpower could not make as great a global impact, as it has in recent years. In life, you are either *on* the way, or *in* the way. Jeff and his entire team at Manpower are definitely on the way to helping others lead more productive lives.

The PAT Principle of Success

While developing an attitude of leadership, you must realize the importance of knowing and applying what I call the PAT Principle of Successful Leadership. PAT is an acronym for Passion, Approachability, and Thoughtfulness. PAT describes Jeff perfectly. He loves what he does and isn't afraid to share his passion.

I am convinced that once you develop the PAT Principle of Success, you can accomplish great things in business. The principle simply says, "It takes passion to succeed, approachability to effectively help others succeed, and thoughtfulness in making sure your decisions have a positive effect on the team."

Ask yourself, "How passionate am I when it comes to my company and its vision? Can others remark that I am approachable whenever issues come up? Do I really care if my decisions affect those around me, as long as the job gets done?"

It takes courage to make adjustments, when you realize you could be a bit more passionate, approachable, and thoughtful when it comes to the organization you represent and the people you interact with daily. The key is to strive toward perfecting what's best for the team, and it begins with perfecting the attitude of leadership.

When it comes to the principles of success, like Jeff Joerres, I believe you must be loyal to your organization's brand, especially as a leader. Loyalty to the brand says, "I am committed to doing whatever it takes to promote the company." It's an inner conviction. I like what Jeff said at his interview for this book: "My job is all about the brand Manpower! It takes passion and relentlessness to always make the organization better." Now that's an attitude of success.

What's your attitude when it comes to leadership and success? You don't have to become a Jeff Joerres to succeed. You simply have to be the best you can be and develop the right attitude. Remember that when you focus only on developing *your* game, and not on helping those around you perfect *their* game, your team or organization can't win big; it will suffer.

The moment you choose to become a leader, the game clock starts ticking. The ball is placed in your hands. You receive the responsibility of taking your squad to the championship. When it comes to the business environment, true championship status does not occur when your organization becomes a Fortune 500 company. Instead, a championship organization is birthed when all the people associated with it run with the vision and do their part in making sure that vision is fulfilled.

Years ago, before Michael Jordan became a superstar, a former coach of his, Coach Dean Smith of the University of North Carolina, told Mike in his freshman year, "Michael, if you can't pass, you can't play." I wonder if the comment inspired Michael to say years later, "Talent wins games, but teamwork and intelligence win championships." Michael Jordan learned the core values of success in basketball by first learning the value of teamwork.

Maximized Relationships . . . Maximized Goals

Imagine waking up every day with the intent of finding ways to express your passion for life and the business. You walk into work with a big smile and your head held high, knowing your attitude of success affects those around you. That kind of attitude benefits the company and ultimately helps you become a better person in the process.

Regardless of whether you are a CEO or small business manager, becoming a better person and positively influencing those around you should be your daily focus. Whether you realize it or not, people are watching you. I am not suggesting that you have spies tracking your every move. What I am saying is that people are examining who you are, what you do, and why you do what you do. While some may be looking on with a critical eye, focus your attention on being a positive example to those who simply want to learn from you. There is something about you that others can benefit from. Why not give them something worthwhile to learn, something worth the effort of cultivating in their own lives?

Over the years, with the help of men like Jeff Joerres, I have learned that a good leader knows how to maximize relationships. Maintaining good relationships is a key to good business. That's where effective communication comes in.

As a team leader, your job should be to clearly communicate your organization's vision and plan for taking it to the next level of success. Jeff believes that poor communication breeds poor relationships. I agree. Poor communication causes problems in business, but Jeff has identified several other factors that can throw a monkey wrench in an organization's plan for success, as well. These factors include:

1. Destructive conflict.
2. Lack of understanding.
3. Distrust.
4. Hidden agendas.
5. Selfishness.

When I look at this list, I see *attitude*. When destructive conflict takes place in a business relationship, it's usually because someone has a poor attitude. Not all conflicts are detrimental to an organization, as Jeff has pointed out. The negative ones, though, will destroy it over time.

Jeff recalls instances where certain individuals within his organization felt as if their projects were not productive. They felt as if their relationship with their clients lacked the proper communication needed to make things happen. In situations like these, a leader makes it a point to step in to identify the problem and come up with a solution. In doing so, he sets himself up as an example of how to resolve conflicts without anyone losing in the process. A leader believes in helping those involved in conflicts move past the uneasiness of conflict resolution, to get on with business.

When conflicts aren't settled in the proper manner, people may leave the table injured, offended, and with a bad attitude. Nothing works when team members and clients aren't making the most of their potential for synergy. In those situations, distrust is born and expressed during the watercooler conversations Jeff mentioned earlier. That's when clients decide to partner with someone else who will give them what they want. That's when hidden agendas take precedence over the order of business.

The point is to do your part to maintain an attitude of leadership for the sake of your family, organization, or company. In business, positive people have no agendas other than to do what's best for the team. I don't know about you, but it's fun coming to work in an energetic environment where everyone is happy and focused on helping those around them become better. I love that! I am all for being around a winning environment where people care enough about the team that they put their selfish desires aside and do whatever it takes to help others.

Synergy Creates Energy

Synergy must be maintained at all costs. The success of your organization depends on it. Do you remember how much fun it was when you were a child and you and your buddies did things together? You played stickball together, swam together, ran together, traded baseball cards, and were probably mischievous together.

Imagine if the "we-do-everything-together" attitude were maintained throughout life and became evident in everything that we did. In the pursuit of individual success, it's easy to forget the value of teamwork. Why is that? Whatever the answer, individual success isn't as meaningful as corporate success.

Henry Ford is quoted as saying, "Coming together is a beginning. Keeping together is progress. Working together is success." That's synergy, and I like it! Mr. Ford deserves a high-five for that nugget of wisdom.

Part of my job as a motivator is to help you, as a leader, rally those around you for the success of your organization. Why? So you can in turn motivate others, so they can motivate someone, until everyone associated with your organization becomes motivated. Being motivated as a leader takes an attitude *adjustment*. Attitude is the motor that keeps your motivation running smoothly; therefore, strive to become the best at what you do, because others depend on your positive guidance. Keep in mind that no one wants to follow a leader with a bad attitude.

ATTITUDE ACTION PLAN

- How can you create an attitude that reflects that you are a part of something bigger than yourself?
- As a leader, you must possess the will to lead people effectively. What are you willing to give of yourself for the sake of the team?
- What sacrifices are you going to embrace for the advantage of your organization/team?
- How strong is your PAT principle (passion, approachability, and thoughtfulness) in your leadership?
- Do you focus on your WIN (What's Important Now)?
- Have you identified all of the problems your team/organization is facing?
- How effective is your conflict resolution strategy?
- Synergy creates energy. What team-building activities are you planning for your team/organization?
- Do you allow your team to create its own team-building exercises?

Brief Biography

Jeffery A. Joerres is chairman, CEO, and president of Manpower, Inc., a world leader in the staffing industry, providing workforce management services and solutions to customers through 3,900 offices in 63 countries. Manpower is a Fortune 500 New York Stock Exchange company, with corporate headquarters in Milwaukee, Wisconsin. Its total sales in 2002 were $11.8 billion.

Joerres was appointed resident and CEO of Manpower, Inc. in 1999, and chairman of the board in 2001. He joined Manpower in 1993 as vice president of marketing, responsible for the company's overall marketing strategy. He then served as Senior vice president of European Operations and Global Account

Management and Development. He is credited with the establishment and growth of Manpower's portfolio of global accounts, which now represents more than $1 billion in annual sales volume. At the same time, Joerres oversaw Manpower's European operations.

Prior to joining Manpower, Joerres was vice resident of sales and marketing for ARI Network Services, a publicly held, high-tech electronic data interchange company. He has also held several management positions within IBM. Joerres holds a Bachelor of Science degree from Marquette University, Milwaukee, Wisconsin.

Do Your Words Match Your Actions?

A. Jeff McLeod, Director of Customer Advocacy and Industry Resource, Kodak Professional Division and Vice President
Eastman Kodak

You've probably noticed that almost all our featured executives address the importance of integrity. It's as simple as this: Employees follow their leader's example. If leaders aren't acting with integrity, employees have no incentive to do so either. When leaders are acting with integrity, employees are more likely to follow suit. What is this trait that everyone agrees is essential to effective leadership? I think you'll like Jeff McLeod's definition.

Be Sure That Your Words Match Your Actions

"I was blessed to grow up in a community of people who role-modeled character, fortitude, and persistence. My father was a laborer in a largely farming-based community. The ethics were simple: Honor God, get up, go to work, get your job done, spend time with your family, and provide a living so your family can do better.

"My father never audibly said, 'You must have integrity.' He simply acted with integrity. Remembering my father's long-lasting influence on me makes me aware of the influence I have on my sons as a parent and on my employees as a manager. I feel I have an obligation to make sure what I say is what I do."

Challenges Are to Be Expected and Accepted

"My father had other sayings that have stuck with me. During challenging times, he often quoted a passage from the Bible, 'If you faint in the day of adversity, your strength is small.' He also used to say, 'That's all in it.' That was his way of saying that challenges are to be expected and accepted. When things went wrong, he didn't get upset; he got busy. To this day, when people ask why I'm so upbeat, I tell them, that my father always said, 'Son, that's all in it.' It was his way of telling me that challenges aren't an obstacle to progress; they are a part of progress, as long as we keep moving."

Value Added

"Several years ago, George Fisher, former chairman and chief executive of Kodak, established six values for the organization to use in its everyday business practices. Those values were:

1. Respect for the dignity of the individual.
2. Uncompromising integrity.
3. Trust.
4. Credibility.
5. Continuous improvement and personal renewal.
6. Recognizing others and celebrating what they have done.

"George was such a visionary. He made a personal commitment to live these values—his words and his actions set the example. Dan Carp, Kodak's chairman and chief executive, reinforces these values. Based on these values, the company has demonstrated that business can grow, adjust, bring in new skills, and restructure operations successfully as long as it is done in good faith.

Leaders Don't Have to Have All the Answers

"Some leaders assume they are expected to know it all. Some are too insecure to admit when the solution to a problem is not readily apparent.

As a result, they fail because they're suffering from 'The Emperor Has No Clothes' syndrome. Employees aren't willing to tell their 'Emperor' (leader) what they think because they assume that he or she does not want to hear it. As the saying goes, 'No one likes a know-it-all.'

"Paraphrasing Dr. Martin Luther King Jr., 'You can walk with kings, but never lose the common touch.' Part of being humble and grounded is asking other people for their input. Asking for help doesn't mean we are weak, it means we are strong enough to know that the best decisions come from seeking feedback.

"I have said on more than one occasion, 'I'm not sure how we're going to handle this. Let's all sleep on it and try it again tomorrow.' The more confident a leader—not cocky, just secure inside—the more open he or she is to accepting other peoples' ideas."

At No Charge

"My firm belief is, 'Whatever we get done, whatever success we have, whatever we achieve, we will do it through people, period.' I believe that people do not care how much we know until they know how much we care.

"I realize that saying may be trite, and it is also true. I do not care how many people there on a team, a leader will only have X number of direct reports. What I've learned over the years is that how you treat your direct reports determines how they treat their direct reports." When we show people he or she cares, they give that extra something in return. I call it the 'At No Charge' Effect. It is the difference between people doing something because they have to and doing something because they want to. "

Leaders Don't Just Say They Care, They Show It

"I always want anyone who I have managed to say, 'He provided me with more than a paycheck. He influenced me in a way that really helped me in my life.' One simple way I try to be a positive influence is to recognize birthdays, wedding anniversaries for employees who are married, and individual anniversaries with the company.

"Many people overlook their work anniversary. I do not mean just their 15th or 20th year, I'm talking about something as simple as their first or third year. This is not company policy. I just think taking the time to write a brief note saying 'Thank you for the job you've done!' is a little thing that can make a big difference.

"I use the company anniversary day to sit down and have a career development discussion with each of my direct reports. We do not talk about problems. This is not a performance appraisal or a disciplinary meeting. We focus solely on how the employee is progressing career-wise. We concentrate on what is working and what's not working, and what the employee can do in terms of professional development to move forward in directions they would like to go."

The Dutch Uncle Discussion

"When I do give negative feedback to an employee, I use the "Dutch Uncle Approach." That's when I sit down with a person and give it to them like it is. I say, 'I'm going to be direct with you, because I care about you.'

"When I tell them what is happening, I do not use the word 'but' because it wipes out what's in front of it. If I say, 'I know you worked overtime on that project, but you did it all wrong' all they will hear is the criticism. Instead if I say, 'I realize you put in a lot of extra time on this, and there are some corrections that need to be made,' they'll hear both the compliment for their effort and the constructive feedback on how to improve their results.

"Instead of saying, 'You've worked here for 10 years and I care about you, but there's no excuse for slacking off,' I would say, 'I care about you, and it seems you haven't been 100 percent lately. What's happening?'"

Leaders Don't Criticize Behavior, They Correct It

"The purpose of these discussions is to hold employees accountable for doing the task correctly, not to make them feel bad for doing it incorrectly. People have sensitivities. My goal is that anyone who interacts with me, directly or indirectly, should be a better person for it. My style is to focus on correcting behavior, not criticizing it."

Wrestle the Issue, Not Each Other

"When struggling with a problem, I enjoy getting my team together and letting them wrestle with it while I listen. If the discussion gets too heated, I balance the views and return our focus to what we can do, not what we cannot do. If the discussion is dying down, I may make a controversial suggestion in order to hear different views and to try to pick out some thread of the solution.

"I believe that a solution always exists. It lies within the problem. A leader may not be able to come up with the answer by himself or herself. Together, the group can. If one has a diversity of people looking at the problem and if they wrestle with it long enough, the answer will come."

To Trust or Not to Trust? That Is the Question

"From 1985 to 1990, I was blessed to live in Malaysia and Singapore. During that time, I traveled almost constantly among 11 countries addressing issues and developing solutions for our business. One thing I learned is that trust has to be earned through honest behavior, and trust transcends any cultural differences which may exist.

"Earning trust is not always easy. While in Malaysia, our company wanted to increase the market share for Kodak film. Film was not being sold in supermarkets in Malaysia. Most consumers purchased their film from photo shops or from one-hour processing businesses. I decided we would start selling film through the grocery store channel, and directed my sales representatives to explore those options.

"During a pilot test, the grocery store was quite successful selling film. The pilot store was also very close in proximity to a major photo shop. What I had not anticipated was that the photo shop manager would become upset with me because he felt Kodak was taking away some of his business."

Leaders Keep the Peace

"The first thing I had to do was tell my sales representative. I told him, 'I encouraged you to do the pilot test for the right reasons. Your reputation is not going to be damaged and you are not going to be hurt in any way.' I wanted to make sure the sales representative felt safe. I wanted him to think, 'When Jeff sets directions, he's not going to leave us hanging. If things get tough, he's going to be right there with us.'

"I have learned that if you have a problem with someone, you have to go to them directly, sit down, and explain your actions so that they understand your motive and purpose, how what you're doing is fair—

while balancing their interests and concerns. That is what I did with the photo shop owner who was upset. My sales representative was motivated to trust me, and Kodak was able to regain the business from the photo shop."

In the End

"Two of the most influential books I have read are the *Bible* and *The Seven Habits of Highly Effective People*. Both books taught me the importance of keeping the end in mind. My priorities in life, respectively, are my relationship with God, my relationship with my wife, my two sons, my relatives and very close friends, and my work obligations.

"I put my sons after my wife because my wife and I are working together to raise our boys. Eventually, my sons will leave (one is already on his own) and then there will be my wife and me again. I never forget, at the end of the day, that my family is my number one priority. That is how I manage to keep things in balance—remembering that it would do me no good to achieve success at work to the detriment of my loved ones.

"I have always valued the exercise of thinking about what people will honestly say about my life after my death. As a result, I try to live my life in a way that if anyone ever said, 'I've always heard that Jeff was a stand-up guy. I always heard you could trust him to act with integrity—no matter what;' my friends, family members, or professional associates would agree and say, 'Yep, that's true, I saw that in his life.'"

Keith's Attitude Check

I first met Jeff in Scottsdale, Arizona. I was the closing speaker at his national sales meeting. I had spoken to Jeff on the phone a couple of times, and was really looking forward to meeting him in person. I wanted to hit a home run with my speech. I always want to do my best, but the respect I'd developed just meeting this remarkable individual over the phone had me extra charged up.

The week before my keynote for Jeff's organization, I was booked for another speaking engagement on the same day but later in the afternoon. That's super fantastic to have the opportunity to give two speeches on the same day. I compare that to a double header in baseball. If you love the game, you just can't get enough of it.

On the morning of my speech, I called the hotel to get directions. My agenda had me speaking to Jeff's group at 8:30 A.M., right after he kicked off the meeting. I usually build in a cushion for Murphy's Law, but that morning there was an accident on the highway, so I arrived at the hotel just 10 minutes before the meeting was supposed to start.

I parked my car and hurried into the lobby to find out where the ballroom was for the group from Kodak. I was shocked when the front desk clerk said in a pleasant voice, "Sorry, sir, we don't have a Kodak meeting here today."

Suffice it to say, I wasn't feeling too positive right at that moment. I said to the hotel clerk, "There must be some mistake." After closely reviewing my notes, I showed her my calendar and asked, "Isn't this the proper address?"

She told me it was and I said, "Then Kodak is supposed to be here." She looked at me and shrugged her shoulders, "I'm sorry, but we don't have a booking for them."

I asked if I could use the phone at the desk so I could call my assistant and find out what was going on. She told me, "Go ahead." Betty answered my office phone and informed me that my talk with Kodak was across town at the other branch of this hotel chain. She told me where I was standing was the hotel for my afternoon presentation.

I quickly looked at my watch. It was now 8:10 A.M. The front desk employee said, "Sir, the hotel you want is located about 40 minutes from here." I grabbed my bag and made a beeline to the door, shouting as I went, "I don't have 40 minutes! Tell me, do I turn right out of the parking lot or left?" She yelled back, "Turn left and go straight until you hit Scottsdale Road. Then turn right, and keep on going."

I'm so glad I had a large rental car that day, because that big boat of a Lincoln Continental was flying like it was a Porsche. I don't think a car that size has ever covered that amount of distance that fast. I pulled into the parking lot at the right hotel, jumped out of the car, threw my keys to the doorman, and bumped into the meeting planner who had come outside to greet me after getting word from the other hotel that I was on my way. She threw the portable microphone around my neck and I walked into the room at 8:29 A.M., just as Jeff started to read my introduction.

I had about 20 seconds to regroup, catch my breath, and thank the Lord. I started my speech explaining to the audience, "I am extremely excited to be there. And when I say excited to be here, I mean that 20 minutes ago I was at the wrong hotel all the way across town looking for you."

Then I paused for a few seconds and got very serious as I shared with them, "As a professional speaker, I never want to be late for a meeting. I never want to disappoint a customer. I also never like to break the speed limit. But today, I had a need for speed."

I explained there'd been a need for me to exceed the posted speed limit because I didn't want to disappoint my friend Jeff McLeod. I went on to say how impressed I had been with Jeff's openness in sharing his faith and core values. I told them I could tell over the phone that this was a man who embodied integrity.

Then, something magical happened. Eight hundred people stood up all at once to give Jeff what seemed like a five-minute standing ovation. I realized that what had touched me about this very special man had also touched them. It occurred to me that Jeff was what this book is all about.

Leaders Strengthen Society

When we're fortunate enough to come into contact with someone who lives his or her values, we can't help but feel blessed. Author John Gardner said, "Some people strengthen society just by being the kind of person they are." Jeff and the other leaders in this book strengthen everyone lucky enough to come into contact with them. Their exemplary behavior strikes a chord within us that says, "That's the kind of person I want to be."

Have you been fortunate to know someone like that in your life? Has there been a manager, coach, parent, or professor you felt blessed to know? Have you worked for or around someone who was a quality person, through and through? Who is that person? How would you describe their long-lasting influence on you?

No Buts About It

Did you already know about the damaging impact of the word *but?* As Jeff pointed out, that word creates conflict because it cancels out what was said before it. Read these sentences and see what happens when we use the word but:

- "I hear what you're saying, but we tried that before and it didn't work."

- "You did a good job on that letter, but you forgot to let them know the board meeting's been changed to 9:30 A.M."
- "I realize I was supposed to call you back yesterday, but we had an emergency."

See how the word *but* usually precedes negative news? People disregard what was said before it, and only pay attention to what follows. If a loan officer tells you, "I know how much you want this loan, but . . . ," you know you're not getting the loan. Using the word *but* set up an "uh oh" effect because listeners know they're about to hear something they'd rather not.

But Creates Conflicts; *And* Creates Cooperation

Now, replace the word *but* with the word *and*. See how the word *and* connects rather than contradicts what is being said? Using the word *and* advances conversations because it acknowledges what is being said instead of arguing with it:

- "I hear what you're saying, and we tried that before and it didn't work. Do you have any suggestions on how we could handle that differently?"
- "You did a good job on that letter, and could you please get back in touch and let them know the board meeting's been changed to 9:30 A.M.?"
- "I'm sorry I didn't call you back yesterday as promised, and I've got that information you requested."

But Argues; *And* Acknowledges

It is particularly important for leaders to role-model the enlightened usage of the word *and*. If you're having a disagreement with someone, you're probably both using the word *but*. Imagine someone says to you, "I know you feel strongly about this, but . . ." Do you hear how contentious that is? That person is essentially telling you your way is wrong, and their way is right or better.

The word *but* sets up a ping-pong debate where people aren't really listening—they're just trying to prove their point of view. The word *but* escalates emotions because it discounts what the other person is saying. As a result, that person will probably repeat what she just said, louder and more vehemently, in an effort to get through.

An associate was shocked to realize she frequently used the word *but* as a space filler. Whenever she paused between phrases, took a breath, or searched for what she wanted to say, the word *but* popped automatically out of her mouth. "I know I said this would only take 15 minutes, but . . ." "That's an interesting suggestion, but . . ." "I'd like to help you with that, but . . ." "I'm sorry that happened, but . . ." She said, "No wonder people think I don't listen. I DO listen, but (OOPS!), you'd never know it from the way I talk."

It's What You Say *and* How You Say It

Bring up the issue of the word *but* at your next staff meeting. Ask employees to give examples of how they might unwittingly be using this word with customers and coworkers. Ask everyone to heighten their awareness of their usage of the word *but*. Determine how you can support each other in your determination to use the word *and* instead.

Perhaps you and your staff can put visual reminders on your phones, by your computers, and on your employee bulletin board so everyone on your team starts using *and* instead of *but*.

The transformation will be amazing. You and your employees will find you can express differences of opinion and move forward to a resolution instead of debating who's right and wrong. Customers and coworkers will feel heard instead of feeling like their point of view is being discounted. Perhaps most importantly, you will be communicating in a way that leads to connection instead of conflict.

What If a Leader's Words/Actions Don't Match?

I was once asked to work with an organization that was struggling with poor morale and lack of productivity. The working environment was extremely negative. Many employees had maxed out their sick days by the middle of the year. Even when visiting this organization, I could feel the weight of doom and gloom the employees seemed to be carrying on their shoulders. It was hard to imagine how I could possibly fix what was broken in this organization in a two-hour speech.

Before the seminar, I had an opportunity to sit down and speak with the president of the company. Within five minutes, it was clear to me what was wrong with the organization. The president's stated values did not match his actions. He wanted his staff to have trust and respect for each other and to be committed to their jobs, but he wasn't equally willing to return those behaviors to them. His previous good nature had disappeared because of the tough economy, and his new attitude was, "They should all feel lucky just to have a job." I could tell he was hoping that my words would be a miracle cure that erased the damage of his long-term mistreatment.

There Is No Miracle Cure

The organization I walked into and the organization I left following my presentation didn't feel like the same place. But, I knew my seminar was only a band-aid for the true source of the problem, and as soon as the next employee was mistreated, the old environment and discontent would settle back into place.

Less than a year later, I received a letter from the new president of that company. She had been in the audience the day I spoke to their organization. She reported that the former president had been fired by the board of directors because turnover had been at an all-time high and productivity had been at an all-time low.

As vice president of her own department, she told me she had used my speech as a springboard to take positive action within her team. Despite the low numbers coming from the rest of the company, her department had managed to surpass the previous year's quota while keeping almost all the same staff. It was clear to me that her proactive leadership, even in the midst of a discouraging situation, had inspired her team members to give their all even when the people around them weren't.

Leaders Can't Always Control Circumstances; They Can Control Their Response

This vice president's determination to be a quality leader, even though her CEO was doing just the opposite, is an example of how we can choose to use our circumstances as an incentive instead of an excuse.

Many people feel Victor Frankl's philosophy, expressed in his classic book *Man's Search for Meaning*, is one of the wisest philosophies ever uttered. Frankl said, "Our greatest freedom is the freedom to choose our attitude." Frankl learned this during his horrific imprisonment during the Holocaust. Frankl observed that even in the midst of their suffering, many of the people in the concentration camps chose to share what little they had and support each other. Frankl, despite witnessing and being a victim of man's inhumanity to man, chose not to become a bitter person. He chose to get on with his life and dedicate himself to making a positive difference for his fellow human beings.

Is Your Attitude an Asset or an Albatross?

Are you in a less-than-perfect work environment? Are you allowing it to depress and disillusion you? Are you allowing it to sap your determination to be a quality person? Do you think, "Why should I care? The people around me don't?"

The message of this book is that IT DOES MATTER what type of person you are. It matters whether you choose to act with integrity. It matters whether you choose to continue to an upstanding individual. Everyone is waiting for someone else to take the lead and set a good example. The people around you need someone to step forward and take the high road. They're hoping someone will transcend the disillusioning circumstances and choose to be a quality person, regardless. Be that person.

ATTITUDE ACTION PLAN

- What are a couple of sayings your parents told you? How have they shaped your life?

- Have you ever worked for a leader who was suffering from "The Emperor Has No Clothes" syndrome? What was that like?

- If you have to discipline an employee, how do you handle the discussion so he or she is receptive to what you're saying, instead of resisting what you're saying?

- Have you traveled to other countries? What do you think is important when working with different cultures?

- Were you aware of the destructive impact of the word *but?* How have you, or how are you going to, work to replace that damaging word in your communication?

- As a leader, how are you going to help your employees start using the word *and?*

- Who is a truly great leader you've had the privilege to work for? How has that person inspired you to be a quality person, regardless of circumstances?
- Do you have a philosophy or motto that keeps you going in tough times? What is it?

Brief Biography

Aaron Jeff McLeod began his professional career with Eastman Kodak Company in 1973 as a technical sales representative.

In 1983, Jeff worked as a marketing planning specialist before becoming manager of Customer and Technical Sales Representative training.

Jeff accepted his first international assignment in 1985 and moved to Kuala Lumpur, Malaysia, as marketing manager for Kodak Malaysia. In 1988, Jeff expanded his international marketing and general management experiences working as manager of marketing operations for the Professional Photography Division for the Asia-Pacific Region based in Singapore.

Upon being repatriated to the United States in 1990, Jeff became director, U.S. Marketing Operations, Professional Photography Division. In 1992, he became national sales manager and vice president, Professional Imaging. In 1996, Jeff was appointed general manager and vice president, Kodak Professional Division, United States and Canada. He was elected a corporate vice president in July 1998.

Jeff is currently director of Customer Advocacy and Industry Resource, Kodak Professional Division.

Born in Dothan, Alabama, Jeff received his bachelor of arts degree in business administration from Morehouse College. He is actively involved in his local church and is the founder of Achievers in Life—a church-based organization dedicated to helping boys, ages 4 to 15, develop physically, mentally, spiritually, and socially in order to reach their fullest potentials. He also serves on the board of directors for the Greater Rochester YMCA and the Rochester Family Mission.

Stay in There and Pitch!

Bob Moawad, Founder and Chairman
Edge Learning, Inc.

Bob is considered one of the pioneers of personal development training. His *Increasing Human Effectiveness* course was one of the first self-improvement programs I took. It helped to change my attitude and, ultimately, helped to change my life. This course has been taught to more than three million people; Bob is a walking, talking role model of the principles he teaches.

Tenacity Is as Important as Talent

"One of my earliest memories is my father telling me to 'Stay in there and pitch.' I had gotten frustrated at something, I can't even remember what it was at this point, and had given up in disgust. He wasn't about to let me quit. He told me to get back to work and try again. I didn't know it then, but that phrase 'Stay in there and pitch' would almost become my life's motto.

"Over the years, I've learned that tenacity is as important, if sometimes not more important, than talent. I've seen plenty of talented people who gave up when the going got tough. As a result, they never amounted to much.

"On the other hand, I've seen people who have persevered and triumphed despite incredible adversity. It's said there's not a lot of traffic on the extra mile, and I've seen that proven again and again. People who are willing to go the extra mile often prevail over more capable individuals."

Don't Tighten Up, Lighten Up

"I think there are too many humor-impaired people walking around the office who are suffering from terminal professionalism. I told Keith jokingly that his first book *Attitude Is Everything* should have been called *The Right Attitude Is Everything*, because many people's attitude is downright lousy.

"Leaders set the mood for the organization so it's imperative for them to maintain a sense of joviality. We need to be able to laugh with others and at ourselves. We can take situations seriously without taking ourselves too seriously.

"I've had an opportunity to practice that the last couple of years as I've been dealing with a very serious health challenge. Believe me, it would have been easy to get depressed or discouraged, but I've found that keeping a sense of humor is the saving grace.

"A while back, I had just had a stem cell transplant when I found this quote by Mother Theresa, 'I know God will never give me more than I can handle. I just wish he wouldn't trust me so much!' I laughed out loud when I saw that, and it helped me keep things in perspective."

Are You Asking or Ordering?

"I'll forever be grateful to Darryl Mudra, from Adams State University, who did his doctoral dissertation on the Expectations of a Division One College Football Program.

"Mudra had what was a radical notion at the time: He proposed that leadership should be player-oriented rather than system-oriented. Instead of 'going by the book,' Mudra suggested that coaches build their game strategy utilizing the available talents of each team member—regardless of the position he played.

"So, if you had a quarterback who couldn't remember plays and a left tackle who was a bright guy, you'd go against tradition and have the left tackle call the plays because he'd be better at it. Not only did this approach work, it worked splendidly.

"No one in the mid-1960s was talking about participative management or employee empowerment, so his work represented a breakthrough. His revolutionary approach came at just the right time, because I needed all the help I could get.

"I had been hired to coach, at the ripe old age of 23, a high school basketball team that was a perennial doormat. This was particularly challenging for me because I'd been an All-State player and captain of a university team that had had a long winning tradition.

"I tried everything I knew to motivate these kids, to no avail. It didn't help that I was using all the autocratic coaching methods I'd grown up with. I was basically giving orders and expecting them to hop to. Didn't happen."

Do It or Else

"Remember, this was the 1960s and teenagers were feeling rather rebellious. I'd tell my team members, 'Do this or else' and they'd say, 'Tell me more about else.' I'd say, 'Either, or' and they'd say, 'I'm leaning toward or.' As you can imagine, I felt like showing them the door.

"After two frustrating years and an embarrassingly bad record, I turned to my former coach and mentor, Dr. Jim Nylander, and asked, 'Do you have any ideas on how I can motivate these young men, because what I'm doing is not working.'

"I had loved playing baseball for Dr. Nylander. He was a wonderful man, a gentle spirit yet very intellectual and with a great sense of humor. He was the one who introduced me to Darryl Mudra's work and suggested I switch to a democratic rather than autocratic style. I started asking instead of ordering. I set up a 360-degree rating program where we rated each other (that included me). The players selected their own squad based on ratings they had given each other. They started designing the offense and defense and making up their own plays.

"In the beginning, it was awkward. They expected me to be the boss, to have all the answers. After a few weeks though, their discomfort was replaced by excitement. I remember one day a player rushed into practice with a play he'd drawn up on a Wheaties cereal box top. That was the day I knew this 'ownership' approach was working.

"What followed was a truly unique three years in which our team went from the bottom of the rankings to three consecutive league championships and a state title. I was asked to coach at another school where I implemented the same system, and that team also established a winning record that stood for more than 25 years.

"At that high school, I was asked to teach a psychology course. I developed a curriculum called Mental Management Skills, and that course became the precursor to the programs I've offered around the world for the last three decades."

Who's Managing Your Mind?

"One of the basic tenets of my program is that if we're given new skills through training, and those new skills are in conflict with our current attitudes and habits, that information will fall on deaf ears. Why? We act in alignment with what we believe to be true about ourselves. To act differently from how we perceive ourselves is in direct contradiction to our subconscious beliefs, and will power alone (the desire to change) is not as powerful as attitudinal belief.

"This is particularly important for leaders to understand because they are often the decision maker on whether to invest money in training programs. Realize that unless employees are educated on how to change their attitudes and habits so they're congruent with the new skills and behaviors, the training won't take. People may find the information interesting, and they may even attempt to learn it or apply it. But if it doesn't mesh with how they see themselves, they'll soon abandon it and go back to being their 'true' self.

"For people to really assimilate material, for them to have a significant learning moment (SLM), that material must fit in with how their mind perceives who and how they are, and who and how they want to be."

Listen Up and Listen Down

"Democratic leadership means asking instead of telling, involving rather than imposing, and consulting rather than directing. One of the best ways to listen down the chain of command is to ask employees for their opinions, and then put a sock in it and listen.

"Listening can be challenging because we often have 10 different things competing for our attention. That's why I think it's important, when someone comes to talk to us, that we put our work aside and focus completely on them. If someone walks in our office and asks if we have a minute, and we say, 'Sure, go ahead' while continuing to shuffle through paperwork, they'll feel unwelcome. They'll think, 'Well, your door may be open, but your mind is closed.'

"You've probably seen the statistics that say that only 7 percent of our message is conveyed by words, 55 percent is conveyed by body language, and 38 percent is conveyed by extra-verbal cues (voice inflection, tone, etc.). One of the best ways we can show people they are genuinely important to us is to give them our undivided attention. That means momentarily setting aside other priorities and concentrating solely on them so our voice doesn't register impatience or annoyance. Only when we're present instead of preoccupied, can we listen to people in a way that makes them KNOW we care."

Footprints or Butt Prints?

"Sometimes people look at my travel and speaking schedule and wonder if I ever burn out. I tell them, 'I've never had that feeling. If I did, I'd just remind myself why I do what I do.' I think most leaders are driven by a desire to make a difference for as many people as possible. If our goal is to add value, then we welcome and appreciate every opportunity to do so.

"A friend of mine, Frosty Westering, is the football coach at Pacific Lutheran University. He had a wonderful slogan, 'The big time is where you are.' I believe that it's our job to make the best of every situation. I live my life by the quote, 'You don't need to accept life the way it comes to you. Design it so it comes to you the way you'd like to get it.'

"If life doesn't come to us the way we like it, it is our 100 percent responsibility to be proactive instead of reactive. We can sit around and moan and groan about how unfair it is and leave butt prints, or we can get up and do something about it and leave footprints. It's our choice."

Keith's Attitude Check

Bob is so right about the power of tenacity. My boss used to tell me, "At the moment of truth, there are either reasons or results." Staying in there and pitching is the key to getting results instead of reasons.

Calvin Coolidge actually expressed this a little more eloquently when he said, "Nothing in the world can take the place of persistence.

Talent will not; nothing is more common than unsuccessful men of talent. Genius will not; the world is full of educated derelicts. The slogan 'Press on' has solved and always will solve the problems of the human race."

Are You Giving Reasons or Getting Results?

Think back to a time in your life you really wanted something, and you had to work hard for it. Did you run into obstacles, setbacks, and disappointments, but you refused to give up? Remember how rewarding that was?

Maybe you went back to college and got your degree while working a full-time job. There were probably times you were so tired you could hardly keep your eyes open to study, but you studied anyway. There were probably professors you didn't like and you were tempted to drop that class, but you attended anyway. There were probably days you couldn't find a parking space and you were tempted to drive back home, but you kept searching until you found one anyway. That's tenacity.

How, as a leader, are you teaching the power of tenacity to your people? Are you holding them accountable for results instead of accepting reasons? A high school teacher used to tell me, "There are two types of people in this world: those who have learned how to work through frustration, and those who wish they had." Which are you? Which are your employees?

Are You an Autocratic or Democratic Leader?

Have you heard of Theory Y and Theory X in regards to leadership styles? The Theory X style of leadership is based on the assumption that people are basically lazy and have to be coerced or threatened by autocratic leaders before they work. Theory Y style of leadership is based on the assumption that people are creative and responsible and will work hard for democratic leaders who encourage them and provide opportunities to participate in organizational decisions.

Would you describe yourself as more of a Theory X (autocratic) or Theory Y (democratic) leader. Or, are you a Theory S (situational) leader?

I agree with Bob that democratically involving employees in decision making helps them own the process and have more of a stake in the outcome. A friend who manages his own business told me he prefers to match his leadership style to the specific person he's dealing with.

Suit Your Style to the Situation

My friend said, "I'm not going to be a participative manager with my new hires. It would be counterproductive to ask for their ideas on how to do things when they just started working here! I think new employees want clear directions. They want to be told exactly what to do so they're not in the dark. It makes them feel secure and well led.

"I do just the opposite with my long-time employees. I have some people who have worked here for 10 years. I'm not going to insult their intelligence and expertise by ordering them around. I frequently ask for their input because they've got frontline, first-hand experience. I encourage their suggestions because they often offer insightful recommendations on how we can streamline procedures and solve problems."

Do you find you get better results when you give precise instructions to new employees and grant more autonomy to long-time workers? I once saw an anecdote about Dave Bristol, the former San Francisco Giants manager who combined the best of both styles. His baseball team had lost their last few games. Instead of berating them and asking what they thought was wrong, he simply announced, "There will be two buses leaving the hotel for the ballpark tomorrow. The 2 P.M. bus will be for those of you who need a little extra work. The empty bus will be leaving at 5 P.M." Well said.

Are We Having Fun Yet?

Bob's statement about keeping our sense of humor—no matter what—was right on. Erma Bombeck essentially said the same thing when she observed, "If we can laugh at it, we can live with it."

How do you incorporate humor in your daily life? Studies repeatedly show that laughing is a great stress-reliever. I once read that 15 minutes a day of heavy deep gut laughter is equivalent to 5 minutes of moderate jogging. Have some fun with yourself tomorrow, get up 15 minutes early, laugh like crazy and get back in bed. What do you do as a leader to encourage your employees to lighten up instead of tighten up?

A friend of mine, Sam Horn, is the author of *Tongue Fu!* (martial arts for the mind and mouth), and her Fun Fu! tips offer ways for us to handle hassles with humor instead of harsh words. Sam had an opportunity to share her Fun Fu! ideas with a group of Internal Revenue Service auditors.

Sam's first suggestion was to take down the punitive signs plastered all over the bulletin board in their lobby. You've probably heard about the research that reveals the long-lasting impact of first impressions, and she felt that the already-nervous people coming through the door were even further intimidated by the "Warning! $25,000 Fine" signs accosting them as soon as they walked in.

By law, these signs had to be posted, but the law didn't say how big the signs had to be. So the IRS employees reduced the signs to a fraction of their former size and replaced them with every cartoon strip, quip, and joke they could find poking fun at the IRS. Their favorites were, "Sorry, we're IN!" and "The secret is to stop thinking of it as YOUR money!"

Did this humor/inspirational wall have everyone holding their sides in laughter? Of course not. It helped though. It helped establish that IRS auditors are human, too, and they deserve to be treated with respect. It helped ease the tension and brought a smile to people's faces. It set a precedent for camaraderie rather than conflict.

When I was at IBM, I started putting up positive affirmations on my office door ever Monday, I noticed after a month that people started walking a different way just to pass by my office door to read my motivational quotes. Over time, other employees started bringing in their favorite motivational messages and we had to move them to the cafeteria wall. Imagine walking into the cafeteria on Monday morning to get a cup of coffee and walking by one wall full of inspirational messages and finding just the words of encouragement that you needed to help you make it through the day.

Could you do something similar in your organization? Why not put up a humor/inspirational wall in your lobby so employees and customers can share a chuckle instead of a curse?

Are You Listening or Waiting for Your Turn to Talk?

A friend of mind was at her dinner table recently talking with her two teenaged sons about their weekend plans. She sensed that her older son was distracted so she asked, "Tom, are you listening to me?" "Sure Mom," he answered. "You have my undivided attention."

Out of the mouths of teens. Bob was so right about the importance of temporarily setting other priorities aside so we can give employees our undivided (versus undevoted) attention when they want or need to talk to us.

I remember a college professor who shared a fascinating study about what people really want from their leaders. This study was unique in that it simply asked employees to finish two sentences. The first sentence was, "I like my manager. He/she _____ (fill in the blank). The second sentence was, "I don't like my manager. He/she _____ (fill in the blank).

The most frequently given answer to the first question was, "I like my manager. He/she LISTENS to me." The most frequently given answer to the second question was (you guessed it) "I don't like my manager. He/she DOESN'T LISTEN to me."

Would your employees say you're a good listener? Why not ask them? If they say yes, find out what you do that makes them feel that way so you can continue doing it. If they say no, find out what you're doing wrong so you can change it.

Are You Making Excuses or Taking Action?

Bob is a humble man so he didn't reveal what a trial these last few years have been for him. In January 2000, Bob's doctor looked him in the eye, told him he had terminal cancer, and predicted that he had, maybe, two and a half years to live. His doctor reported he'd had 57 patients over the past seven years with the same type of cancer that Bob had.

Bob being Bob asked, "Doc, how many of those patients are still alive?" The doctor answered, "One out of 57." Bob replied, "Make that two out of 58."

Why I'm sharing this is because of what Bob did after receiving this devastating news. He took action. Bob needed a stem cell transplant, and he needed one soon. What he discovered though, is that the donor list for stem cells is very limited. In fact, his medical team searched for a year and a half for a match. Once they found a candidate, there was still only a 20 percent chance this individual would have the necessary 10 antigens. Fortunately, the donor, a 51-year-old German male, did. They flew over the stem cells and Bob got his transplant.

Leaders Don't Wait, They Initiate

Since then, Bob has dedicated himself to bringing the need for stem cell donors to light. That's what leaders do. When they encounter a problem, they don't whine or complain about it; they go to work correcting it. They don't wait around for someone else to fix it; they initiate action to fix it themselves.

In every presentation, Bob dedicates five minutes to educating participants about how easy it is to register. It's as simple as going to your local blood bank and volunteering to be a bone marrow donor. Chances of being called are slim; however, if needed, your stem cells can be harvested through a transfusion-like process and flown across the country to, as Bob says, "save the life of a 4-year-old or a 40-year-old."

Bob explains it's not like being an organ donor where you need to die and give up parts of your body. The procedure is nonintrusive and it's life-saving. Tens of thousands of people die annually because they cannot find a matching donor. Bob's goal is to motivate a million more people to register for this life-giving service.

Take the Lead

I saw a sign once that said, "If you see a problem, it's yours. If you think somebody should do something about it, remember, you're as much a somebody as anybody."

Is there a problem in your community? Could you initiate action to correct it? Could you, like Bob, launch a campaign to raise awareness for a good cause? That's what leaders do—they take the lead in changing the world for the better.

ATTITUDE ACTION PLAN

- Are you someone who has learned to work through frustration? Describe a time you tenaciously worked to achieve something as a leader.

- On a scale of 1 to 10 (1 being nonexistent and 10 being you're a Robin Williams clone) how would you rate your sense of humor? Describe a time humor was your saving grace.

- What do you do to help your employees lighten up instead of tighten up?

- What style of leadership do you use primarily?

- Which style are you more comfortable with?

- Who is someone who really listens to you?

- How does that person make you feel?

- What do they do that makes you feel they're giving you their undivided attention?

- In what way are you "taking the lead" to solve a problem or campaign for a worthy cause?

Brief Biography

Bob Moawad is founder and chairman of Edge Learning Institute. From the frontlines of American education to the boardrooms of some our nation's most prestigious Fortune 500 companies, Bob Moawad has earned a well-deserved reputation as a tireless teacher, coach, leader, speaker, author, innovator, benefactor, visionary, consultant, "edutainer," and friend.

Bob received his bachelor's degree in education from Central Washington University in 1964. He received his master's in education from Central Washington University in 1967.

Bob began his career as a high school educator and coach utilizing a unique democratic coaching process to set school records at three high schools, including coaching a state championship basketball team. As a high school psychology teacher, he developed a six-week unit on mental management skills, and at the request of parents whose students had not taken his class, began offering weekend seminars. Since then, he has developed a thriving organization—Edge Learning Institute—with headquarters in Tacoma, Washington. Edge is a professional development firm dedicated to assisting organizations to maximize their human assets, increase productivity, manage change without distress, and achieve higher levels of customer satisfaction. Edge processes have earned international recognition and acceptance for pioneering practical new insights into individual and team effectiveness. Bob travels throughout the world fulfilling teaching and speaking engagements ranging from a few dozen corporate executives to keynote addresses before thousands of people.

Bob and his wife, Andrea, are active in community councils and boards throughout the Tacoma/Pierce County, Washington area. In 1988, Bob received the Small Business Person of the Year Award, and in 2002 received the Pierce County Rotary Club Community Service Award. He served as president of the National Association for Self-Esteem from 1994 through 1996. He is also in the Central Washington University Athletic Hall of Fame and received the prestigious Distinguished Alumnus Award.

Bob continues to play tenor saxophone and sing in two 1950s/1960s rock-and-roll groups. He resides in Lakewood, Washington with his wife, Andrea, and has two grown sons.

Lagniappe: "A Little Something Extra"

My uncle, Dr. Bill Harrell, recently retired from Texas Southern University after 50 years teaching pharmaceutical science. He told me about a word he used in his lectures to keep students focused. They paid close attention when they heard the word, because what followed would often be key information for the next exam.

The word he used was *lagniappe*. He explained that lagniappe is a Cajun word that means a little something extra, a little something more.

This final chapter is not followed by an exam, but I wanted to give you a little something extra, a little something more—a lagniappe. This chapter gives you additional wisdom and leadership insights from other leaders. If you find yourself with limited time to read or review a previous chapter, you can turn here to pick up a little something extra, a little something more, and continue to lead with the attitude of leadership.

Thick-Skinned, but Tender-Hearted

Rolfe Carawan, President and CEO
LifeMatters International

I first met Rolfe in Cabo San Lucas, Mexico. We were both keynote speakers for the Cadillac Conference of top sales managers. Rolfe is one of the top business speakers in the country, and when I asked for his insight on leadership, here's what he said:

"It is important for leaders to remember that all team members are equally important, but often they are not equally valued. The coach or leader of every team is responsible for knowing the strengths and weaknesses of each team member and then putting each person in a position to succeed."

No Bad Teams, Just Bad Leaders

"I've seen it over and over again in business; leaders complain that their manager and employees don't 'get it.' Then I find that their people are just bored and disgusted. They don't feel challenged or appreciated. They have the sense that what they do doesn't matter. How does a leader turn a team around? He gets to know its members as individuals. If it's a large corporation in which it is impossible to know everyone, then it is the leader's job to get to know the managers who do know the people. It's the leader's job to understand what motivates, excites, and unites people to achieve a common goal. It is the leader's job to convey the message and the vision that drives the organization or the team."

Effective Leaders Need Humility

"Leadership is the ability to inspire others to accomplish mutually desirable goals and to execute in any situation. It is entirely possible, even fairly common, for individuals who are not in leadership positions to be leaders. Your ability to attract followers is based on who you are, not on your title or position.

"Humility—the ability to put others first while living under the discipline of proven principles—is what was sorely lacking in the lives of the leaders at Enron and Arthur Andersen and in others who lacked it. In the business world today, there are many competent people who can strategize and set goals, but they are sometimes so consumed with self-interest that they cannot lead others to execute those goals. They are leaders in name only, because they lack followers. Lacking compassion and empathy, the success they seek is their own. Instead of understanding the human drive to succeed and supporting it, they attempt to lead, unfortunately, by capitalizing on human frailties and weaknesses. They become thin-skinned and callous-hearted.

"Humility just may be the most overlooked attitude of leadership. When leaders yield to the temptation of arrogance and pride they fail to garner the loyalty necessary to execute during difficult times, yet true leaders, by putting others first, are able to perform the impossible."

Keith's Attitude Check

There are no bad teams, just bad leaders. I've seen it in sports and in business. You read about a team firing a coach, because the team couldn't win, and they bring in a new coach, with the same players, same uniform, same schedule, and soon they are playing for the championship.

At IBM, when I was there, we had a manager who didn't seem to care, and the team had low morale. None of us thought we could make our sales quota. The following month, a brand-new manager came in with a brand-new attitude that became contagious, and he led us to record sales.

Let Go of Your Ego

Humility is the key for an attitude of leadership. I was told a long time ago that ego stands for Edging God Out. If you actually want to serve and have impact, you can do it only with a humble attitude. Whether you are in the mailroom or in the boardroom, everybody plays a critical role in helping a team or company achieve success.

One year I spoke at the Eclipsys Company's Annual Sales and Support Meeting in Atlanta, Georgia. When Chairman Jim Hall handed me his business card, I noticed he didn't have his title on his business card. I asked: "Why don't you have your title on your business card?"

His response was, "At this company, we are one team. Titles don't mean anything, everyone in this company is the same, everyone plays an important role in helping us provide the very best products and services to our customers. We are one team making a big difference."

ATTITUDE ACTION PLAN

- How does your team performance reflect your leadership? Who is coaching you to be a better leader?

- As the leader of your team, what can you do today to inspire, connect, and motivate each team member?

- Is your ego edging out your ability to connect to your organization/team?

Take the Blame—Give the Credit

George E. Cates, Retired CEO and Chairman
Mid-America Apartment Communities

When I spoke at the Mid-America Apartment Communities annual meeting, even though I hadn't personally met George Cates, I felt like I knew him personally. I heard so many wonderful things about him. Many of his former employees said they wish I had a chance to meet him. "He's such a wonderful human being, such a great leader," they said.

When you get several people coming up to you within a few minutes telling you the same thing, you know the person they are talking about has to be special.

"If you pinned me down and made me identify the most important role of a business leader, I'd say it is to define and encourage a culture in which people are trusted, respected, and given the chance to fail and learn from their mistakes.

"I acquired this attitude from a mentor. He called me into his office one day and said, 'Here's the deal; you are going to report to me, and I'm going to give you all the rope you want. You are going to make mistakes, but don't worry about them. I'll cover for you. We'll share the blame, but I'll give you the credit for anything you do well. I just want you to learn from your mistakes and not repeat them. Any time you need help, you can come to me. If you don't come to me, I'm going to assume you don't need help.'"

No Fear, Step Up

"Even though we are now going through a tough time in our market because of the low interest rates that are leading more people to move out of apartments and buy their own homes, there is no fear in our company. People may put pressure on themselves to make something happen in an overwhelmingly negative market, but there is no concern that some corporate bear up in the executive offices is going to chew them up if they make a mistake.

"During tough times, it's the leader's responsibility to step up and tell the people in the organization that there is no reason to panic or to be fearful. It's important that people understand that we've been here before. It's important for them to hear that loud and clear. 'It's not going to be a very enjoyable time, and I don't expect you to enjoy it, but don't lose sleep over it. Business is cyclical. We've been through this before. Stay calm and do your jobs.' That is the message you want to send through the company."

Keith's Attitude Check

George Cates' attitude of leadership is based on mutual respect, trust, and a willingness to "take the blame and give the credit."

He's a humble man who finds it difficult to talk about himself. He told me he was an engineer, not a romantic or a visionary or a poet. He is not a big reader of business manuals or motivational books. He doesn't even read the *Wall Street Journal* regularly, yet within a few minutes of conversation with him, I clearly understood that when it comes to leadership, George Cates gets it.

Goethe said, "Treat people as if they were what they ought to be, and you help them to become what they are capable of being." True leaders create an entire company of leaders whose talents and energy are multiplied many times. They let people know they want them to succeed and that they will support them, rather than pouncing on them when they make mistakes. Fear may work in a traditional command-and-control environment, but not many successful businesses operate that way anymore.

ATTITUDE ACTION PLAN

- Are you willing to take the blame, but give the credit?
- Are you willing to let your people make mistakes and learn from them?
- What fears could inhibit you from encouraging risk taking?
- If you quelled those fears, how much more could you and your team accomplish?

The Power of the Parable

Judge Nelson A. Diaz
City Solicitor, Philadelphia

Although good leaders are active leaders, not all are activists; that is, they don't necessarily spend their time trying to change systems outside of their immediate control. Judge Nelson A. Diaz, though, a Latino who grew up in Harlem, had a calling to make a difference in the world, and he has earned many honors and awards for the work he has accomplished.

"I studied every speech Martin Luther King ever made, whether it was in a church in Harlem or on the steps of the Lincoln Memorial. He was one of our nation's greatest communicators, and I wanted to understand why he was able to galvanize people with his message. One of the reasons he was so mesmerizing as a speaker was because he preached such universal truths. He wanted to see unity among people. He wanted people to leave the pews and take their religion into the world and use it in their everyday interactions, to achieve peace. He never read his speech; he spoke from conviction and used parables, so listeners could relate to his material.

"As leaders, I think the use of metaphors helps us get our message across. If we're talking about teamwork, we can use the body as an example. The body has many parts, and each has its function. We can't all be the head, or the hands, or the feet. We can't all get the glory and have the glamorous jobs. Some of us have to be the digestive system. It's important to understand that the digestive system allows the body to live and is just as important as every other part. Yes, the illustration is simplistic, but the example resonates with inescapable truth. It's a way to illustrate that the frontline worker is as important as the accountant, who is as important as the CEO. Any one of them can bring down the team; every one of them can build up the team."

The Power of Someone Believing in You

"I grew up in Harlem in difficult circumstances. I never knew my father, until I was 10. We lived in public housing, and my mother, who worked all day, let me out of the house from sunup to sundown. Fortunately, fate in the form of Leroy Otis intervened when I was 10. Leroy had played in the Negro League. He saw me play baseball one day and asked me to join his team. I played for him until I was 17, and with his help and the guidance of David Wilkerson, I went from being a troublemaker and a struggling D student to graduating at the top of my class with a B+ average.

"I attended college at St. John's in Queens, partly because I wanted to go to a campus that had grass. All I had known in Harlem was concrete and asphalt. I worked at Gimbel's Department Store during the week and caddied on the weekends to pay for school. The chairman of the St. John's University accounting department suggested I go to law school and Peter Liacouras recruited me to Temple University. The idea hadn't even occurred to me, because there were absolutely no Puerto Ricans in law school, and only 35 of the 35,000 students at Temple were Hispanic.

"Thanks to that man's initiative and belief in me, I did enroll at Temple. Once there, I discovered that only four blacks had graduated from the school in the previous eight years, even though the university was in our neighborhood, and the majority of residents were black or Hispanic. I felt a need, like Martin Luther King Jr., to instigate change, and, thus, began my life of peaceful advocacy. I became the first Puerto Rican to pass the bar in Pennsylvania, and I started organizing, picketing, and filing lawsuits to correct the inequities I saw everywhere around me.

"I'm grateful to Charles Bowser, who took me aside and told me I needed to be 'downtown' if I wanted to be effective. He was the one who opened my eyes to the fact that we are more likely to induce change by working within the establishment, instead of fighting against the establishment. That's one of the reasons this former troublemaker from Harlem—me—became the first Latino judge in the state of Pennsylvania. As one of the only individuals of Hispanic origin in a high government position, I felt people were looking to me for leadership. I felt I had a responsibility to fight for the rights of underrepresented minorities."

Some Challenges Never Go Away

"The challenge of being a minority never goes away. I continue to face stereotypes and prejudice. I'm never Latino enough, black enough, or good enough. Some people assume I've achieved my positions because of Affirmative Action. Some people perceive me as a token. I keep running into walls, and, yes, it tests my faith. That's when I think about Martin Luther King Jr., Leroy Otis, Charlie, and the others who intervened on my behalf, and I rededicate myself. I realize I can't go back; I have to move forward. Everything I've done is about uplifting the community. Instead of worrying about what people think about me, I get to work proving my competence, so people judge me on my results, not my race.

"I had a calling. I felt I had to supply the leadership that was lacking, until others were prepared to fill that gap and take the lead. At one time, I was the only Latino lawyer in the state; now there are thousands. That's the power of leadership, the ability to create opportunities where none existed.

"One thing I'm grateful for is my children now seem to understand my lifelong fight for justice, even though it meant I missed many of their activities. The National Bar Association arranged to have my portrait painted to honor my work. The portrait-hanging ceremony was televised, and a reporter asked my son, 'What do you think of your dad?' My son said, on camera, that he was proud of me for developing the community. That was the nicest thing he's ever said about me, and it meant the world to me."

Keith's Attitude Check

My family instilled in me the belief that a positive attitude is important. Having the right mind-set makes a difference, and if you take responsibility for improving yourself, you can have what you want and be who you want.

Life Knocks You Down, It Doesn't Knock You Out

My life mission involves instilling that belief in others, so they, too, can overcome whatever obstacles they face and become who they want and achieve what they want.

One of the interesting things about Judge Diaz is that he refused to become a victim of his difficult childhood circumstances. I've noticed an interesting trend as I've traveled the country and interviewed dozens of successful leaders. The ones who grew up in difficult circumstances chose to use their challenging childhood as an incentive, rather than as an excuse. Their situations became a springboard from which they dived into life with enthusiasm and made a difference to themselves and to others. When life knocked them down, it didn't knock them out.

Victor versus Victim, It's a Choice

Surely, we all know people who say the reason they haven't accomplished what they've wanted is because they grew up in a dysfunctional family. They say they came from a broken home, or their parents went through a devastating divorce, or their mom or dad was an alcoholic. These people blame their problematic upbringing for disallowing them to achieve their potential. That's like saying that something you ate 10 years ago is giving you a stomachache today. Each day is a new opportunity, a new chance to put a fresh foot forward. Our past can only hold us down if we let it. Would you lie on a railroad track while the train was coming, and moan about being tied down? You might, if your hands were bound, but what if both hands were free? All you would have to do is reach down and unwrap the ropes around your stomach. Would you stay there, bemoaning your fate, until the locomotive ran you over? Some people live like they have no options; others live like they have no limits. Which way do you live? Each of us holds the key to unlocking our future.

True leaders choose not to let difficult beginnings define them; instead, they defy their difficult beginnings. They take responsibility for overcoming adversity, instead of letting adversity overcome them.

ATTITUDE ACTION PLAN

- How effectively do you use parables and metaphors when you communicate?

- Describe your childhood. Reframe it into how you would like your adulthood to be. Victor or victim.

- Was there someone who intervened on your behalf? Who believed in you, and what did he or she do for you?

- What injustice have you encountered and how are you committed to changing it?

- What change are you trying to instigate? Are you working within the system or fighting against the system?

- If unfair assumptions are made about you, how do you keep them from blocking your progress?

- What do you do to rededicate yourself to moving forward?

Loving What You Do

Gerri Elliott, Corporate Vice President
Microsoft Corporation

Do what you love, and you will never work another day in your life. When Gerri Elliott has a bad day at work, she goes out to see a customer. It changes her outlook. It changes her attitude.

"At school, my son was interviewed about what he wanted to be when he grew up. I worked for IBM at the time, and my son answered the question by saying, 'I want to be an IBMer.' When asked why, he said, 'Because Mom and Dad are both IBMers, and they love what they do. I'd like to do that, too.'

"When I heard that story, I was thrilled. I thought, 'Thank God we have always made everything we do positive, from a work perspective. What he saw was always positive. Mom and Dad are happy. They love their company. They love what they do.'

"He'd say the same thing about Microsoft right now. 'Mom loves what she does.' I speak highly of it and let my son and daughter know that what I do is a good thing. They know the amount of hours Mom works on this stuff is a good thing, because it makes her happy. It's a positive experience.

"It was years ago when my son was interviewed, but if he were interviewed again and answered the same way, I'd be elated, because I'd know what I do has always been a positive experience for my kids. They've never seen Mom and Dad work because they have to. Of course, we have to, but to the kids, it's been Mom and Dad work because they love what they do. That's amazing to me."

Some Things Are Nonnegotiable

"In my way of balance, my family comes first. My kids come first. The only reason I do what I do is for the family, and whenever I can, I schedule my family time. I set hard guidelines that brand certain appointments nonnegotiable. Literally, at the beginning of the year, I schedule family time on the calendar. I put all of my children's vacations and major events on the calendar the minute I know about them. My secretary knows those dates are sacred. She also knows that dinnertime and bedtime and the time around certain evening events are sacred, also. Halloween is nonnegotiable. My kids' birthdays are nonnegotiable. My kids' holidays are nonnegotiable. It would take an act of God to get me to change any of those on the calendar, and everybody knows it.

"I am courageous when it comes to guarding my family time. If Bill Gates said, 'Gerri, you have to be in this meeting, or you're fired' (Bill would never say this by the way), and it fell on my daughter's birthday, I'd be looking for employment the next day.

"Granted, work doesn't stop at 5:00 P.M. every day. It just doesn't happen, so I sign back onto the system every night after my kids go to bed. I have my routine, and folks know they can count on me, because I'll be connected, either via e-mail or phone; and they can always get to me. But family comes first."

Maximizing the Minute

"Probably one of the best books I've ever read is *One Minute Manager*. I loved it because its premise was to take the time when you recognize somebody doing something good and let him or her know. When you recognize somebody doing something not so good, let him or her know, also. You communicate both, right away, in the same respectful, positive way. You convey both equally. You don't focus on the negative more than the positive or vice versa.

"I think I'd just become a manager when I read that book, and the principles, such as respect and other leadership insights, have stayed with me all these years."

Keith's Attitude Check

After I spoke to a group at Microsoft in Las Vegas, some of the employees came up to me and said, "You remind us of our CEO, Steven Ballmer. Have you ever heard him give a motivational speech?"

"No," I replied.

"His enthusiasm, his energy, and his passion are second to none. No one prepares and works harder in crafting every word of a speech than he does.

"Being our leader, Steve wants to make sure each word has the maximum impact on us, and that it touches and motivates every Microsoft employee. After he delivers his state-of-the-business address, people feel like they could climb Mount Everest! If you ever get a chance, Keith, to hear him speak, you would be in for a real treat."

This attitude of leadership is obviously contagious within Microsoft, because most of the leaders I've met have it, and Gerri Elliott is one of them.

Gerri's job satisfaction and enthusiasm is evident in her passion for connecting with her team, and her customers. Her enthusiasm is even displayed after hours. Enthusiasm is contagious, even her kids are catching it!

I have a trademark introduction that I do when I speak. I tell my audience how I visualized them being my best audience ever, and that when I was introduced they were standing on their feet giving me a standing ovation. I then tell them I am going to bring that vision to life. I leave the stage, reintroduce myself, and the audience responds by standing up and applauding. That sets the tone for the rest of my speech. I later explain to them that if you want your best, you've got to be willing to give your best.

The last four letters of the word enthusiasm, *i-a-s-m*, means "I am sold, myself." Gerri is sold on Microsoft, and her people are sold on her. Are you sold on the company you work for? Are your people sold on you?

Enthusiasm also means "I am seriously motivated." Are you seriously motivated for the company you work for? Your enthusiasm is contagious. Without enthusiasm, you have no energy. Who wants to follow a leader with no energy. Remember, a dead battery can't jump a dead battery.

ATTITUDE ACTION PLAN

■ Consider your enthusiasm level. Are you seriously motivated? Are you sold on your company? As a leader, what tone are you setting for the organization? How does your family view your company?

■ Are you making the most of your minutes? Are you connecting with people in your organization? How? What changes can you make to ensure you provide ongoing coaching and encouragement?

■ Some things in life, should be nonnegotiable. What core values and activities have you set aside as nonnegotiable? Are you courageous enough to stand by them 100 percent, no matter the consequences?

Follow the Golden Rules

Terry Burman, CEO
Sterling Jewelers, Inc.

This organization is one of the most enthusiastic, leadership-driven, and committed group of individuals who all strive for a common goal: To be the best, and to be profitable.

"Enthusiasm and focus are very important. I don't know if they are the most important things we have, but they should be in the top tier of the things we project as leaders. All businesses are made up of people, the decisions that those people make, and the execution of those decisions. The tone you set at the top is going to filter its way down to all operating levels of the business. People skills are very important. What are people skills? They go right back to the fact that you're establishing a culture in a business—getting people to work as a team, getting people to collaborate, getting people to treat each other properly, getting people to work their best and not settle for anything less than the best—in terms of working out problems. It's part motivation, part collaboration, and part teamwork getting people to do those things. I think the most important part of it is establishing values about people, publicizing those values, and consistently sticking with them, even when it's uncomfortable to do so.

"If we have a store manager who is 30 percent over plan for the past three years, but he or she sexually harasses somebody in the store, we don't find an excuse not to fire that person if it is proven that he or she did, indeed, sexually harass somebody. If you don't stick to the principles, you lose credibility. The infraction becomes more known more than the supportive evidence. You need to say what you mean, mean what you say, and stick to it.

"It's zero tolerance. The offenders are gone. Sometimes it takes a little more courage to stick by the values you establish. Once you do establish the values, it's kind of like a collaboration, also, making sure you don't level people because they say something that is opposed to your ideas or because they come up with something you consider a stupid idea."

CEOs Are People, Too

"Some companies have a culture that if anybody disagrees with the CEO, it's open warfare, so you have to establish a culture where collaboration is okay, where people challenging each other is okay, including the CEO of the business. You must be comfortable doing that.

"You must have the confidence to see that the system actually works. Soon employees see that if they want to participate in a meaningful way, that's how they are going to have to participate.

"The history of the company wasn't necessarily such that people were willing to challenge an open forum, so in my first few months I was here, I had to put people on the spot. I had to change the culture, so I challenged people to challenge me. 'Do you think that's okay?' 'Well, what about this?' 'If I were you, I would ask this question or that question. Why aren't you asking it?'

"You can push people out of their shells, depending on the culture. You have to do it, and then you can't jump down their throats, because they don't have a good idea."

Keith's Attitude Check

As a leader, you are what you say; you are what you do. The biggest mistake any leader can make is to talk out of both sides of their mouth, to voice one opinion to one person, but an opposite opinion to another. Remember, words never die. If you can't follow through, don't put it out there.

Nobody's perfect, but when somebody does something wrong or something goes bad, as a leader you need to take the appropriate action. It's not always easy, but for the sake of the team, organization, and all those involved doing the right thing is a must.

Zero tolerance is extremely important. I feel it's the foundation that helps holds everything that is good about a company together. It helps keep your core values intact. Action always speaks louder than words, whether it's doing what's right or fixing a situation that went wrong.

ATTITUDE ACTION PLAN

- Zero tolerance, what action do you need to take?
- When life knocks you down, it doesn't have to knock you out. Get up and rally the troops by putting the right people in the right place. Reward the effort when objectives are met.
- Challenge people to challenge you. Are you learning from everyone? What call to action, strategies, and training do you need to implement to create an unstoppable organization/team?

Feet Washing Leadership

Mark Ganz, President
Regence Blue Cross Blue Shield of Oregon

I first met Mark when he picked me up from the hotel in downtown Portland to take me to dinner, because as a leader he wanted to meet me and get to know me prior to my speaking to his organization. He also paid for my dinner. Mark's attitude to serve works around the clock, 24/7.

Leadership Is Not Management

"The essence of a true leader is reflected when you step down from the pedestal and serve your people, rather than pushing or pulling them. He noted that Jesus was probably the prototype for the servant-leader."

"One of Jesus' messages on how to live and lead was never better expressed than when he washed the feet of his apostles during the Last Supper. I think of my job as serving the people who are the foundation of this company every day, the frontline employees, the people who answer the phones, and the people who pay the claims, too. They are the ones who have the real impact on this company day in and day out. My job as president of the company is to support them. It's really the inverse approach to the typical command-and-control form of leadership.

"I see my job as a support position. I recognize that as the leader of the company, I have the power to influence, inspire, and move people to a vision. People pay deference to the president, but I think leadership is less about the position and more about the person. I want to stay true to the person I am, rather than thinking, 'I'm the president, so I guess I should be this way.' I deal with people in the same way, whether it is someone on the frontline in the lowest pay rank or a senior vice president just below me on the scale. They get paid differently and they have different roles that justify the difference in pay, but essentially we're all links in the chain that serves our customers.

"It's important for the people on the line to feel connected to the leadership, so they feel free to express their concerns and promote their ideas.

"Leaders can develop people skills, but it really starts with the heart and ends with the heart. You have to care about people. You can't fake that or learn that.

"Listen to those being led.

"It's impossible for a leader to be effective without listening to those who follow. A good leader needs to meet people where they're coming from, start from where they are, and then lead them to the 'promised land.'"

Keith's Attitude Check

I connect with Mark spiritually, and I agree that Jesus was the perfect role model of how to serve and lead people. A servant-leader removes all bias, prejudice, and emotional baggage. Mark clearly demonstrates the importance of a 24/7 attitude of leadership lifestyle. Whether he's working or relaxing at home, serving others is a lifestyle.

Servant Leadership

Have you ever seen the TV commercial about the rent-a-car company where a car is being driven and it's all wrapped up in brown paper, that's Enterprise Rent-a-Car. When I think about having the attitude to serve like Mark talked about, I think about Enterprise.

If you ever experience an interaction with an Enterprise Rent-a-Car employee, you'll know firsthand they have a positive attitude to serve. Whether it's picking you up at your home, your office, or one of the managers having to wash your car just to make sure it's perfect for you, each leader within Enterprise is trained and experienced to serve. Their servant leadership starts at the top with the chairman and CEO, Andy Taylor, and flows throughout the organization. Andy learned the value of servitude from his father. In 1957, Jack Taylor, former founder and CEO began with a simple mission: Take care of customers and employees, and profits will follow.

Andy's primary responsibility as a leader is to ensure that his company never strays from its mission of serving its customers and employees first. His goal is to create an environment that supports employees' development, provides opportunities for their growth, and compensates them for their achievements. Andy Taylor, his management team, and all employees always go the extra mile to deliver exceptional customer service. Service for them is an attitude, operating 24 hours a day, seven days a week.

ATTITUDE ACTION PLAN

- Who, in your opinion, is the perfect role model to model your leadership qualities?

- What changes in behaviors do you need to embrace to feel comfortable serving others?

- What does serving others mean to you, feel like, and look like? What obstacles are hindering you from developing a 24/7 service attitude?

Leaders Want the Ball

Allan L. Schuman, Chairman of the Board and CEO
Ecolab, Inc.

I think some of our greatest leaders are the ones who stepped up to the plate in times of need. Churchill went through horrendous times personally, but when his country was being bombed, he took charge in a commanding way that gave his people hope. New York Mayor Rudy Guilani did the same thing in the hours and days following September 11, 2001.

During challenging times, people pray that someone will step forward and "take the helm." When times are tough and we are under attack, people desperately want their leader to be strong and to role-model courage.

Leaders are like sports champions in that they rise to the challenge. In the final minutes of a close game, the best athletes say, "Give me the ball." Chokers, on the other hand, say, "DON'T give me the ball." Al is a leader who has always asked for the ball.

"True leaders don't wilt under pressure, they welcome pressure. I learned this at an early age because my parents were immigrants who worked very long, hard hours. I was pretty much left on my own, so I learned to provide my own direction. I think it taught me resourceful-ness. I played football, edited the school newspaper, and was elected president of both my high school and college senior class. I was even elected master of my fraternity lodge."

Leaders Don't Settle for Status Quo

"Because no one 'gave' me anything, I learned that if I wanted some-thing, it was up to me to make it happen. That's the proof of the pud-ding: When the chips are down, instead of waiting for somebody to come to your rescue, are you the type of person who takes charge and takes responsibility for making things happen? There was no one push-ing me, so I learned to push myself.

"This ability to go out on the edge has served me all my career. I've been in this industry for 45 years so I know it very well. There have been times I had the courage to go against 'corporate thought processes' because I knew our markets well enough to recommend that we do things differently. It would have been easier to play it cool, keep a low profile, and not gamble my reputation. But leaders don't shirk from opportunity, they embrace it. I was comfortable 'taking the ball of lead-ership' and showing them that this new strategy was going to work and that it wasn't good business to just go with the status quo. As a result, those bold moves paid off for our organization and for myself.

"I never stop. I'm never satisfied. I'm always thinking there's got to be a better way. I have this fire in me, this energy to make things happen."

Are You Swift?

"Of course, you never know how you're going to perform in a crisis. I think one way to increase the odds that we'll rise to the occasion in-stead of run from it is to learn how to think swiftly. By thinking swiftly, I mean maintaining a mental alertness so we're acutely aware of what's happening around us. Staying on our mental toes gives us the ability to respond quickly when something needs to be attended to in-stead of being slow to react.

"Thinking swiftly means learning from trial and error the first time instead of repeating mistakes ad infinitum. It means being able to meet people and put them at ease while quickly 'sizing them up' and figuring out the best way to proceed. Thinking swiftly means never being satisfied to say, 'There's nothing we can do.' It's believing, 'There's GOT to be something we can do. There's got to be a better mouse trap.'

"The ability to be 'swift' is one of the first things I look for when hiring people. In the interview, I'll actually ask, 'Are you swift?' If the applicant is slow on the uptake and says in a confused voice, 'I don't know what you mean,' I conclude, 'Uh oh, they're out of here.' When I ask an applicant, 'Are you swift?' and s/he immediately picks up on it and runs with it an answer like, 'Do you mean, am I quick on my mental feet?' I think, 'We're in business!'"

Good Move

"One of the keys to being a swift thinker is constantly observing and learning from other people. For example, my grandson was playing with his GameBoy. I had no idea what it was or how to play it. However, I watched him, and whenever he made a move, I made the same move. Whatever he did, I mimicked. After a while, he looked at me, impressed, and said, 'Wow. You're pretty good at this.'

"Now, I didn't know what the heck I was doing. But I progressed fairly quickly simply because I observed and followed his example. That type of 'best practice' learning, where we study people who are good at what they do, and apply their expertise to accelerate our own, is another example of 'swift thinking.'"

Trust Fund

"I think another prerequisite to being a good leader is 'Can you trust him or her?' Whether or not we're trusted comes down to whether or not we're a straight-shooter. Do we keep our promises? Are we honest? I tell people when they're not doing things right. They may not like it at the time, however they never have to wonder where they stand with me. They know I'm going to tell the truth, and in the long run, that's much better than having to read between the lines and second-guess whether your boss really 'means' what he or she is saying.

"In keeping with that policy, anyone in our company is welcome to argue with me. I love it when people argue with me because sometimes they bring up things I don't know. I admire people who stand up for what they believe, because it shows they're willing to take a chance and it shows they have their courage of their convictions.

"Some people, especially managers from European countries, are shocked at the fact that I encourage dissent. However, I'm very clear that if we talk something out, they're either going to convince me I'm wrong or I'm going to convince them they're wrong. Either way, we'll have a better decision.

"There is also such a thing as being TOO outspoken. Being honest doesn't mean saying what you really think about everything. You have to choose your spots. It's important to ask yourself, 'Is sharing my opinion going to help or hurt?' If it's not going to help and it could hurt, it's better to keep your mouth shut."

Stay in Touch

"If leaders want employees to feel any type of loyalty, it's crucial to stay in touch through almost constant communication. I do all sorts of things, from leaving messages on the entire sales team's voicemail, to writing columns for our monthly corporate publications, to sending a monthly letter to all employees asking them to let me know of their progress, obstacles, and successes. One of our most popular events is our annual CEO 'call-in.' Anyone in the world can call me that day. I'm on the phone for six, seven, eight hours straight; answering questions and fielding calls from around the country.

"I do anything my management team asks. I show up in training classes, and I'm probably one of the only CEO's that actually works our company booth in our industry trade show. Our customers see that and think, 'Ah, he is taking an interest in this show, which means he is taking in interest in his people, which means they're going to take an interest in me.' That's what I'm here for, to set up that circle where everyone feels valued and appreciated. We have 20,000 employees and millions of customers, but they are not numbers to me. I treat them like they're like my brother or sister. People want to be well-led. And that means acting in a way people can trust and respect you."

Keith's Attitude Check

Al, who described himself as being a 66-year-old guy with a 25-year-old brain is definitely a swift thinker. You get energized just talking with him. Have you trained yourself to think swiftly? Or, is your motto, "I'm undecided and that's final."

One way to speed up your decision-making process is to give yourself a time limit for reaching a conclusion. Studies actually show that, past a point, mulling over a dilemma for days doesn't necessarily help you make a wiser choice. Vacillating can become a bad habit just as swift thinking can become a good habit. Which are you going to cultivate?

Who's Got the Ball?

Be honest with yourself. Are you one of those people who, when the game's on the line, says, "Give me the ball." Or, are you hoping the ball goes to someone else? The word "resourceful" is defined as "capable of devising ways and means; able to meet situations."

What's your resourcefulness quotient? Have you cultivated the ability to figure things out on your own? Do you welcome challenge as an opportunity to test yourself, or do you back away from challenges because you're not sure you're up to the test?

A friend took a weekend drive through the countryside to visit "horse country." She was on an isolated road when her back left tire went flat. She was able to pull over to the side of the road safely, but then she just sat there, waiting for someone to come along. She had never changed a tire before and had no idea how to even start.

After an hour, it was starting to get dark, and she realized that the "White Knight" was probably not going to show up. She didn't have her cell phone with her to call AAA or a friend, and there wasn't a house in sight. She reluctantly realized she was going to have to fix her tire herself.

She looked in the glove compartment, found the manual for the car, and started following instructions. Forty-five minutes later, she was back on the road, having fixed her own tire. She told me how good she felt about herself. She realized that for some people, changing a tire was not a big deal, but for her it was a statement about how she could take care of herself and handle a crisis, if she just put her mind to it.

Gear Up

Are you facing a challenge right now? Are you waiting for someone to come along and rescue you? Could you figure out how to resolve it, all by yourself? Doing so will not only build your own resourcefulness, it will role-model for your employees and/or children that when we're in trouble, we should first look to OURSELVES to resolve the situation, instead of standing by, helplessly, wringing our hands.

Charles Schulz, creator of the famed Peanuts cartoon strip, said, "Life is like a ten-speed bike. Most of us have gears we never use." As Al pointed out, leaders don't shirk challenges, they welcome them. Vow to yourself that you will gear-up and face your next challenge head-on. You will probably discover, as Al did, that when you do, you will discover you have resources you never knew existed.

ATTITUDE ACTION PLAN

- Who is someone you respect for being good in a crisis?
- Were you "given" things when you were a child, or did you have to make your own way? Did that help or hurt your ability to learn resourcefulness (the ability to be self-sufficient)?
- On a scale of 1 to 10 (10 being highest), how would you rank your ability to "think swiftly?"

Keith's Final Attitude Check

Walking in Love

The most important element of an attitude of leadership is an attitude of love. The wisdom and character these successful leaders demonstrate in their life and share in this book can be boiled down to one powerful word *love*. When you think about it, isn't that what the attitude for leadership is all about? Cultivating the principles shared by these leaders is really about cultivating or developing character, and character is rooted in love.

My pastor and mentor, Dr. Creflo Dollar, has taught me much about character through his own leadership, challenges, and opportunities. From his teaching and leadership examples, I have learned about the power of love and how to exercise love in challenging situations. He says, "Love finds the pause button, allowing you to gain control of your emotions when you'd rather lose your temper.

"Love is coachable, teachable, and doesn't get offended at correction. Love cares more for others than for self. The opposite of love is selfishness. A selfish leader manipulates rather than motivates, influences rather than inspires, controls rather than coaches."

My love was tested several times while writing this book. People were assigned certain projects, who committed to getting things done at a certain time and with a certain level of professionalism, and they didn't always come through. Some people overpromised and underdelivered. As a leader, when we overpromise and underdeliver you place yourself in a position of weakness. Your defense is usually driven by a series of excuses, rather than being accountable for your commitment, your actions, and most importantly your attitude.

An important lesson I learned is not to take accountability for other people's actions but be willing exhibit love and forgive others when they don't follow through, mislead you, and don't end up fulfilling their end of the deal. Exhibiting love as a leader is not always easy, I'll be the first to admit this situation was hard for me. But what I learned was that when someone does something wrong to you, you must set your mind and attitude to do something good for them. Remember, if you don't have love as a leader, you are a useless leader.

As a leader embracing an attitude of leadership, you should strive everyday to pass the test for maintaining your "love walk."

I had another opportunity to pass the test and strengthen my love walk. I was on my way to the hotel from the airport in a taxi, and the driver got lost. When we finally arrived at the hotel, the fare for the taxi was double the usual amount. "Okay, Keith," I said to myself, "get it together." I found my personal pause button, paid the full fare, and tipped the driver. Then I asked him to wait for a second, because I had something inside the hotel I wanted to give him. When I returned, I handed him a map. "Just in case you are the taxi driver who takes me back to the airport," I said.

Kindness and goodness are aspects of love. Kindness prepared the heart of the taxi driver to receive the good I had for him, even when it was in the form of a map.

When you are tested in your love walk, just remember what goes around comes around. Don't give up, cave in, or quit.

Change Is Not Change until *You* Change

The attitude of leadership transcends titles, positions, race, or gender. There is no special difference between the attitudes required to lead a company, organization, or individual. Leadership is leadership. Taking the lead and keeping it, however, will require you to embrace an attitude of love, and an attitude of continuous improvement. It requires change, and change produces growth, but as Dr. Dollar quotes often, "Change is not change until you change."

To encompass the principles presented in this book, you must embrace change. Change begins with a quality decision and requires diligence to bring about the transformation. Often individuals and organizations set their sails for change, yet never fully transform, because they lack the due diligence and discipline required to stay on course. Dr. Dollar reminds me often, "Consistency is the key to the breakthrough, doing something one time won't do it." The attitude for leadership demands a little something extra from you and a little something more of you every day.

The following quote reflects what an attitude of leadership is all about:

A leader is patient, kind, and walks in love.

A leader is not jealous, conceited, or proud.

A leader is not ill mannered, selfish, or irritable.

A leader does not keep a record of wrong things done to them.

A leader is proactive, not reactive.

A leader is not happy with evil, but is happy with the truth, honest, and integrity.

A leader is steadfast, focused, and committed to their vision.

A leader is ever ready to believe the best of every person, and treats everyone with respect.

A leader's hopes are fadeless under all circumstances, and a leader endures everything without weakening, caving in, or quitting.

Remember, on the day you were born the potential for leadership was also born. I applaud you for investing time in your personal development by reading this book. I encourage you to apply what you've learned and share it with others. It is my hope that you will stay inspired and motivated to take the lead of leadership in your life, helping you to make a difference in someone else's life.

INDEX